Land and Leasing

Second Edition

by

Dan McCue and Deborah Hubbs

published by

THE UNIVERSITY OF TEXAS AT AUSTIN

Continuing & Innovative Education

PETROLEUM EXTENSION SERVICE

2013

Library of Congress Cataloging-in-Publication Data

McCue, Edward Daniel, 1958–
Land and leasing / by Dan McCue and Deborah Hubbs. — 2nd ed.
p. cm.
Rev. ed. of: Land and leasing / by Judith Eubank ; edited by Jodie Leecraft. 1984.
Includes bibliographical references and index.
ISBN 0-88698-263-4 (alk. paper)
1. Oil and gas leases—United States. 2. Leases—United States. 3. Land tenure—Law and legislation—
United States. I. Hubbs, Deborah Frances, 1967- II. Eubank, Judith. Land and leasing. III. Title.
KF1865.E93 2013
346.7304'6823—dc23

2012012986

DISCLAIMER

Although all reasonable care has been taken in preparing this publication, the authors, the Petroleum Extension Service (PETEX) of The University of Texas at Austin, and any other individuals and their affiliated groups involved in preparing this content assume no responsibility for the consequences of its use. Each recipient should ensure he or she is properly trained and informed about the unique policies and practices regarding application of the information contained herein. Any recommendations, descriptions, and methods in this book are presented solely for educational purposes.

First Edition published 1984. Second Edition 2013.
Printed in the United States of America

Catalog No. 1.00120
ISBN 0-88698-263-4
978-0-88698-263-8

No state tax funds were used to publish this book.
The University of Texas at Austin is an equal opportunity employer.

Editor: Virginia Dosher
Graphic Designer: Debbie Caples
Cover Art: E. K. Weaver

Contents

Figures vi
Tables viii
Foreword ix
Preface xi
Acknowledgments xiii
About the Authors xv
Introduction 1

1 Privately Owned Land 3
  Private Ownership 3
    Types of Ownership 4
    Rights to Mineral Ownership 5
    Limitations on Mineral Ownership 7
  Landowners and Types of Estates They Own 11
    Surface Owners and Mineral Owners 11
    Life Tenants and Remaindermen 12
    Cotenants 12
    Married Persons 13
  Landowners as Agents of the State 14
  Representatives of Mineral Estate Owners 15
    Fiduciaries 15
    Executors and Administrators 15
    Guardians 16
    Trustees 16
    Persons Acting under Powers of Attorney 16
    Representatives of Unknown or Missing Heirs 17
  Summary 17

2 State and Federal Lands 19
  State Lands 20
  Federal Lands 22
    Public Domain Lands 23
    Acquired Lands 25
    Indian Lands 25
    Offshore Lands 26
  Summary 28

3 Land Measurement and Land Description 29
  Units of Measurement 30
  Methods of Description 32
    Metes and Bounds 32
    Public Land Survey System 35
    Urban Subdivisions 38
  Completeness of Description 39

	Summary	39
4	**Preparations for Leasing**	41
	Preliminary Explorations	41
	Geologists and Geophysicists	42
	Landmen	43
	Lease Brokers	44
	Preliminary Title Checks	44
	Purpose	44
	Sources of Information	45
	Preliminary Negotiations	49
	Concerns of the Landman	49
	Concerns of the Landowner	51
	Summary	53
5	**Elements of the Lease**	55
	Lease Forms	55
	State and Federal Forms	56
	Forms Published by Private Companies	56
	Forms Prepared for Individuals and Associations	59
	Elements of the Lease	60
	Title	60
	Date	60
	Parties	60
	Consideration	62
	Granting Clause	62
	Description	64
	Mother Hubbard Clause	64
	Habendum Clause	66
	Royalty Clause	67
	Shut-In Royalty Clause	69
	Drilling and Delay Rental Clause	70
	Dry Hole, Cessation of Production, and Continuous Drilling Clauses	72
	Pooling and Unitization Clause	72
	Surrender Clause	76
	Damage Clause	76
	Assignment Clause	77
	Warranty and Proportionate Reduction Clauses	78
	Force Majeure Clause	78
	Legal Effect Clause and Lessor's Signature	79
	Acknowledgment	79
	Summary	79
6	**Execution of the Lease**	81
	Final Negotiations	81
	Special Terms and Provisions	82
	Execution and Acknowledgment	85
	Variations in Proper Execution	85

	The Importance of Proper Acknowledgment	86
	Recording of the Executed Lease	86
	Memorandum of Lease	86
	Bonus Drafts	87
	Recording Procedures	87
	Ratification	88
	Summary	88
7	**Preparations for Drilling, Producing, and Selling**	91
	Examining Titles	92
	Title Examiners	92
	Title Opinions	92
	Curing Titles	96
	Affidavits	96
	Other Kinds of Documents	98
	Permitting and Drilling	100
	Executing Division Orders	100
	Summary	103
8	**Agreements to Explore and Develop**	105
	Support Agreements	107
	Dry-Hole Contribution Agreements	108
	Bottomhole Contribution Agreements	109
	Farmout Agreements	110
	Letter Agreements and Formal Contracts	112
	Joint Operating Agreements	113
	Model Forms	114
	Special Provisions	115
	Summary	117
9	**Pooling, Unitization, and Release of Oil and Gas Leases**	119
	Pooling	120
	Voluntary Pooling	120
	Involuntary Pooling	123
	Unitization	123
	Private Lands	124
	Federal and State Lands	125
	Release	126
	Summary	128
References		131
Appendices		133
Figure Credits		167
Glossary		171
Index		197

Figures

1.1 The first page of a form oil and gas lease for Texas from the American Association of Professional Landmen (AAPL) 6

1.2 East Texas saw the consequences of the rule of capture, unchecked by regulation. 9

1.3 The water lines of a fracturing operation, or "frac job" 10

1.4 In most of the oil-producing nations outside of the United States, rights to minerals are owned by the central government. 14

2.1 In Alaska, land in private ownership outside of native lands makes up less than 1% of the total land. 20

2.2 Management of federal lands by U.S. government agencies 22

2.3 The Bureau of Indian Affairs administers 56 million acres of land held in trust for Native Americans and Alaskan Natives. 25

2.4 Lands off the shore of the United States are owned by the government: from the shore to 3 or 9 nautical miles out by state government, from 3 or 9 nautical miles out to the 8,000-foot depth line by the federal government. 27

3.1 It was once common for English surveying equipment to include a measuring chain. 30

3.2 Modern equipment used in conducting land surveys includes Global Positioning System (GPS) devices. 31

3.3 This drawing demonstrates how the direction of each boundary line of a property is measured for a metes and bounds description. 33

3.4 This simple plat shows the bearings and distances of the property lines as they are typically identified by surveyors. 33

3.5 Small, oddly shaped surveys in a Texas county 34

3.6 A map showing principal meridians and base lines of U.S. public land surveys. 35

3.7 Township numbers are vertical, and range numbers are horizontal. 36

3.8 A plat of a sectioned Congressional township 37

3.9 A subdivided section 37

3.10 Blocks and lots form regular patterns in urban subdivisions. 38

4.1 An abstract of title traces the history of ownership of a property. 45

4.2 A landman searching for records at the county clerk's office 47

4.3 A landman should consider approaching the landowner for information about a land's legal history. 48

5.1 A Producers 88 lease form 57

5.2 A typical lease begins with a title that names the subject of the agreement and a statement of the effective date, the names of the parties, and the consideration promised. 63
5.3 A granting clause, a land description, and a Mother Hubbard clause 64
5.4 A habendum clause fixes the primary term of the lease. 66
5.5 A royalty clause states the percentage of production to be received by the lessor. 68
5.6 A producing well being shut in with a workover rig 69
5.7 A delay rental clause allows extension or termination of the lease if a well is not drilled during the primary term. 71
5.8 A pooling and unitization clause allows the lessee to combine tracts with others in a pool or a unit for the purpose of drilling. 73
5.9 A damage clause addresses how the lessee will compensate the surface owner for such things as losses resulting from accidents. 76
5.10 An assignment clause allows the lessee to assign the lease rights to another party and specifies how notice of assignment should be given. 77
5.11 A force majeure clause keeps the lease in force even though delays specified in the lease prevent the lessee from meeting its obligations. 78

6.1 An aerial photo of a ranch 82
6.2 There can be lease provisions that protect domestic animals or compensate the owner in the event that animals are harmed by operations carried out on the land. 84
6.3 A recordation stamp 87
6.4 A sample ratification of an oil and gas lease 89

7.1 A sample form for a title opinion 93
7.2 A runsheet mapping the ownership of mineral rights 95
7.3 A sample division order 101

8.1 The AAPL joint operating agreements for offshore operations are available through the Web site for the OCS Advisory Board (www.ocsadvisoryboard.org). 114

9.1 The areas outlined in red on the map represent tracts that have been pooled to form drilling and spacing units. 121
9.2 A form for a release of an oil and gas lease 127

D.1 A form for a memorandum (memo) of oil and gas lease 142

Tables

1.1 Types of Law Affecting Mineral Leasing 7
1.2 A Typical Descent and Distribution Scheme 15

2.1 Leasing Agencies for State Lands 21
2.2 Leasing Authorities for U.S. Public Lands 23

4.1 Summary of Preparations for Leasing 49
4.2 State Regulatory Agencies for the Top Ten Oil-Producing States 52

5.1 Types of Standard Lease Forms 55
5.2 Parts of a Standard Oil and Gas Lease 61

8.1 Types of Exploration and Development Agreements 106
8.2 Advantages of a Dry-Hole Contribution Agreement for Both Parties 108
8.3 Advantages of a Bottomhole Contribution Agreement for Both Parties 109
8.4 Advantages of a Farmout Agreement for Both Parties 110

9.1 Comparison of Pooling and Unitization 123

Foreword

Just over 30 years ago, the Association of Desk and Derrick Clubs (ADDC), an organization of employees of the petroleum and other energy industries in the United States and Canada, approached PETEX about creating a series of books that give a basic overview of the oil and gas industry using an approach that laypeople understand. The first edition of *Land and Leasing* was one book in the series designed to aid accountants, bankers, insurance agents, executives, and others to understand subjects outside of their specialization but of interest to those in the industry. The first book and anchor in the series, *Fundamentals of Petroleum*, gives a broad view of the entire industry, where *Land and Leasing*, 2nd edition, offers a survey of the legal aspects of land ownership and leasing in the context of oil and gas exploitation. The technologies of horizontal drilling and hydraulic fracturing, largely developed in the 1950s, have made it possible for producers to recover oil and gas from shale with a profit. Since the original publication of this book, those technologies, along with other supporting equipment invented for the purpose of recovering native fluids from shale, have been applied in the field. The rapid development of domestic shale formations in the United States has brought with it a flurry of leasing on lands with shale deposits. Plays such as the Marcellus, Haynesville, and Barnett frequently appear in the news, creating an interest in the general public to learn about the topic, in landowners to lease their land, and in others to develop a career as a land professional.

As it is the mission of PETEX to provide up-to-date, quality training and publications, this second edition of *Land and Leasing* was designed to respond to that renewed interest in the subject. The book has been thoroughly updated with current information. It has stayed close to its original concept, however: simplifying a technical and complex subject for the non-expert.

Land and Leasing has traditionally been used as a reference for professionals in the industry and as a reference in PETEX training courses on Professional Land Management. It is also suggested as a library reference and a textbook for college courses in oil and gas law.

In the past few years, there has been a realization about the extent of gas reserves in domestic shale plays. These massive reserves, along with the sizable oil reserves in plays such as the Monterey, Bakken, and Eagle Ford will make certain that the topic continues to be an important one for readers.

Preface

As the need for hydrocarbons grows around the world, the need for exploring new oil and gas reserves also grows. Integral to the exploration for oil and gas in the United States is the need to know who owns the minerals and how to lease from them so that oil and gas exploration companies can drill for new reserves. Land professionals are an integral part of the exploration effort. There has been an influx of new land professionals into the business in recent years, and they need to know the basics of land work. PETEX, in its book *Land and Leasing*, provides the basic knowledge a land professional needs to begin his or her land career.

Land and Leasing, 2nd edition, addresses everything—from types of land ownership to basic land contracts. The most common contract in the oil and gas industry is the oil and gas lease, which *Land and Leasing* discusses paragraph by paragraph. In addition, *Land and Leasing* addresses negotiation of the lease, title checks at the county clerk's office, units of land measure, and methods of curing defective titles.

Land and Leasing is a basic handbook that every new land professional should have. Thanks, PETEX, for accumulating such a wealth of necessary knowledge in one accessible place.

Alan H. Morgan, CPL
Vice President-Land
Remora Oil Company
Houston, Texas

Acknowledgments

PETEX wishes to extend its sincere thanks to the following individuals for their generous gifts of time and expertise in the matter of oil and gas leasing.

L. Rae Connet, Attorney at Law, Senior Land Advisor and Managing Partner, PetroLand Services, Hawthorne, California

Barry Myhr, CPL and Senior Land Negotiator, Noble Energy, Inc., Denver, Colorado

Joseph Munsey, RPL and Senior Land Advisor, Southern California Gas Company (SoCalGas), San Clemente, California

Dora Soria, Staff Landman at ConocoPhillips Alaska, Inc. and National Director of the Alaska Association of Professional Landmen, Anchorage, Alaska

Scott Stone, CPL, Spartan Resources, L.L.C., Oklahoma City, Oklahoma

Jack Wilhelm, CPL and Attorney at Law, Austin, Texas

PETEX would also like to express appreciation to the following individuals, associations, agencies, and companies for furnishing forms and illustrations.

American Association of Professional Landmen (AAPL)
Atascosa County Clerk's Office
Bret Boteler and EnerMax, Inc.
Briscoe Center, The University of Texas at Austin
L. Rae Connet
J. G. Domke
Five State Land Services, Inc.
GeoSouthern Energy Corporation
Billy Hefton and the *Enid News & Eagle*
Deborah Hubbs
Dan McCue
National Atlas of the United States of America
O'Connor Center for the Rocky Mountain West
Pound Printing Company
Ted W. Walters & Associates, L.L.P.
Texas General Land Office
U.S. Bureau of Land Management
World Resources Institute

Thanks to Debbie Caples for design, layout, and production; E.K. Weaver for illustrations; Leah Lehmann for photo research; Josh Bauermeister and Dewey Badeaux for additional editorial review; and Debby Denehy for managerial support.

Lastly, we would like to acknowledge the contributions of many professionals in the field to the first edition of the book, and particularly the contributions of the members of the Association of Desk and Derrick Clubs (ADDC) who guided the project and reviewed the manuscript.

Virginia Dosher, Editor
PETEX
The University of Texas at Austin

About the Authors

Deborah Hubbs
General Counsel
Business Development Manager
GeoSouthern Energy Corporation
The Woodlands, Texas

Deborah Hubbs serves as General Counsel and Business Development Manager for GeoSouthern Energy Corporation. In her role at GeoSouthern, Deborah oversees the Legal, Environmental, Health and Safety, Information Technology, and Regulatory Groups. Deborah also looks for new oil and gas opportunities for GeoSouthern to invest in as the company seeks to expand its portfolio in new basins around the United States. Prior to working at GeoSouthern, Deborah worked as a Land Team Lead for the Appalachian Basin business unit at Anadarko Petroleum Corporation. During her tenure at Anadarko, Deborah was on the Board of Directors for Women's Energy Network™, serving two years as the Northside Program Director. Currently, Deborah is the Vice-Chair for the Oil and Gas Committee Newsletter for the Environment, Energy, and Resources Section of the American Bar Association.

Deborah received a B.A. degree from Southern Nazarene University and a J.D. degree from the University of Oklahoma College of Law. She is licensed to practice law in the State of Texas.

Deborah would like to thank PETEX and Dan McCue for giving her this opportunity—and for their patience throughout the project. She would also like to thank Owen Anderson for teaching her the fundamentals of oil and gas law. Finally, she would like to thank Meg Molleston for her mentorship and teaching her about "all things land."

Dan McCue
Senior Land Negotiator
BP America Production Company
Houston, Texas

Dan McCue obtained a B.B.A. in Petroleum Land Management from The University of Texas at Austin. Afterwards, he spent 18 years with Amoco Production Company as a Senior Land Negotiator, assigned to various regions of the United States including Alaska. He then served Spinnaker Exploration Company as Senior Landman. While at that company, from 1998 to 2007, he was responsible for the acquisition of leases, the negotiation of commercial deals, the drafting of operating, farmout, and production handling agreements, and the coordination of competitor analysis for federal lease sales in both shelf and deepwater Gulf of Mexico (GOM). Following the sale of Spinnaker Exploration Company to Norsk Hydro ASA, Dan joined newly formed Beryl Oil and Gas, L.P. as Vice President of Land in 2007. There, he was responsible for creating Beryl's Land Department for the integration of newly acquired Gulf of Mexico assets. In 2009, Beryl was sold to Dynamic Offshore Resources, L.L.C. Prior to joining BP America Production Company, he served as Director of Land Management for Calera Corporation of Los Gatos, California.

At the BP office in Houston, Dan is Senior Land Negotiator. In addition to his regular professional work, since 1995 he has been an instructor at the PETEX Learning and Assessment Center-Houston, where he teaches Petroleum Fundamentals: Aspects of Oil and Gas Leasing and Introduction to Offshore Operations: Offshore Leasing Acquisition, courses that focus on onshore lands in the United States as well as offshore lands of the Outer Continental Shelf (OCS). Dan has contributed to another PETEX book, *Fundamentals of Petroleum*, 5th edition.

Introduction

Before a petroleum company can develop oil or gas reserves on land belonging to someone else, it must acquire the legal rights to explore, drill, and produce on that land. How these rights are acquired and from whom differ from country to country. In most oil-producing nations, mineral resources are owned by the national government, and petroleum companies must negotiate with government representatives to secure contracts for mineral development. The complexity, cost, and, in some cases, the instability of these arrangements can be very great.

This book focuses on land management in the United States. (Appendix J treats briefly the subject of mineral leasing in Canada.) In the United States, as in other countries, much of the land and mineral wealth are publicly owned. But, in addition to the resources belonging to state and federal governments, vast amounts of land—about two-thirds of onshore territory—are privately owned. The mineral rights to this privately owned land are also commonly owned by individuals. So companies that wish to exploit domestic oil and gas reserves must often acquire the rights to do so from private citizens. The legal instrument that both the government and private owners use to grant those rights is the oil and gas lease. The term *oil and gas lease* is a generic term and as used in this book also implies the terms *oil, gas, and minerals lease* and *oil, gas, and associated liquid hydrocarbons lease.*

The legal obligations established by an oil and gas lease differ markedly from those set up by an ordinary commercial lease. Because the relationship between the landowner and the oil and gas company under a lease is highly interconnected—both legally and economically—regular monitoring is needed to ensure that all the provisions of the lease are met. Companies have responded to the complexities of the leasing relationship by hiring personnel with more legal training than in the past; today, many of their employees are attorneys. Private landowners, for their part, are increasingly aware of the complexity of the arrangement and the value of their mineral resources.

They often employ specialists of their own—attorneys, accountants, financial analysts, and estate planners—to make informed decisions about the leasing of their mineral rights. State and federal governments, of course, use their own specialists to assess the value of publicly owned mineral wealth.

A grasp of the basic legal issues and terms, as well as some attention to the economic and social complexities, is essential to understanding how the petroleum industry leases and develops mineral reserves in the United States. To facilitate that understanding, related topics are grouped in sequential chapters in this book. Chapters 1 to 3 deal with land ownership: who owns land and minerals, who may lease, and under what conditions. Chapters 4 to 7 describe the leasing process: how oil and gas leases are acquired, and by whom. Chapters 8 and 9 discuss a number of related arrangements often needed to exploit leased minerals effectively—operating agreements, joint ventures, and unitization, for example. These last arrangements frequently involve the same company personnel who help to secure leases.

Terms that appear in italics are defined in the glossary at the end of the book. Throughout, the word *landman* is used to refer to the professional in the petroleum industry who negotiates leases with landowners and production agreements with operators in the field. In spite of how it appears, it is intended as a gender-neutral term: Today, the profession counts many women in its ranks. In the coming years, another term such as *land professional* or *land negotiator* may take its place, but the original term is still overwhelmingly used in the industry today.

In this chapter:

- Limitations to the rights of landowners to use and dispose of their property
- Severance of estates: surface and mineral estates
- Definitions of oil and gas lease, lessor, and lessee
- Government restrictions on oil and gas operations
- Disputes between parties under an oil and gas lease
- Types of land ownership in the context of the oil and gas lease
- Powers of fiduciaries with respect to oil and gas leases

1 Privately Owned Land

PRIVATE OWNERSHIP

The word *landowner* describes a person who holds the title to a specific piece of property. Some people think a property owner can do almost anything with the land he or she owns—sell or lease it, build on it or dig into it, plant it, or leave it to anyone in a last will and testament. Many laws affect what the landowner may do with his or her property, however. Besides federal and state laws and regulations, city ordinances might also influence the owner's actions. Zoning ordinances, for example, might prohibit an owner from drilling a well in the backyard. It would seem that a rural landowner would have fewer restrictions than a landowner in an urban area and could explore, develop, and profit from his or her property without hindrance. But is the rural landowner unhindered either? And does that landowner's property include anything that might be found beneath the surface of the land as well as whatever is standing or growing on top?

A "fee" is an estate or interest in land.

The answer to such questions might be yes or no, depending on a wide variety of circumstances. American property law is complex, and much of it is *case law*, or *common law*, that varies from state to state. Such law is composed of many court decisions made over the years on individual cases. Common law is fundamental to land ownership in all of the states, with (arguably) the exception of Louisiana. There, the Napoleonic Code serves as the basis of *statute law*, or *civil law*, which governs real estate ownership. Statute law, unlike common law, originates in the laws established by a legislative or other governing body. Both of these types of law—common law and civil law—have long histories and are full of numerous statutory additions and variations. Statutes often vary from state to state; common law itself is complex and diverse. Both types of law make use of terminology that can be confusing.

One common-law term very frequently applied to the private ownership of land is *fee*. A property owner might hold land in *fee simple*; the oil and gas lease just signed constitutes a *determinable fee* in the same land; the lawyer who has just explained the lease will certainly expect a handsome fee for his services. All of these fees seem to be connected, yet they are clearly not the same. The various usages, in fact, can all be traced back to the Middle Ages in England, when a fee, or *fief*, was land held under a feudal lord. At that time, land was granted with the expectation that the *grantee* provide goods or services to an overlord. By extension, a "fee" came to mean almost any payment or service rightly due to a superior. Eventually, the term was applied to the compensation for professional services, to the sum charged for a license or an admission ticket, and even to a tip or gratuity. In common usage these days, it can be almost any sort of payment, but in common law, "fee" still means, basically, an estate or interest in land. The landowner is a fee holder; the land is the fee; and the land is held in fee.

Types of Ownership

A twentieth-century American fee holder, although subject to state and federal laws, still enjoys considerable freedom in the use and disposal of his or her property. One important freedom is the right to inherit and to *devise*, or will, the fee. (An owner is said, legally, to "devise" real property and to "*bequeath*" personal property to heirs.) The designation "fee simple" indicates that there are no restrictions on how the owner may convey the land, and particularly none on how the owner may devise it. In nearly all states, a holder of fee simple property can leave an estate to a spouse, children, or anyone—even a stranger. Sometimes, though, property is *entailed*—that is, there are restrictions on how the owner may pass property in a will. If, for example, the land is held in *fee tail*, the landowner can leave it only to "heirs of his body." Entailed property is rare in this country; fee simple holdings are far more common. For that reason, references to the landowner in the following pages can be understood to mean the free holder of fee simple property unless the term is qualified in some way.

Rights to Mineral Ownership

An unqualified landowner is one with no restrictions on what he or she may do with the land. That person has the right to:

- Divide, or *sever*, the estate into separate estates
- Exploit and benefit from the estate
- Lease the estate
- *Convey* the estate (and specifically, devise the estate)

After an estate is severed, there are two estates:

- Surface estate
- Mineral estate

The unqualified owner holds title to the surface of the land, the space above it, and the subsoil below it, along with title to *minerals* contained in the land and—along with them—the rights to explore, develop, produce, and benefit from minerals on the estate. Because his or her rights to the land are exclusive, such a landowner can prevent other people from entering the property and taking its minerals or otherwise benefiting from it.

Of course, there is no truly unqualified owner. In the United States, as elsewhere, state and federal laws as well as local ordinances restrict the use and sale of land. But an owner of land in fee simple, subject to government restrictions and restrictions brought about by private agreements (such as contracts), does have the rights named above.

An owner in fee simple, for example, may sell an entire interest (all legal rights) in the land, sell only the surface and retain the minerals, or sell only the minerals (or only certain minerals) and keep the surface (becoming owner of the *fee in surface*). If the owner does sever, or separate, his or her interests, a *surface estate* and a *mineral estate* are created. These are then legally considered to be separate estates. They might be sold to separate owners, leased to separate companies or individuals, and divided again and again as they are conveyed (transferred) for various purposes. Mineral estates are especially subject to complicated divisions. An owner, for example, can sell all or a specified portion of interest in the minerals or all or a specified portion of interest in the proceeds from the minerals.

The legal instrument that gives an organization or individual the right to enter someone else's property, to search for oil and gas, and to produce and profit from them is the *oil and gas lease* (fig. 1.1). Its legal definition varies from state to state, and even within a given state, no actual document or lease form can be regarded as standard.

AAPL FORM 658-85

OIL, GAS AND MINERAL LEASE
TEXAS

THIS AGREEMENT made this ___________ day of ______________________________, 20______, between ______________________________, Lessor (whether one or more), whose address is ______________________________, and ______________________________, Lessee, whose address is: ______________________________.

1. GRANT. Lessor, in consideration of a cash payment and other good and valuable consideration in hand paid, of the royalties herein provided for, and of the agreements of Lessee herein contained, hereby grant, leases and lets exclusively unto Lessee the land described in paragraph 2 below, hereinafter referred to as leased premises, for the purposes of investigating, exploring, prospecting, drilling and mining for and producing oil, gas (the term "gas" as used herein includes helium, carbon dioxide and other commercial gases, as well as hydrocarbon gases), sulphur, fissionable materials, and all other minerals, conducting exploration, geological and geophysical surveys, core tests, gravity and magnetic surveys, for introducing or injecting fire, air, gas, steam, water, salt water, chemicals, and fluids or substances into any subsurface stratum or strata which is not productive of fresh water for primary, secondary and other enhanced recovery operations.

2. LEASED PREMISES. (Description)

in the County of ______________________________, State of Texas, containing ____________________ gross acres, more or less, including all riparian rights and any interests therein which Lessor may hereafter acquire by reversion, accretion, prescription or otherwise. In consideration of the aforementioned cash payment, Lessor agrees to execute at Lessee's request any additional or supplemental instruments to effect a more complete or accurate description of the land so covered. For the purpose of determining the amount of any rentals or shut-in payments hereunder, the number of gross acres above specified shall be deemed correct, whether actually more or less.

3. TERM. Subject to the other provisions herein contained, this Lease shall be for a term of ______________________________ years from the date hereof (called "primary term") and as long thereafter as oil, gas, sulphur, fissionable materials or other mineral is produced in paying quantities from the leased premises or land pooled therewith, or this lease is otherwise maintained in force and effect pursuant to other provisions herein contained.

4. RENTAL PAYMENT. Subject to the other provisions herein contained, if operations for drilling or mining are not commenced on said land, or on acreage pooled therewith as hereinafter provided for, on or before one year from the date hereof, this Lease shall terminate as to both parties, unless on or before such date Lessee shall pay or tender, or make a bona fide attempt to pay or tender, to Lessor, or to the credit of Lessor in ______________________________ at ______________________________, which depository and its successors shall be Lessor's agents and shall continue as the depository for all rentals payable hereunder regardless of changes in ownership of said land or rentals, the sum of ______________________________ Dollars ($______________________), hereinafter called rentals, which shall cover the privilege of deferring commencement of drilling or mining operations for a period of twelve (12) months. In like manner and upon like payment or tenders annually the commencement of drilling or mining operations may be further deferred for successive periods of twelve (12) months each during the primary term hereof. All payments or tenders may be made in currency, or by check or by draft, and such payments or tenders to Lessor or to the depository by deposit in the U.S. Mails on or before the rental due date in a stamped envelope addressed to the depository or to the Lessor at the last address known to Lessee shall constitute proper payment. If such depository, or any successor depository, shall fail, liquidate or be succeeded by another depository, or for any other reasons fail or refuse to accept rentals or any other payments, Lessee shall not be held in default for failure to make such payments or tenders until 60 days after Lessee has received from Lessor a proper recordable instrument naming another depository as agent to receive such payments or tenders. If Lessee, in good faith and with reasonable diligence, timely attempts to pay a rental but fails to pay, or incorrectly pays, any portion thereof this lease shall not terminate if Lessee properly pays such rental within thirty (30) days after written notice from Lessor of Lessee's error or failure. Failure to make proper payment shall not affect any other interest under this lease for which proper payment was made. The cash payment is consideration for this Lease according to its terms and shall not be allocated as mere rental for a period. Lessee may at any time or times execute and deliver to Lessor, or to the depository above named, or place of record a release or releases of this lease as to all or any part of the leased premises, or as to any minerals or horizons under all or any part thereof, and thereby be relieved of all obligations as to the land or interest released. If this lease is released as to all minerals and horizons under only a portion of the leased premises, Lessee's obligation to pay or tender rentals and other payments shall be proportionately reduced in accordance with the net acreage interest retained.

5. ROYALTY PAYMENT. The royalties to be paid to the Lessor are: (a) On oil, 1/8th of that produced and saved from said land, the same to be delivered at the wells or to the Lessor's credit into the pipelines to which the wells may be connected. Lessee shall have the continuing right to purchase such production at the wellhead market price then prevailing in the same field (or if there is no such price then prevailing in the same field, then the nearest field in which there is such a prevailing price) for production of similar grade and gravity. Lessee may sell any royalty oil in its possession and pay Lessor the price received by Lessee for such oil computed at the well; (b) For gas (including casinghead gas) and all other substances covered hereby (i) if used off the leased premises or used in the manufacture of gasoline or other products, the market value at the well of one-eighth (1/8) of the gas so used, or (ii) if sold on or off the leased premises, one-eighth (1/8) of the amount realized from such sale, provided the amount realized from the sale of gas on or off the leased premises shall be the price established by the Gas Sales Contract entered into in good faith by Lessee and gas purchaser, provided that on gas sold by Lessee the market value shall not exceed the amount received by Lessee for such gas computed at the mouth of the well; (c) If a well on the leased premises or lands pooled therewith is capable of producing oil or gas or any other substance covered hereby but such well is either shut-in or production therefrom is not being sold or purchased by Lessee or royalties on production therefrom are not otherwise being paid to Lessor, and if this lease is not otherwise maintained in effect, such well shall nevertheless be considered as though it were producing for the purpose of maintaining this lease, whether during or after the primary term, and Lessee shall tender a shut-in payment of One Dollar per acre then covered by this lease, such payment to be made to Lessor or to Lessor's credit in the depository designated above, on or before 90 days after the next ensuing anniversary date of this lease, and thereafter on or before each anniversary date hereof while the well is shut-in or production therefrom is not being sold or purchased by Lessee or royalties on production therefrom are not otherwise being paid to Lessor. This lease shall remain in force so long as such well is capable of producing and Lessee's failure to properly pay shut-in payment shall render Lessee liable for the amount due but shall not operate to terminate this lease. The intermittent production from any well during such year shall not render necessary any new or additional shut-in payments with respect to such well or the acreage ascribed thereto.

Figure 1.1 The first page of a form oil and gas lease for Texas from the American Association of Professional Landmen (AAPL)

Limitations on Mineral Ownership

Any sales or leasing agreements that the owner of a mineral estate might wish to make are limited by legal and economic considerations. For example, a state might set limitations on such agreements in its court system, where cases interpret the state's concept of mineral ownership. Other legal limitations come from statutory law, especially from the rules enforced by the regulatory commissions created for that purpose by state legislatures. These rules vary from one state to the next, but, in general, they concern such matters as well *spacing* (legal requirements for distance between wells), each well's allowable daily production, and field rules for production practices. (A summary of types of law affecting mineral leasing appears in table 1.1.)

Economic considerations—especially the tremendous amounts of money required to drill for and produce hydrocarbons—also influence the owner's decision to sell or lease a mineral estate. These legal and economic limitations influence what the owner of a mineral estate can do, and both the owner and any person or company with whom he or she enters into an agreement concerning the mineral estate must have a clear understanding of the constraints on that estate.

Table 1.1
Types of Law Affecting Mineral Leasing

International Law	International agreements govern economic zones. For example, the United Nations Convention on the Law of the Sea prescribes the exclusive economic zone (EEZ) around each nation, determining rights to offshore production of oil and gas. See Chapter 2 for information on federal offshore lands.
Constitutional Law	Principles established in the U.S. Constitution and the constitutions of individual states govern fundamental rights to minerals—for instance, the right of a landowner to lease out the land or to explore and develop on the land.
Statutory Law	Laws at the state and federal level and even local ordinances govern many aspects of oil and gas leasing, including procedures for leasing public lands and safety regulations for pipelines.
Administrative Law	Rules and regulations of federal and state agencies govern everyday concerns of those leasing for mineral development, including obtaining permits, conducting testing, and disposing of pollutants.
Common/Case Law	Cases in the courts, especially in top oil-producing states, interpret statutes and create new law when there are no statutes. Important cases such as ones deciding whether an owner can drain the oil under a neighbor's land serve as precedent for later cases that are similar.
Private Law	Private agreements (usually written contracts) govern many business relationships. Under an oil and gas lease, one party is bound to a promise made to another for the use of land to drill a well and produce the minerals underneath the surface.

Mineral ownership theories:
- Nonabsolute ownership
- Absolute ownership

Legal Limitations

Oil and gas exploration and production are now among the most heavily regulated of American industries. Many of the legal constraints on the use and disposal of subsurface minerals have their origins in early English common law, which said some useful things about mining hard minerals but offered little guidance on the subjects of oil and natural gas. American state courts realized that petroleum was not a stationary resource like a coal seam and observed, in fact, that oil wandered around rather freely, migrating across property lines and behaving very much like an underground river or a free-ranging wild animal. Because oil and gas were migratory and (until produced) invisible, the courts in some states such as Oklahoma and Louisiana decided that such minerals could not actually be owned until they had been "captured" and reduced to possession. This concept has been referred to as the *rule of capture.* In states that adopted this view (variously called *nonabsolute ownership*, *nonownership*, or *nonownership in place*), the person who owns a fee simple estate cannot own subsurface oil and gas until these minerals have been separated from their natural habitat and reduced to possession. Instead, he or she owns the land's surface, the exclusive right to drill for minerals, and the right to retain any minerals produced. The rule of capture, as first enunciated by courts in nonownership states, gave a landowner title to all the oil and gas that could be produced from wells on the estate—even if it could be proved that some of these minerals had been drained from under a neighbor's land. The unlucky neighbor had no recourse except to drill wells and capture oil as fast as possible on his or her own estate.

The courts in other states such as Texas and West Virginia took a different view, one that affirmed the ownership of minerals "in place"—that is, under the surface of the land. This theory is called *absolute ownership*, or *ownership in place*, and it states that oil and gas are part of the land and can be fully owned even before they are produced and are visibly flowing from a well. Even states with an absolute ownership view of minerals, however, acknowledge that oil and gas can move around under the surface in ways impossible to control. So, oil that travels across a property line and moves to a well on the other side leaves its owner, who loses title to it. The new owner acquires title until someone adjacent drills a well and drains away the property in turn.

In practice, then, neither theory of mineral ownership prevented neighbors from draining each other's property. So long as the rule of capture was applied in disputed cases—as it was in nearly all states—a landowner's only real protection for a mineral estate was to drill his or her own well. When it finally became apparent that drilling practices were leading to overproduction corresponding to a crash in prices and destruction of the landscape, as it did in the East Texas oilfield (fig. 1.2), state legislatures were forced to pass conservation laws to regulate production and create agencies to enforce the laws. The kinds of laws enacted varied from state to state. For example, Texas, which had imposed martial law for several weeks in the East field in an attempt to control the overproduction occurring there, found it

***Figure 1.2.** East Texas saw the consequences of the rule of capture, unchecked by regulation. In that place, contractors established wells side by side in a race to drain the reservoirs, causing a crash in the price of oil and the destruction of the water drive—the natural mechanism of the reservoir that draws in water as oil is drawn out so that pressure is maintained.*

advisable to pass fairly strict laws about well spacing. West Virginia, on the other hand, left the spacing of shallow wells relatively unregulated. Many of these conservation laws were challenged in the courts, but most were upheld. State regulatory agencies such as the Texas Railroad Commission (TRC or RRC) and the Oklahoma Corporation Commission (OCC) came to be charged with the responsibility for enforcing sound conservation rules, preventing waste of valuable resources, and protecting landowners' *correlative rights.* (Correlative rights are the rights of the owner of each property in a pool to produce without waste a just and equitable share of the oil and gas. Two landowners with tracts over the same producing reservoir should both enjoy benefits from it—in proportionate measure to the size of their parcels of land.)

Limitations on mineral ownership:

- Legal limitations
- Economic constraints

Today, several state and federal agencies involve themselves in regulatory questions. For example, though the landowner might never deal directly with the *Environmental Protection Agency* (*EPA*), this agency can certainly affect his or her legal transactions, particularly where the use of chemically treated water is used to hydraulically fracture the oil and gas reservoir underneath the subsurface, thus raising concerns about contaminating the underground supply of fresh water (fig. 1.3).

Further, both state and federal government agencies such as the *Bureau of Land Management* (*BLM*) might own minerals adjacent to a landowner's minerals and may limit whether the landowner's minerals can be pooled with the agency's minerals to form a spacing unit. This leaves the offsetting landowner no choice but to have a well of his or her own to avoid drainage by those agencies.

Courtesy of EnerMax, Inc. Photo by Bret Boteler

***Figure 1.3.** The water lines of a fracturing operation, or "frac job"*

Economic Constraints

The other constraints upon a mineral estate owner are chiefly economic. No matter how potentially valuable the minerals under the land, a private individual often lacks the money required to explore that land, drill it, and capture the minerals. Even a mineral estate owner who succeeded in raising the money would still be dependent upon the highly specialized technical knowledge and skills of geologists, engineers, drilling and production crews, and (in most cases) marketing and legal personnel. Under present circumstances, oil and gas resources are more difficult to produce than before at a profit and sophisticated techniques and equipment are increasingly used. It is not surprising that landowners generally allow someone else to search for and produce the minerals beneath their property.

LANDOWNERS AND TYPES OF ESTATES THEY OWN

Once a landowner has decided to lease, is he or she free to do so? A landowner can usually *execute* a valid oil and gas lease if the land is held in fee simple. Property can, however, be held by types of ownership other than fee simple, and even a fee simple arrangement can be complicated if the owner severs the surface from the mineral estate. The type of ownership of a tract of land directly affects how it may be leased for the purposes of mineral exploration and production. The most common types of owners of land with production potential are surface owners and mineral owners. With respect to leasing, surface and mineral owners might be restricted in what they can do with the type of estate they own, as explained in the sections that follow.

Surface Owners and Mineral Owners

The owner of a surface estate has historically had little say about the leasing and production of subsurface minerals. Surface owners still have little say about who leases minerals, but they have begun to assert themselves more vocally about the techniques used to produce the minerals, as techniques can affect the surface estate directly. The mineral estate owner, on the other hand, subject only to the limitations of the deed and various laws and regulations, can enter the property, use as much of the surface as is reasonable to explore for oil and gas, and produce the minerals for his or her own profit. The owner of the mineral interest might also have the right to execute an oil and gas lease (thereby becoming the *lessor*). The *lessee* (an oil company, for example) in turn receives the right to enter the property and the right to explore, conduct drilling and operating activities, build roads, and install gathering lines, tanks, and other aids to the reasonable development of the mineral estate.

Rights of the lessee:

- Explore
- Build roads
- Install equipment
- Operate
- Produce

Whether or not there is any cooperation and consultation between surface and mineral estate owners, the courts usually uphold a lessee's rights to enter and develop leased property. By law, surface owners can generally do little to restrict these rights. Any surface owner who turns back the drilling trucks at the gate risks a court judgment that allows damages to a lessee denied access. These damages can include the increased costs of drilling and any loss of oil and gas from drainage to production on adjoining land. If, on the other hand, surface and mineral owners are on good terms that they wish to maintain, the mineral estate owner might wish to provide pre-agreed surface damage compensation to the surface owner in the oil and gas lease. In some areas, lessees might even give surface owners small *royalty* payments to which they have no legal claim but that offer some compensation for damaged surface property.

A royalty is a percentage of production paid to the mineral owner, either as cash or as a part of the minerals.

The surface owner in all states is normally entitled, at a minimum, to reasonable compensation for damage to the surface estate that is the result of drilling operations. Some states such as Oklahoma have also passed statutes that affect the relationship between the mineral estate owner or the lessee and the surface owner. Therefore, parties to a lease should review the laws of the state where the well is to be drilled to determine whether unusual requirements exist before operations are begun and, of course, the oil and gas lease itself to determine if the lessee has a contractual duty for damage to the surface.

Life Tenants and Remaindermen

A *life tenant* does not have full legal title to property but rather the exclusive right to possess and use it during his or her lifetime, and cannot leave the property to heirs. A *remainderman* has a future interest in the property and will come into possession of it upon the death of the life tenant. Because they share interests in the land, both the life tenant and the remainderman should, under ordinary circumstances, execute an oil and gas lease together. If the remainderman does not execute the lease along with the life tenant or at least *ratify* (approve and confirm) it, the lease will expire when the life tenant dies. That possibility could become an unpleasant and expensive reality for a lessee if the death were to occur in the middle of production.

With all the needed signatures available, the lessee's only problem is how to pay rentals, royalties, and *bonuses* to the parties concerned. Some states have statutes that determine who is entitled to receive the payment of rentals, royalties, and bonuses. For example, the life estate owner might be entitled to rentals only, while the remaindermen are entitled to the actual bonus and royalty payments. Absent any statutory or common-law requirements, these payments should, ideally, be specified in the lease itself, and the lease should be signed by both the life estate owner and the remaindermen. Failing any agreement between life tenants and remaindermen, the matter should be referred to an attorney for advice.

Cotenants

Types of cotenancy:
- Tenancy in common
- Joint tenancy (with a right of survivorship)
- Tenancy by the entirety

Cotenants (also known as *co-owners*) are people who own land together. The two most commonly recognized types of cotenancies are the *tenancy in common* and the *joint tenancy* with a *right of survivorship*. With both types, cotenants are entitled to equal possession and use of the land. But only joint tenants may also exercise a right of survivorship—that is, inherit the interest of another cotenant when that cotenant dies. Under a tenancy in common scheme, when a cotenant dies, the interest passes to devisees in a will or to the cotenant's heirs.

Whether one cotenant of a joint tenancy can lease the land without the consent of fellow owners is a disputed point. Some states do not permit a co-owner to lease without such consent. A number of states do permit that, while stipulating that a lease obtained from a single co-owner applies only to that owner's interest and cannot be held to bind anyone else. A lessee then becomes, legally, a tenant in common with the other owners and as such may enter the land and search, drill, produce, and so on. In a small number of states, if the lease obtained by a company does not have signatures from all the cotenants (including those who own very small fractions of interest), the company may not be able to obtain a drilling permit or might be considered to be in trespass when it enters upon the property to drill a well.

In a majority of states, cotenants who did not sign the lease cannot be held responsible for the costs of exploring and drilling a well that proves to be dry. Should a well prove productive, nonjoining co-owners do receive a share in the profits after the drilling party has recouped the costs of drilling, development, production, and marketing that can be attributed to the nonjoiners' shares.

Once a lease has been signed, nonjoining cotentants might later decide to ratify (confirm) the lease rather than share the ongoing costs of producing wells and additional development. It is also fairly common, especially when many cotenants are involved, to have one cotenant sign a base lease and all the others sign a lease *ratification*. Finally, some states have *forced pooling* statutes that require unleased cotenants to join in drilling a well on pooled land or to lease their interests to the lessee. The terms of such leases are set down by the relevant governmental authority.

Married Persons

U.S. systems of marital property ownership:

- Community property
- Tenancies by the entirety

Anyone seeking an oil and gas lease from a married person would be prudent to have both spouses sign the lease. There are still situations—and states—that require both signatures, particularly states with the type of ownership for married couples called *tenancy by the entirety*. In states where that type of ownership is recognized, both spouses' signatures are required to sell or encumber the property in any way. Some states that recognize *community property* (such as California) and most noncommunity property states require both spouses to sign, as well. (Community property is shared property, or property acquired after the marital community has been formed; what each spouse owned before marriage remains his or her separate property provided that it is not commingled, or mixed with the community property so that it cannot be distinguished.) In addition, if the land to be leased is part of the homestead and its leasing will cause the homestead to be encumbered, both husband and wife are required to sign the lease. *Homestead property* consists of the land, house, outbuildings, and sometimes other things (tools, for instance) that are occupied or used by the owner and his or her family. Where homestead property is recognized, it cannot be seized by creditors (people or companies owed money) except under special circumstances.

LANDOWNERS AS AGENTS OF THE STATE

In Texas, owners of mineral-classified lands share proceeds from mineral leasing with the state.

In many countries, the government is the sole owner of all subsurface minerals, and anyone wishing to produce those minerals must deal directly with the government concerned (fig. 1.4). In Texas, the same situation once existed. In its first constitution, the Republic of Texas followed the legal examples of Spain and Mexico that declared all minerals under the land to be property of the crown, or state. Later, the state of Texas changed its laws to conform to the English model of private and fee ownership. Then it gave its land commissioner the power to classify land at the time of *patenting*. (Patenting is simply the granting of land by the sovereign—that is, by the state power that holds the title.) The land commissioner classified property according to its use, and those tracts that were *mineral-classified* remained, so far as their minerals were concerned, the property of the state of Texas. A citizen who obtains the patent to a mineral-classified tract can fence it, farm it, and enjoy all the rights of fee ownership except the right to fully control leasing and fully profit from its minerals.

Certain lands patented in Texas between 1895 and 1931 were mineral-classified. The state still has the title to any minerals found under those lands. In 1919, however, Texas passed the Relinquishment Act, which was interpreted by the court in *Greene v. Robinson* (Tex. 1928), to mean that the surface owner of a mineral-classified tract is—for leasing purposes—the agent of the state. The surface owner can execute an oil and gas lease on his or her land and receive 50% of all the economic benefits from that lease. The other 50% goes to the state. If a Texas landowner is in any doubt as to whether his or her land is mineral-classified, the Commissioner of the *General Land Office* (*GLO*) in Austin, Texas, can provide information. Oil and gas leases on such property must be executed on official forms supplied, filled in, and approved by the General Land Office.

Figure 1.4. In most of the oil-producing nations outside of the United States, rights to minerals are owned by the central government.

REPRESENTATIVES OF MINERAL ESTATE OWNERS

Fiduciaries

A *fiduciary* is a person in a special relationship of trust who acts in a legal capacity solely for the benefit of another on a particular task. The following types of fiduciaries are ones that are commonly involved in managing the estates of others.

- *Executors* and *administrators* of estates
- Legal *guardians*
- *Trustees*
- *Attorneys-in-fact* (persons acting under *powers of attorney*)
- Representatives of unknown or missing heirs of a mineral estate

Generally, the ability of each type of fiduciary to execute a valid oil and gas lease on the behalf of the other depends upon the laws of the state in which the property is located and the specific provisions of the instrument that empowers him or her to act.

Executors and Administrators

When a landowner dies *intestate*, or without leaving a valid will, the court appoints an administrator to oversee the deceased owner's estate. An administrator can generally execute oil and gas leases with the authority of the court. Gaining the court's approval depends upon procedures that vary from state to state. When the deceased landowner's heirs take possession—according to the state's laws of *descent and distribution* (table 1.2)—those heirs may then execute valid leases on their inherited property.

Table 1.2
A Typical Descent and Distribution Scheme

The following descent and distribution scheme represents a typical one, rather than a particular one for a given state. Statutes for each state determine how property passes when a person dies intestate. Consult a particular state's probate code to find the relevant statutes for any given situation.

Heir(s)	Share of Estate
Spouse	100%
Children	Equal shares amounting to 100%
Parents	Equal shares amounting to 100%
Siblings	Equal shares amounting to 100%
Descendants of siblings (nieces, nephews)	Equal shares amounting to 100%
Grandparents	Equal shares amounting to 100%
Remaining descendants of grandparents (aunts, uncles, cousins)	Equal shares amounting to 100%
Next-of-kin (remaining relatives)	Proportionate shares according to degree of relationship to deceased amounting to 100%
Escheat to state	100%

The table shows the order of eligibility of each class to take property. If there is no surviving member in a class, the property is distributed to the next class of takers in the row below. If there is a surviving member in a class, no property passes to the next class.

In another situation, a landowner dies, leaving a will that names someone to carry it out. That person named, the executor, is not usually able to execute mineral leases unless the will under which he or she acts expressly allows it. In some states, even an independent executor with court authority cannot execute an oil and gas lease unless the will explicitly gives him or her the power to do so.

Guardians

Guardians manage property for persons legally unable to manage it themselves—for minor children or the mentally incompetent, for example. Whether appointed by the court or named in a will, guardians have the power—when acting under court order—to execute oil and gas leases. They need to be familiar, however, with the state statutes that regulate leases granted on behalf of persons in special legal categories. Many states have enacted laws that make leasing the property of minors and the legally incompetent considerably easier than it once was, but the prospective lessee—as well as the guardian—should examine these laws carefully for special procedures and provisions.

Trustees

A *trust* conveys property to a *legal person* (who is defined as an individual, a partnership, or a corporation) for the benefit of a third party.

It is always desirable that a trust instrument give trustees the power to execute oil and gas leases. If a trust agreement is silent on this point (in other words, it does not address it), state law might still permit a trustee to grant leases, particularly if the trustee is authorized to sell the property. If the trust merely allows the trustee to mortgage the property, the power to lease is not automatically carried as an additional right. In Texas, for instance, a trust instrument that explicitly invokes the Texas Trust Act gives trustees quite liberal powers to execute leases. In other states, the appropriate language can similarly empower trustees to grant mineral leases.

Persons Acting under Powers of Attorney

When a legal document is recorded, it is entered into public records.

A power of attorney is a legal instrument giving written authority to a person to act for another. An attorney-in-fact, or person acting under a power of attorney, cannot, in most instances, execute oil and gas leases for the other. Other powers—to bargain, sell, grant, and convey property—do not carry the right to grant mineral leases unless that additional authority is explicitly set out in the instrument. A power of attorney must be executed and recorded according to state statutes. Finally, a power of attorney ends with the death of the person who granted it unless it is drawn so as to survive disability, which can include death. Before accepting a lease from anyone acting under such a power, the lessee should examine the instrument's specific provisions, its execution, and its *recording* (if recording is required). The lessee should also ascertain the current status of the holder.

Representatives of Unknown or Missing Heirs

It sometimes happens that mineral owners or heirs remain unknown or simply cannot be located even after diligent efforts to find them. In such a case, some states allow a judicial *transfer* or judicial *determination of ownership* by the filing of an application at court to appoint a receiver to represent the missing owner and to execute oil and gas leases on the property.

SUMMARY

- A landowner has many rights, but they are not unlimited. Constitutional provisions, federal and state statutes, administrative rules and regulations, case law, the type of land interest possessed, and any legal agreements that the owner has entered into might restrict how land can be used, conveyed, or taken away.
- An unqualified landowner holds title to the surface of the land and to minerals such as oil and gas that lie beneath it. That means that he or she may sever the estate, or divide it into surface and mineral estates. He or she may, by the same measure, lease the subsurface to another party, who can produce the minerals.
- An oil and gas lease is the legal instrument that grants the right to search for oil or gas and produce them on someone else's property. With such a lease, the owner of the mineral land is the lessor and the party that will make use of the estate is the lessee. The surface estate and the mineral estate can be leased independently.
- Court holdings did not prevent the destructive frenzy of well construction that took place in some fields as owners of adjacent tracts of land competed for the same underground resources. So regulatory agencies at the state and federal levels have been granted powers to restrict mineral production.
- Traditionally, when a dispute has arisen between a surface owner and a mineral owner or lessee, the law has often favored the one involved in developing minerals, although it has acknowledged claims by surface owners for reasonable damages.
- Type of ownership determines the terms under which an estate can be leased. The owner may hold the estate in fee simple (with the fewest restrictions), as a life tenant (until death), as a remainderman (after the death of the life tenant), or as a cotenant (sharing an interest in the estate along with others). The owner may share the estate under marriage, as well.
- When the estate is held by a life tenant, the lessee has an interest in getting both the tenant and remainderman to execute the oil and gas lease to avoid a situation where the lease ends abruptly during production because the life tenant dies. When a lease is sought from someone who might share property, such as a married person or a cotenant, it is advisable to seek signatures from other co-owners and be informed of how co-ownership affects the leasing relationship.

- In Texas, some lands are called "mineral-classified," which means that the surface owner can execute an oil and gas lease but must share half the proceeds with the state because the state owns the minerals.
- Fiduciaries acting on behalf of a landowner may or may not be able to execute an oil and gas lease. For example, the administrator of an estate generally has the authority to do so, while an executor only has that authority if it is explicitly granted in the will. Guardians and trustees often have the authority, while persons acting under a power of attorney do not.

2

State and Federal Lands

In this chapter:

- Obtaining information on leasing state lands
- Types of federal leased lands: onshore public domain land, acquired land, Indian land, and offshore land
- Government agencies involved in leasing federal lands: the Bureau of Land Management, the Bureau of Indian Affairs, and the Bureau of Ocean Energy Management
- Procedures for leasing each type of federal leased land

While much of our nation's oil and gas is located on privately owned land, large amounts of both are to be found on state and federal lands. (Extensive private ownership of mineral resources is the exception, not the rule, among nations. See Appendix J to learn about mineral ownership in Canada.) The various state legislatures, as well as the United States Congress, have made provisions for the leasing of some (though by no means all) of this publicly held land to the petroleum industry. Chapter 1 discusses one set of conditions—in Texas—under which a mineral estate severed from the surface estate can be leased by the surface owner acting as agent for the state. On such mineral-classified lands, the government and the private citizen may share the economic rewards of successful mineral development. When the government owns both surface and mineral estates, leasing might still be possible if the appropriate procedures are carefully followed.

STATE LANDS

The *Texas Register* is a journal that posts notices about rules and regulations of Texas state agencies.

The leasing of state lands is a matter of separate, rather piecemeal legislation, instead of a uniformly applicable code (fig. 2.1). Each state has a board or an agency to handle applications for mineral leases. Competitive bidding is commonly conducted on state-supplied forms. However, specific procedures, lease terms, and expected payments for a successful venture vary widely among the states, as does the maximum acreage that any individual or corporation may lease. Table 2.1 lists the leasing agencies for state lands. The prospective lessee should also understand that leasing procedures and terms are subject to change from year to year. Anyone planning to lease from a state agency should request a copy of the Lease Sale Notice and become very familiar with its instructions, procedures, and terms.

In Texas, for example, a bidder can read the state's leasing regulations in the *Texas Register*, which is available online. The state's General Land Office can also help with interpreting the regulations. A truly thorny legal question might best be put to the Texas Attorney General's Office. These same sources can provide information on how to lease from cities, counties, school districts, and other political units of the state. Veterans' land tracts are governed by special rules, and these rules—along with lease forms—may be obtained from the Veterans Land Board in Austin.

Figure 2.1. In Alaska, land in private ownership outside of native lands makes up less than 1% of the total land. The rest is owned by the state, the federal government, or native peoples.

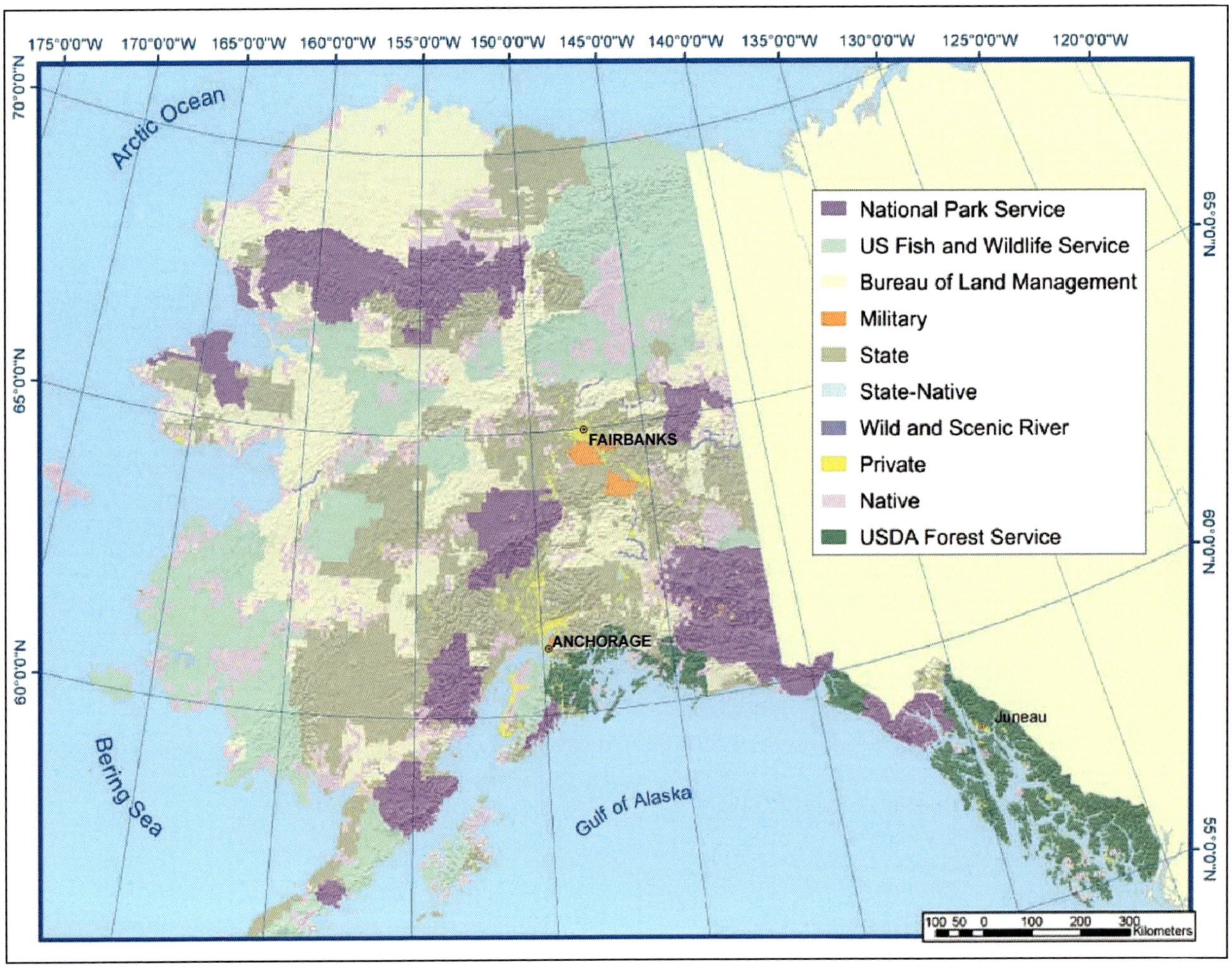

Courtesy of World Resources Institute

Table 2.1
Leasing Agencies for State Lands

Alabama	Department of Conservation and Natural Resources
Alaska	Department of Natural Resources
Arizona	State Land Department
Arkansas	Department of Environmental Quality
California	Department of Conservation
Colorado	Department of Natural Resources
Connecticut	Department of Energy and Environmental Protection
Delaware	Department of Natural Resources
Florida	Department of Environmental Protection
Georgia	Department of Natural Resources
Hawaii	Department of Land and Natural Resources
Idaho	State Land Board
Illinois	Department of Natural Resources
Indiana	Department of Natural Resources
Iowa	Department of Natural Resources
Kansas	State Conservation Commission
Kentucky	Department for Natural Resources
Louisiana	Department of Natural Resources
Maine	Department of Conservation
Maryland	Department of Natural Resources
Michigan	Department of Natural Resources
Minnesota	Department of Natural Resources
Mississippi	Department of Environmental Quality
Missouri	Department of Natural Resources
Montana	Department of Natural Resources
Nebraska	Department of Natural Resources
Nevada	Department of Conservation and Natural Resources
New Mexico	Energy, Minerals and Natural Resource Department
New York	Department of Environmental Conservation
North Carolina	Department of Natural Resources
North Dakota	Department of Trust Lands
Ohio	Department of Natural Resources
Oklahoma	Commissioners of the Land Office
Oregon	Division of State Lands
Pennsylvania	Department of Natural Resources and Conservation
South Carolina	Department of Natural Resources
South Dakota	Department of Environment and Natural Resources
Tennessee	Department of Environment and Conservation
Texas	General Land Office
Utah	Department of Natural Resources
Vermont	Agency of Natural Resources
Virginia	Department of Conservation and Recreation
Washington	Department of Natural Resources
West Virginia	Division of Natural Resources
Wisconsin	Department of Natural Resources
Wyoming	Office of State Lands and Investments

States not included in the table are ones without significant oil and gas resources.

FEDERAL LANDS

Federal lands cover approximately one-third of the United States and are managed by the U.S. *Department of the Interior* (*DOI*) (fig. 2.2). These lands include national parks, military properties, and wildlife refuges, which are generally not made available for mineral exploration. The federal government, as land owner, leases in accordance with its specified rules of care for the environment, orderly development of national resources, and receiving a fair-market value for the use of its lands. The Bureau of Land Management (BLM) is responsible for onshore lands except those controlled by Native Americans; offshore lands fall under the jurisdiction of the *Bureau of Ocean Energy Management* (*BOEM*). For the purpose of mineral leasing, the federal government classifies tracts that are leased into several categories, including the following:

- *Onshore public domain lands*
- *Acquired lands*
- *Indian lands*
- (*Federal*) *offshore lands*

Table 2.2 provides a summary of the leasing authorities for each type of public land.

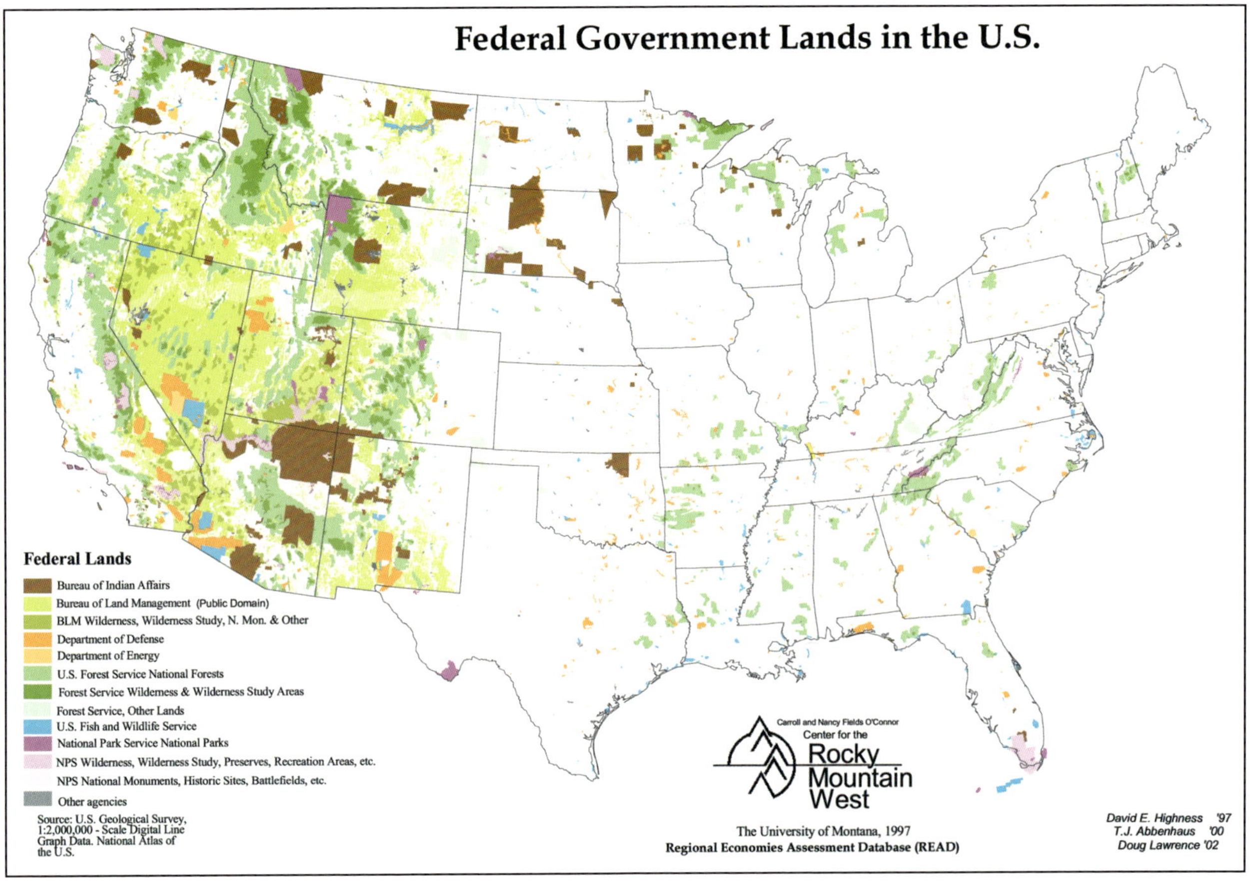

Source: O'Connor Center for the Rocky Mountain West, 2002

Figure 2.2. Management of federal lands by U.S. government agencies

Table 2.2
Leasing Authorities for U.S. Public Lands

State Lands	See Table 2.1 for a list of state leasing agencies.
Federal Lands	
Onshore public domain lands	Bureau of Land Management
Acquired lands	Bureau of Land Management
Indian lands	
Tribal lands	Bureau of Indian Affairs and the relevant tribal council
Allotted lands	Bureau of Indian Affairs
Offshore lands	Bureau of Ocean Energy Management

Public Domain Lands

The *Code of Federal Regulations* is a collection of the rules and regulations of the federal government organized by subject.

Land in the public domain is land originally owned by the United States that has not subsequently been disposed of (granted to another owner). Both the surface and the mineral estates of those lands belong to the United States. The federal government has also reserved the mineral rights to some property patented to individual citizens, just as the state of Texas has with its mineral-classified lands.

When oil and gas leases were first obtained for public lands, back in the 19th century, existing mining laws were applied to the transactions. These laws proved so unsatisfactory, though, that in 1920, Congress passed the Mineral Leasing Act specifically to authorize leasing federal lands for the development of minerals. Although the Act has been amended a number of times, it still governs the leasing of onshore federal lands in the public domain. Leasing procedures for those onshore lands are controlled by the U.S. Department of the Interior and by the BLM. The bureau will supply copies of its regulations upon request; questions should be sent to the appropriate state office. Most federal lands in Texas, New Mexico, and Oklahoma, for example, are supervised by the New Mexico BLM office in Santa Fe, although some fall under the jurisdiction of the BLM in Cheyenne, Wyoming. The detailed terms for onshore leasing can also be found in Title 43 of the *Code of Federal Regulations*, Part 3100—available online, in law libraries, and in many large public libraries. Prospective lessees must be aware that the rules for leasing can change and might not be consistent in different BLM offices across the states. The BLM uses two types of leases for oil and gas exploration: competitive and noncompetitive.

Competitive Leasing

The Federal Onshore Oil and Gas Leasing Reform Act of 1987 requires that public lands available for oil and gas leasing be offered by competitive leasing first. Once the BLM has offered the lands competitively and not received a bid,

The primary term is the initial period of time within which a well must be drilled to keep the lease in force.

it is allowed to issue non-competitive leases. Each lease sale is publicly announced and widely advertised. The Lease Sale Notice will detail the special terms and conditions associated with the leases offered and contain a detailed description of the lands available for leasing. The BLM conducts lease sales using auctions. Leases are awarded to the highest qualified bid submitted; the agency has a right to reject bids that do not meet certain criteria.

To qualify, bidders must be adult U.S. citizens—whether bidding as individuals or in groups—or corporations formed under federal or state laws. Corporations whose stockholders include a specific percentage of aliens (non-citizens) must furnish the BLM with special information as outlined in that agency's regulations. Aliens may not themselves hold leases on federal lands, and no person may hold leases, whether competitively or noncompetitively acquired, on more than 246,080 acres in any state, with the exception of Alaska. The Alaska limit is 300,000 acres in each of its two leasing districts. (See Appendix C for more information on leasing in Alaska.)

Lease terms are established by each individual BLM office and can vary. A California BLM lease sale held in 2009 provided for a minimum bonus bid of $2 per acre, a 10-year *primary term*, a 12.5% royalty, and annual rentals of $1.50 per acre for years 1 through 5 and $2.00 per acre for years 6 through 10. Successful commercial production extends the life of a lease beyond the end of the primary term. Once production ceases or the lease is relinquished by the lessee, the BLM is able to lease the land again.

Noncompetitive Leasing

Lands that do not receive a bid at the lease sale are made available on a first-come, first-served basis to those who file either a noncompetitive presale offer or a noncompetitive day-after-sale offer. A qualified bidder can obtain forms for each type of noncompetitive offer from the BLM office.

An interested party can submit a presale offer by completing the appropriate paperwork accurately describing the lands as shown in the Lease Sale Notice and by paying a filing fee and the first year's rental. If the BLM does not receive a bid on that particular tract, the offer will be accepted and a lease issued. A presale offer has priority over any day-after-sale offer.

Submitting a noncompetitive day-after-sale offer is similar to the presale offer, except that it can be submitted on the day of the lease sale or any day thereafter. Day-after-sale offers submitted on the day of the sale or the day following the sale are considered to be simultaneously filed. In this case, a drawing will be held to determine the winner. After the day-after-sale drawing, any remaining tracts are available for a period of two years.

Because it is common for lessees to subsequently wish to transfer, or *assign*, all or a portion of their interest in a lease, they should be aware that all assignments of federal leases must be approved by the BLM before any such assignment is effective.

Acquired Lands

Acquired federal lands, as their name indicates, were obtained by deed from previous owners. In 1947, the Mineral Leasing Act for Acquired Lands gave the Secretary of the Interior the authority to lease acquired lands in much the same way that public domain lands are leased. However, acquired lands have an additional safeguard against possible damage: The government agency with jurisdiction over a particular piece of property must consent to the leasing of that property's minerals. The agency can also set up special rules to protect the land's primary purpose. Finally, lands located within national parks and monuments—or inside incorporated cities, towns, or villages—are excluded from the act and therefore cannot be leased.

Indian Lands

Title 16, Section 470bb(4) and Title 42, Section 12511 of the *United States Code*, the compilation of federal laws, defines lands of Native American peoples or lands held in trust by the United States for native peoples as "Indian lands" (fig. 2.3), using the term that goes back to the era of the original legislation. Leasing those lands can present special problems and, once again, requires that the lessee be thoroughly familiar with federal regulations. The procedures involved differ somewhat, depending on whether the land in question is tribal land or allotted land. *Tribal land* is land within a reservation or land that is

The *United States Code* is a collection of the federal laws of the United States organized by subject.

Courtesy of the National Atlas of the United States of America

Figure 2.3. The Bureau of Indian Affairs administers 56 million acres of land held in trust for Native Americans and Alaskan Natives. The map depicts the largest land units administered by the BIA—ones that are at least 23,000 acres in size.

Types of Indian lands:
- Tribal lands
- Allotted lands

owned by a Native American tribe, group, or band. *Allotted land* has been legally defined so that a specific individual uses it, but the United States retains control over any leases or conveyances affecting it. In either case, a person should conduct a very careful *title check* before making an application for a mineral lease on Indian land. The required records might be found in one of the following offices: the relevant state office of the *Bureau of Indian Affairs (BIA)*, the office of the Director of the BLM (both in Washington, D.C. and in the state where the land is located), and the office of the *county clerk* for the relevant county. All of these sources should be checked. If the land has a leasing history, it should also be carefully examined to make sure that all federal regulations have been followed and that no question about title is likely to affect a new application.

Whether the prospective lessee wishes to bid on tribal or on allotted land, the rules to be followed can be found in Title 25 of the *Code of Federal Regulations*, Chapter 1, Subchapter I. For tribal lands, permission to lease must be sought from the tribal council; for allotted lands, requests go to the BIA. The BLM serves in an advisory capacity to tribes on the matter of leasing but it does not lease minerals on Indian lands. Notice of Lease Sales for both kinds of land is published well in advance of the sale. Bids are made according to guidelines set out by the Secretary of the Interior, and successful bidders must provide required bonds with each lease.

There are some reservations in Oklahoma, Wyoming, and Montana that have their own separate rules for mineral leasing. A bidder planning to deal with one of these reservations should consult the subchapter of the *Code of Federal Regulations* cited in the previous paragraph.

Offshore Lands

The submerged lands of the Outer Continental Shelf are controlled by the federal government.

The *Outer Continental Shelf (OCS)* can be defined, for practical purposes, as the submerged land seaward from state-owned lands to a distance extending approximately 200 miles from the coast. Offshore lands stretching from the shoreline seaward for 3 nautical miles belong to the coastal states. Texas and Florida—on its west coast—own the land to a distance of 9 nautical miles from their shores. Between the 3- or 9-mile lines and the 8,000-foot depth line lie the federally controlled areas of the Outer Continental Shelf (fig. 2.4). These federal offshore lands are leased according to the terms set out in the Outer Continental Shelf Lands Act of 1953, which has been amended several times in subsequent decades. The guidelines for opening OCS lands to exploration and development are established by the Bureau of Ocean Energy Management. The BOEM is charged with the management of the nation's natural gas, oil, and other mineral resources on the Outer Continental Shelf.

The OCS Lands Act provides that all lease sales must first be included in a Five Year Program. The current program approved by the Secretary of the Interior covers lease sales through 2017. Each program can take years to receive final approval, due to a lengthy process that requires extensive review from bordering states, state and federal agencies, and environmental

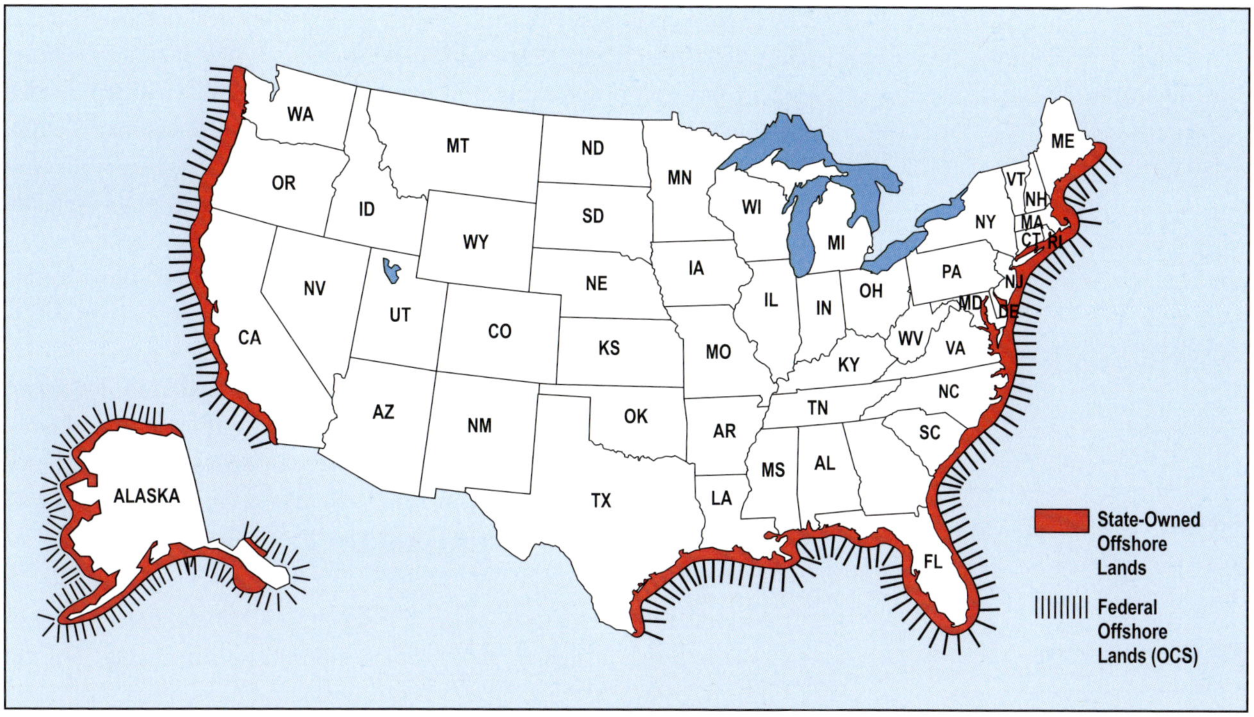

Figure 2.4. Lands off the shore of the United States are owned by the government: from the shore to 3 or 9 nautical miles out by state government, from 3 or 9 nautical miles out to the 8,000-foot depth line by the federal government.

impact study groups. Public hearings are also conducted on the programs prior to final approval by the Secretary of the Interior.

If a program is approved and a sale is held, the process of bid submission, lease terms, and restrictions are detailed in the Final Notice of Sale (FNOS). The bid form is also included in the notice. Bids are completed and then submitted in a sealed envelope. The minimum acceptable per-acre bonus, primary term, annual rental, and royalty are set and published in the notice. Bids are evaluated by the BOEM based solely on the bonus offered in the sealed bid. Some terms vary based on water depth. In the Gulf of Mexico, from shallow water to deep water, the current minimum acceptable bonus ranges from \$144,000 to \$216,000, the rental ranges from \$7 to \$11, and primary terms range from 5 to 10 years. Royalty is fixed at 18.75%. For example, 56 companies submitted bids for Central Planning Area Sale 216/222, which was held in 2012. There were 593 bids submitted on 454 blocks; 90 blocks received multiple bids. Although the minimum acceptable bid was \$216,000 per block for deepwater blocks, the high bid at the sale was \$157,111,000 for a 5,700-acre lease covering Mississippi Canyon Block 718. The sum of all high bids was \$1,704,500,995.

Companies are allowed to bid alone or form partnerships in order to submit a joint bid. Companies on the BOEM list of Restricted Joint Bidders are not allowed to bid together in partnerships. Those are companies that produce at least 1.6 million barrels of oil equivalent on a daily basis worldwide. The sale is open to the public, and bidding begins at 9:00 a.m. the day of the sale.

The BOEM then evaluates each bid in a 90-day process to determine if it is adequate, as the agency is charged with ensuring all bids meet fair-market value. Companies submitting bids must declare if they own any pre-stack depth migrated seismic data over a block for which they submitted a bid. Following the sale, the BOEM might request a copy of this seismic data to determine bid adequacy. If a bid is rejected, the block then becomes available for the next lease sale, which is likely to take place one year later.

SUMMARY

- In the United States, there are many types of federal land, including national parks, wildlife refuges, Indian land, and offshore federal land. Among these types of lands, many can be leased for the production of oil and gas. The type determines, in each case, what agency is charged with the administration of leases and what procedures must be followed to lease the land.
- Procedures for leasing in individual states vary widely. Each state has its own board or agency that handles applications for leasing, and the process commonly takes place as competitive bidding on forms supplied by the agency. State lands are typically onshore, although coastal states have offshore lands up to a certain distance from their shores (where the Outer Continental Shelf—and the limit for federal lands—begins).
- Tracts of federal land available for leasing are designated as onshore public domain land, acquired land, Indian land, and offshore land.
- The Bureau of Land Management administers the leasing of federal onshore lands except for Indian lands. These include onshore public domain lands and acquired lands. Lands for lease are first offered for competitive bidding; if no bids are received, the BLM is allowed to accept offers that meet minimum requirements such as meeting market price.
- The Bureau of Indian Affairs administers the leasing of Indian lands. The BLM assists the BIA in its tasks in various ways, such as by supervising operations on those leased lands and offering advice to the BIA and tribes that own lands for lease.
- The Bureau of Ocean Energy Management administers the leasing of offshore federal lands. These are the lands of the Outer Continental Shelf between state offshore lands and the lands underlying international waters.
- The procedures for leasing federal lands are determined by rules in the *Code of Federal Regulations* and rules of the respective DOI agency charged with leasing.

In this chapter:

- Purpose of the land description
- Units of measurement used in land descriptions
- Types of land descriptions used in the United States
- Metes and bounds land descriptions
- Public Land Survey System land descriptions
- Descriptions of urban subdivisions
- Importance of having a complete description of property

3 Land Measurement and Land Description

To be valid, a conveyance of land—by lease, by deed, or by will—must include a *legal description* of the property being transferred. An adequate description, whether it appears in the conveying instrument or in an earlier document cited by the instrument, should permit the tract to be identified on the ground; it should also distinguish the tract from neighboring properties. In the United States, however, this task of describing land is somewhat complicated by history. The fact that various parts of U.S. territory were acquired from other countries—gradually, and by means ranging from purchase to conquest—means that there is often not a single, consistent method of identifying and describing land. There is no single, uniform set of measurements for setting out the lengths, breadths, and areas of individual pieces of property. Most landowners know the dimensions of their tracts in acres, feet, and miles, but to obtain those measurements, some owners—particularly in the southwestern states—must convert various traditional Spanish or French units of measurement to U.S. customary units. Many landowners will identify their property by means of the U.S. government's *Public Land Survey System* (*PLSS*), but some must use a considerably older method known as *metes and bounds*,

A legal description is one that situates the property geographically so that it can be located.

even when their land has been surveyed and recorded on an official *plat*, or surveyor's map. The discussion of units of measurement and of methods used to divide and describe property must include these variations on the standard systems.

UNITS OF MEASUREMENT

Traditional European units of measurement in land surveys:

- Varas
- Links, chains, and rods
- Arpents

Descriptions of land originally claimed, possessed, and surveyed by the English will generally be set out in feet, yards, miles, and acres. Thus, property owners in Massachusetts or Virginia, for example, will commonly find—when they investigate old documents that describe their land—these familiar English units of linear and square measurement. They might also find slightly more esoteric units of the kind once employed by surveyors in the British Empire: the *links*, *chains*, *rods*, and so on that have their origins in particular pieces of surveyor's equipment. (Figures 3.1 and 3.2 show traditional and modern surveying tools. Tables in Appendix L set out traditional English measurements for land and their customary U.S. equivalents.)

Many property titles, however, do not go back to English claims. They derive instead from so-called *foreign grants*, or property originally granted to an individual landowner by Spain, France, or Mexico when those nations still owned territories that were incorporated into the United States. Titles are based upon such grants in parts of Florida, Louisiana, Colorado, Utah, Nevada, California, Arizona, New Mexico, and Texas. In the last four states, anyone who goes to the county courthouse to look up the legal documents pertaining to a piece of land might find—at the far end of the title chain—a grant set out in Spanish *varas* rather than in English units of measurement.

Figure 3.1. It was once common for English surveying equipment to include a measuring chain. The actual length of the surveyor's chain was used as a measure of distance across land.

Figure 3.2. Modern equipment used in conducting land surveys includes Global Positioning System (GPS) devices.

Similarly, a person who undertakes such a search in Louisiana might find a grant using French *arpents*. Use of the arpent is especially common in southeastern Louisiana; in Texas, the Spanish vara is more likely to be applied to land in the southern and eastern portions of the state.

A problem for anyone wishing to translate French and Spanish measurements into English ones is the degree to which they vary—the vara from state to state and the arpent from one Louisiana parish to another. (Tables in Appendix L provide customary U.S. equivalents for traditional Spanish and French units used to measure land.)

Finally, something should be said about the International System (SI) of Units, the modern form of the metric system of measurement. Not many landowners or lessees will encounter land descriptions given in *metres* (the basic linear unit) or *hectares* (the basic square unit). Several states have considered adopting SI/metric measurements, but surveys continue to be measured in customary U.S. units. Many government agencies, including the Bureau of Land Management (BLM) and the Bureau of Ocean Energy Management (BOEM), have not yet converted to the SI system. (Tables in Appendix M show how to convert SI/metric measurements into their customary U.S. equivalents.)

International System (SI) units such as metres and hectares are not commonly used for land surveys in the United States.

METHODS OF DESCRIPTION

Settlers in what is now the United States often did not survey land or record those surveys. They simply took possession, moved in, and began clearing and farming their new property. Only later did they realize the advantages of laying out tracts according to a regular system. By that time, land ownership in much of New England and the frontier states resembled a patchwork quilt. Even tracts inside the 6-square-mile townships that were laid out in parts of the 13 colonies (and in Vermont, Maine, Kentucky, and Tennessee) were sometimes of varying sizes and shapes. Surveying and recording these tracts did not make them any neater. On the contrary, surveying land after it has passed into private hands merely acknowledges the patchwork pattern—or lack of pattern. Tracts of the patchwork variety can be described, however, by a method called "metes and bounds."

Metes and Bounds

"Mete" comes from a root word meaning "to measure" and is closely related to another root meaning "post" or "tree." "Bound" is simply a limit or boundary. A description of land by metes and bounds, then, relies on natural and artificial monuments such as riverbeds, stream courses, rocks, roads, ridges, and even fences that often serve to delimit one piece of property from another to establish the perimeter of a property. In other words, a metes and bounds description is one of the shape of a property as defined by its boundaries.

The place of beginning is the point where a metes and bounds survey starts.

The metes and bounds technique begins with a fixed reference point, called the *place* or *point of beginning* (*POB*), and follows the property perimeter, describing the *bearing*, or direction, of each survey line in terms of the cardinal points on the compass and degrees of a circle (fig. 3.3) along with the distance that the survey line continues in that direction. The bearing can be given with greater precision if minutes (1/60 of a degree) and seconds (1/3600 of a degree) are added. A perimeter line might be described, for example, as South 13 degrees, 44 minutes, and 40 seconds West, 185.83 feet (S 13°44'40" W 185.83'). Metes and bounds also allows a surveyor to measure more organic boundaries with a subset of sophisticated techniques using arcs of a circle. A property that is correctly measured using the technique will have a perimeter that "closes," so that the description ends at the place of beginning (fig. 3.4). If that is not the case, it is an indication that there is a discrepancy in the measurements.

The bearing of a survey line is its direction of travel.

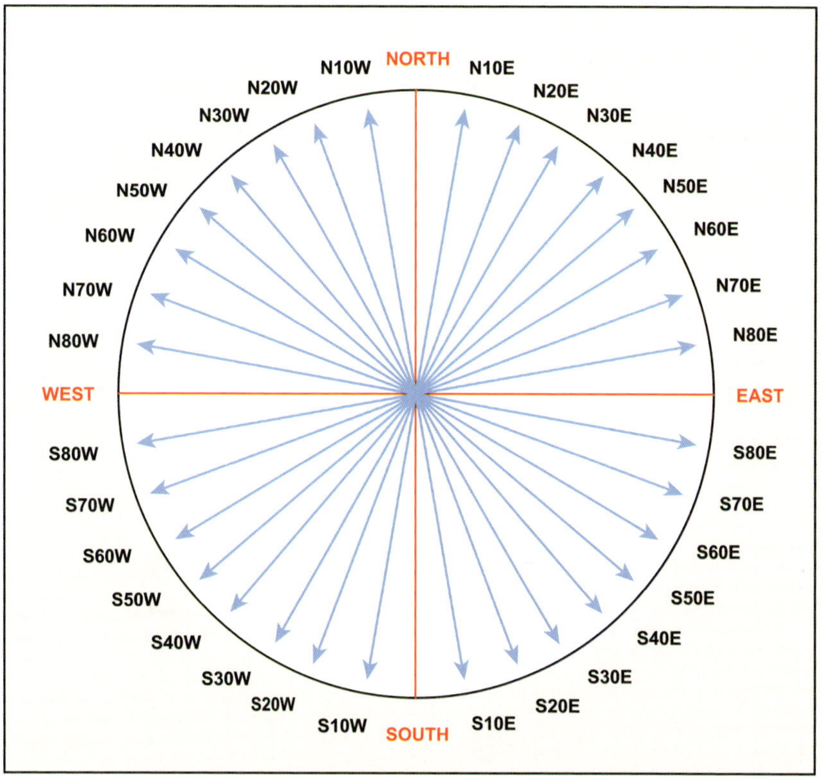

Figure 3.3. This drawing demonstrates how the direction of each boundary line of a property is measured for a metes and bounds description. Comparing an individual property boundary to the lines with a similar bearing on the compass will allow an estimation of the measurement.

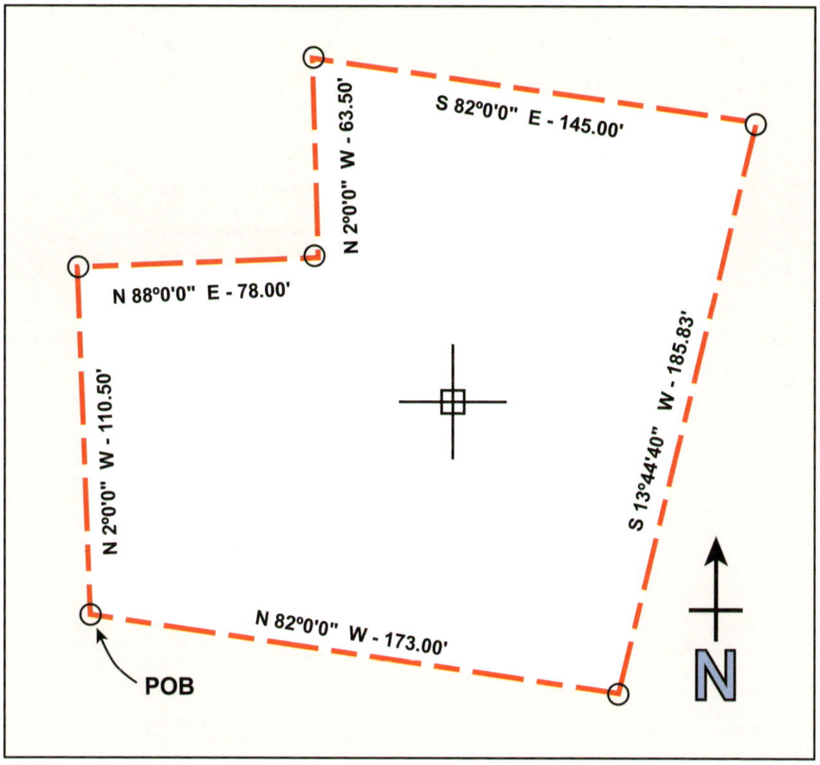

Figure 3.4. This simple plat shows the bearings and distances of the property lines as they are typically identified by surveyors. It also shows the conventional abbreviation for place of beginning, POB. Note that the perimeter of the property closes at the place of beginning.

SOURCE: WWW.IAMMEA.ORG/GGINGRAS

Metes and bounds surveys use natural objects such as rocks and streams as markers, even though those markers might move over time.

Descriptions by metes and bounds are still used, not only in the states we have mentioned, but also in parts of the South and Southwest, where the French, Spanish, and Mexican governments often granted land in tracts of irregular shape and size. Such foreign grants in California have now been integrated into the U.S. Public Land Survey System, but Texas—which kept title to its public lands when it came into the Union—has never been part of that system. Areas of Texas, therefore, have their own survey pattern, and still consist of small, irregular tracts that must be identified by county and individual survey (fig. 3.5). Where land has been surveyed in parcels, as in many Texas counties, and a given piece of property does not fill up an entire survey, descriptions must rely to some degree on markers such as trees, streams, rocks, and so on. Thus, if a property is coextensive (in other words, it has the same boundaries) as the land in a survey conducted by the J. J. Puffin Railroad Company, describing that property is quite simple. If, on the other hand, that land consists of a small wedge-shaped tract in the northeast corner of the survey, a description of it might require mention of two small streams, a protruding piece of granite, a mesquite tree, and a neighboring stock tank.

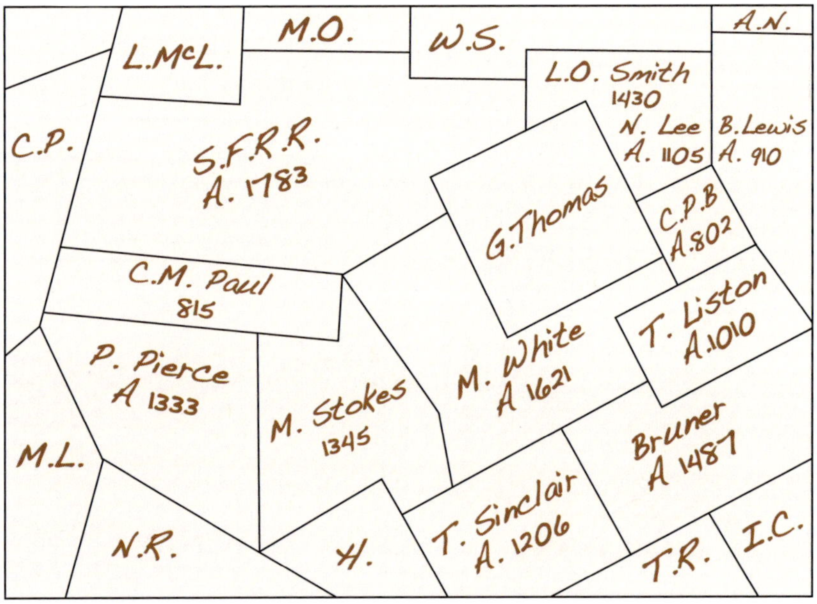

Figure 3.5. Small, oddly shaped surveys in a Texas county

Public Land Survey System

In 1785, the Continental Congress adopted an ordinance calling for a rectangular system of land management to be used in all newly acquired territories lying north of the Ohio River. That system is now known as the Public Land Survey System. Ohio was the first state to benefit from the system; later, the rectangular survey system was used in Alabama, Florida, Mississippi, the states north of the Ohio River, and those west of the Mississippi River (with the exception of Texas).

Public Land Survey System:

- A Congressional township is a square unit of area.
- Meridians and base lines are lines.
- Ranges and townships are columns and tiers.

The basic unit of the system, a square 6 miles wide and 6 miles long, is called a *Congressional township*. (Its dimensions were clearly suggested by the colonial township mentioned earlier.) To cut a region up into Congressional townships, surveyors start from the intersection of a north-south line called a *principal meridian* and an east-west line called a *base line*. Figure 3.6 shows the principal meridians and base lines of the United States. Additional parallel lines are marked off and numbered at 6-mile intervals on either side of the principal meridian and the base line. A region is thus divided into east-west (horizontal) tiers commonly referred to as *townships* and north-south (vertical) columns called *ranges*; the intersections of these townships and ranges form 6-mile squares.

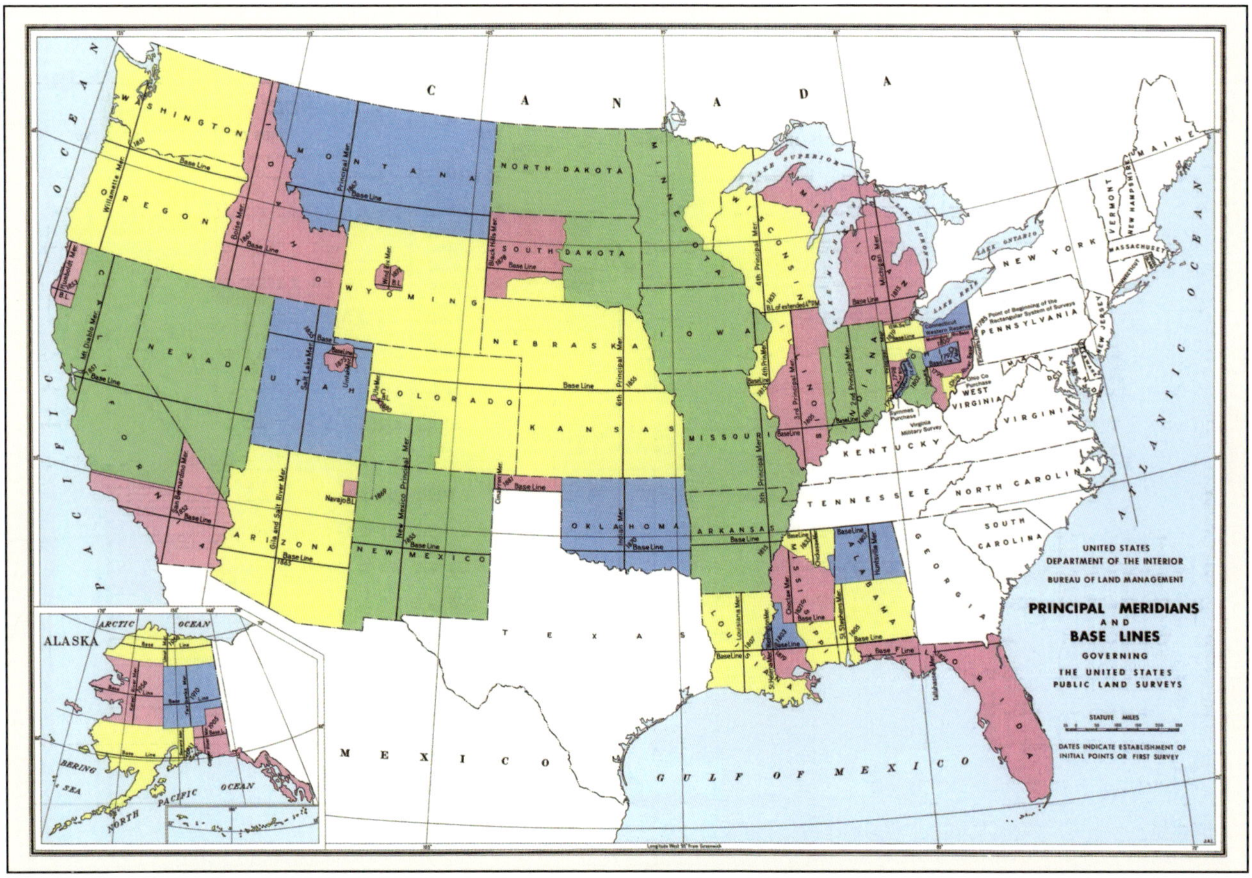

Source: U.S. Geological Survey

Figure 3.6. A map showing principal meridians and base lines of U.S. public land surveys. States that are not shaded in color on the map are ones that have not historically been part of the Public Land Survey System; land descriptions in those states are often in metes and bounds.

Figure 3.7 illustrates this pattern of townships and ranges; it also shows the first step in identifying a particular tract by locating the Congressional township in which it lies.

Each Congressional township is further divided into 36 sections of a square mile, or 640 acres. These sections are numbered from 1 to 36, starting in the northeast corner with number 1 and going straight west to number 6, then dropping down one tier and going straight east to number 12. The pattern is repeated until the southeast corner (section 36) has been reached. Figure 3.8 shows a plat of a Congressional township with the shaded sections representing the 6-mile square itself and the lighter rows representing adjoining sections of neighboring Congressional townships. (It should be noted that not all Congressional townships are precisely 6 square miles, owing to the convergence of lines marking ranges that follow the curvature of the Earth.)

Finally, each section of a Congressional township is subdivided into quarters of 160 acres and smaller fractions like eighths (80 acres), sixteenths (40 acres), and so on. The trick to reading a subdivided section number is to remember that each division stands in the same relation to the quarter as the quarter stands to the section as a whole. Each subdivision, that is, will be indicated by letters and numbers that locate it within the section, the quarter section, the quarter-quarter, and so forth. Figure 3.9 locates a 20-acre tract in

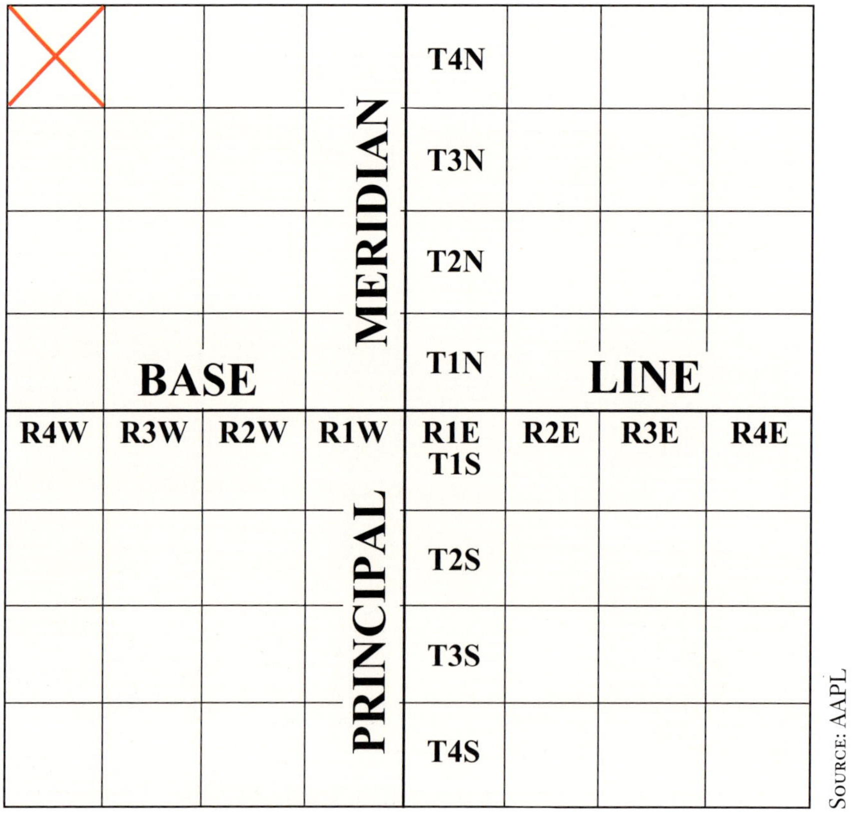

Figure 3.7. Township numbers are vertical, and range numbers are horizontal. A Congressional township is located at Township 4 North, Range 4 West (in the 4th tier north of the base line and the 4th column west of the meridian).

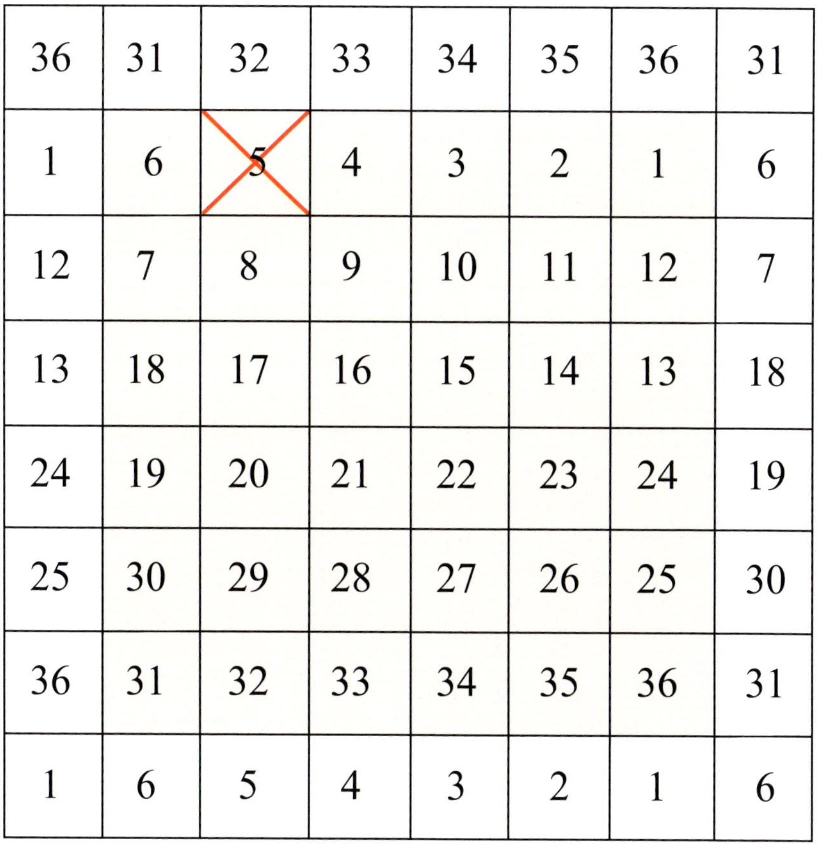

SOURCE: AAPL

Figure 3.8. A plat of a sectioned Congressional township. A hypothetical tract lies in Section 5, and its legal description can be extended to read section 5 T4N R4E.

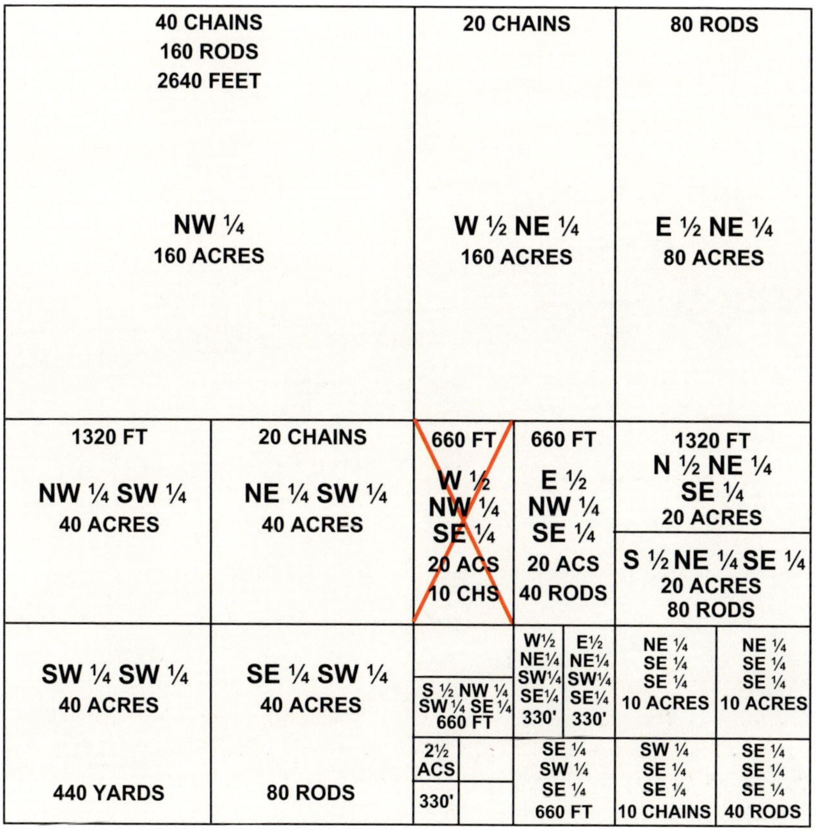

SOURCE: AAPL

Figure 3.9. A subdivided section. An X marks the 20-acre tract that can be fully described as W ½ NW ¼ SE ¼ of section 5 T4N R4E, Tornado County, Kansas.

the southeast quarter of a divided section. It further pinpoints the location by specifying the northwest quarter of that quarter—and the west half of that quarter-quarter. To locate a small parcel of land within a subdivided section, then, read the numbers backward.

One caution for reading subdivisions: Look carefully for commas. They indicate separate tracts and can make a great difference in the number of acres under discussion. For example, a reading of S ½, NW ¼ indicates two tracts—the first amounting to 320 acres (one-half section) and the other 160 acres (one-quarter section). The total number of acres is 480. Without the comma, the description would run S ½ NW ¼, describing a single tract of 80 acres.

Urban Subdivisions

Individual lots, often small, make up the blocks of a typical town or city subdivision (fig. 3.10). These lots are usually quite easy to find on a subdivision plat; all the blocks are numbered and each lot on a block is also numbered. After a housing subdivision (generally owned by one person or company) has been surveyed, the entire tract is mapped to show the arrangement of streets, blocks, and lots. The legal description of a lot ready for sale might read: *Lot 10, Block 6, of the J. D. Hepplewhite Subdivision to the City of Dallas, per plat on file in Book..., page..., of the Map Records of Dallas County, Texas.*

Figure 3.10. Blocks and lots form regular patterns in urban subdivisions. They are differentiated by numbers on plats.

COMPLETENESS OF DESCRIPTION

In any transfer of land, a clear and complete description of the property is essential; the description should allow a property surveyor to actually locate the property on the ground. Confusion as to what land has been conveyed can lead to title problems and even to litigation. To be clear and complete, a legal description should include the following items: the names of the county or parish and the state in which the land lies; details of any known survey plat, with its date, surveyor's name, and recording information; and the date (with book and page references to the recording of the transaction) on which the present owner acquired the land. If the land appears in the U.S. government's public system, the section, portion of the section, township, and range should be listed. If more than one meridian runs through the state, the name of the relevant meridian should be given, as well. Property not included in the public system must be carefully described by metes and bounds with the names of the bounding owners, a description of all bearing marks, and any other information needed for unambiguous identification. For urban property, a description should include the names of the subdivision and the city, the lot and block numbers, and a reference to the surveyor's plat with the name of the surveyor, date of the survey, and details about the recording.

SUMMARY

- To be valid, a conveyance of land must include a legal description of the land being transferred or refer to a previously recorded document that contains a legal description. The description must allow a person to identify the property on the ground and distinguish it from other properties. A complete property description can prevent litigation.
- Because various areas of the United States once existed as territories whose inhabitants used different systems of measurement, traditional measurements appearing in land descriptions often vary from region to region and from conventional measurements used today. English survey systems have traditionally used links, chains, and rods; French systems, arpents; and Spanish and Mexican systems, varas.
- There are two primary methods of land description currently used in the United States: the metes and bounds method and the Public Land Survey System method. Modern plats of urban subdivisions are derived from coordinates of one of the methods previously described but typically add lot and block numbers.
- Land described in metes and bounds can form an irregular pattern. The method is based on the principle of describing the overall shape of a tract of land. A survey begins at a fixed location, the point of beginning (POB), and then measures the distance traveled and the bearing along the perimeter back to the POB. Natural and artificial monuments, such as trees, rocks, and markers placed by the surveyor, are used as reference points when a property is surveyed for a description.

- The Public Land Survey System is made of a grid of lines corresponding to longitude (meridians) and latitude (base lines). Additional parallel lines are added between those that form units 6 miles wide by 6 miles long, called "Congressional townships." Each unit is subdivided into 36 sections, with each section covering 1 square mile and 640 acres. The system allows its users to identify where the tract is located within the system of meridians and base lines.

In this chapter:

- Preliminary explorations before a company attempts to negotiate leases
- Roles of geologists, landmen, lease brokers, and attorneys early in the leasing process
- Preliminary title checks
- Sources of information for title checks
- Concerns of the landman and of the landowner in negotiating a lease

4 Preparations for Leasing

PRELIMINARY EXPLORATIONS

When negotiating an oil and gas lease in preparation to explore for hydrocarbons, many operators find that they must take into account a greater degree of business savvy and bargaining power on the part of mineral interest owners than was once the case. Whether these owners are public agencies or private citizens, today more of them are treating their mineral rights as assets to be rationally managed rather than as unfathomable mysteries best managed by others. Private owners, for example, are organizing themselves into groups like the *National Association of Royalty Owners* (*NARO*) to keep up with relevant tax laws, plan lobbying strategies, and exchange information on everything from accounting systems to the going royalty rate in the area and the royalty language in a lease. Not all owners are this concerned about their minerals, of course, and some mineral owners are still unaware that they even own mineral interests outside their home county or state. Nevertheless, owners have responded to a variety of conditions—including a series of highly publicized energy crises and a shaky national economy—by becoming better-informed custodians of their mineral resources. The work of geologists and geophysicists, landmen, and lease brokers in identifying and leasing oil and gas properties has become correspondingly more sophisticated and challenging.

Geologists and Geophysicists

Resources for company geologists and geophysicists:

- Maps
- Published data
- Well logs
- Well production figures
- Professional associations
- Private scouting companies
- State regulatory agencies
- Seismic studies

The decision to acquire leases in a given area—along with related decisions about how much to offer, what to concede in the way of special conditions and clauses, and so forth—rests upon the best geophysical or geological information that a company can procure. In a "hot" area, information about the subsurface and its possible oil- or gas-bearing formations could be relatively scarce. There can be frenetic leasing activity in new areas, for instance, even though data is lacking. Speculation can be rife in such areas, precisely because there has not yet been the opportunity to gather clear information. Producing areas, on the other hand, might offer information in easily accessible forms. Company geologists or geophysicists can often do quite a bit of exploratory work from their offices—using maps and other kinds of published data, as well as logs and production figures from existing wells. Further information can be gleaned from professional associations (such as the *American Association of Petroleum Geologists*, or *AAPG*), from private scouting companies, from well-log libraries (most of which charge their members a fee and provide them with various data services), and from state regulatory agencies. When seismic information must be obtained on the land, a petroleum company will seek the consent of the landowner before conducting tests. The two parties might enter into a contract known as a *seismic option agreement* that allows seismic exploration for a specified price per acre. The company can then set up its equipment, generate underground vibrations, and measure them to learn about subsurface formations. Once enough information has been gathered, the company can then lease the acreage that seems most promising for a price agreed upon in the contract (assuming a lease has not already been signed by the parties).

The larger the company, the more time and money it can generally afford to spend on exploration. Large companies can also invest in the latest technological refinements to improve their information, although even small companies can now take advantage of automated systems for data storage and retrieval, computerized mapping, and computerized risk estimates. No matter how large the operation, however, or how ample and sophisticated the information obtained for it, an element of guesswork always remains. The hunch often plays its part, especially in areas where production is not yet under way. The question persists: How much information is enough to justify leasing? Or, as one operator put it, "Do we lease as much as we can and then finish our homework? Or do we gather data until we're just about certain and then try to lease what's left?" Most companies try to strike a balance between timely acquisition of leases and reasonable completeness of information. There is always the risk, on the one hand, of losing *prospects* to rival operators; on the other hand, no one wants to commit precious capital to a venture that, with a little more exploration, would have revealed itself as unpromising. Therefore, a company might be interested in obtaining oil and gas leases and seismic agreements simultaneously.

Landmen

A prospect is an area that is considered to have production potential.

Once the geologists have identified a prospective area of interest, they outline it on a plat or map that goes to the company land department. A *landman* must then find out whether the tracts lying within the area of interest are available for leasing and, if they are, who owns the relevant mineral rights. During a preliminary check of the records (to be described later in this chapter), the landman might discover that all of the desired tracts are already under lease. If, however, some promising land is still available, the landman will obtain company management authority to acquire leases and go on to the next stage of the work—contracting with landowners and offering to lease their property. After the leases have been acquired and before actual drilling begins, a more intensive examination of records and titles will be necessary. A part of this work might also be undertaken by the landman. Finally, an oil company's land department must monitor the continuous development of its leased properties, oversee royalty and other payments, and make day-to-day decisions on matters of major and minor concern. For example, if a portion of the prospective area is currently leased by another company, a landman might need to arrange complicated joint ventures with the other oil company before drilling can proceed; he or she might similarly need to pacify an angry surface owner who claims to have lost 10 heads of cattle from circumstances relating to well operations.

To accomplish their various tasks, landmen should have a good working knowledge of the law—especially of property, inheritance, oil and gas, and tax law. They should be familiar with the drafting, executing, and recording of certain kinds of legal instruments; and they should be able to do certain kinds of legal research. Some landmen are, in fact, attorneys, although more hold degrees in business or petroleum land management. Landmen need, in addition, a thorough familiarity with the state and federal regulations that affect their work. State agencies such as the *Texas Railroad Commission* (*TRC or RRC*) or the *Oklahoma Corporation Commission* (*OCC*) formulate the rules that govern well spacing, well density, *pooling* procedures, and other crucial details. To be uninformed of any such rules—or of conditions that might warrant an exception being granted to one or more of them—is to risk losing opportunities to lease.

Finally, to be successful, landmen must be persuasive, socially adept and adaptable, well-informed, and comfortable in meeting, talking, and negotiating with a wide variety of people. Unless they can convince landowners to sign leases (assuming that the prices the company will pay are reasonable), they will fail at the primary task.

Lease Brokers

A *lease broker* is, essentially, an independent landman. He or she often works with several operators or companies in a given area; a company landman might coordinate the efforts of one or more independent brokers, relying on them to do much of the legwork of preliminary record checks and the "people work" of preliminary or even concluding negotiations. Brokers often live in the areas where they work for a period of time. Their intimate knowledge of the local situation—its land, its people, and its resources—can be very valuable to representatives of large companies. This local knowledge, when accompanied by the proper experience, can make the broker more effective in the field than a company landman; the company landman can then become more nearly an administrator and a negotiator with other companies. The lease brokers report back to the company landman on the status of title checks or lease negotiations. In many cases, a broker will need authorization from the landman to pay a higher bonus or royalty to a mineral owner.

PRELIMINARY TITLE CHECKS

Purpose

Types of title studies conducted by lessees:

- Preliminary title checks
- Examinations of title

A runsheet is a list and brief description of all the documents pertaining to a land's title.

A preliminary check of the records, or title check, performed by a landman or lease broker before a lease is signed should not be confused with the much more detailed *examination of title* performed by a lawyer after a lease is signed. In the first instance, the landman wants to know the names and addresses of the current mineral interest owners so that he or she can negotiate a lease. The landman also wants to learn who owns the surface of the land that is of interest, whether the property (both surface and subsurface) is already leased or otherwise encumbered, and whether any of the owners of that property are legally unable to execute a lease. The job of the landman at this point is to clear the way for a new lease.

The more information that the landman can collect in this preliminary search, the better. It will save steps later on. It could also uncover problems that, had they come to light only after a lease was agreed upon, could have caused the company considerable difficulty. The landman does not usually aim, however, at establishing which owners have good title to land. A good title is one that can be sold or successfully defended in court. A lawyer who specializes in title work will establish who holds good title—along with the full legal status of the land in question—once a lessee has decided to drill a well. As part of the preliminary work, the landman will learn the owners of record, try to look at all the documents in the land's history of ownership, and briefly describe these documents in a *runsheet*, which can later be handed over to an attorney who plans to make a full examination of title.

Sources of Information

The *statute of frauds* is a term referring to many laws across the states that require certain kinds of contracts to be evidenced in writing to be enforceable. Among these contracts are ones for real estate. The "paper trail" created by the requirement facilitates research for anyone who wishes to learn the history of a tract's ownership. The instruments relating to that history (or copies of them) are nearly always recorded and filed in public county offices. Portable copies of such tract ownership records are called *abstracts of title* (fig. 4.1). The landman in search of information about a given tract approaches the following sources to find records:

- State and federal agencies
- *Abstract companies* or *title companies*
- County clerk offices
- Landowners

Most real-estate transactions are evidenced as written documents because of the requirements of the statute of frauds.

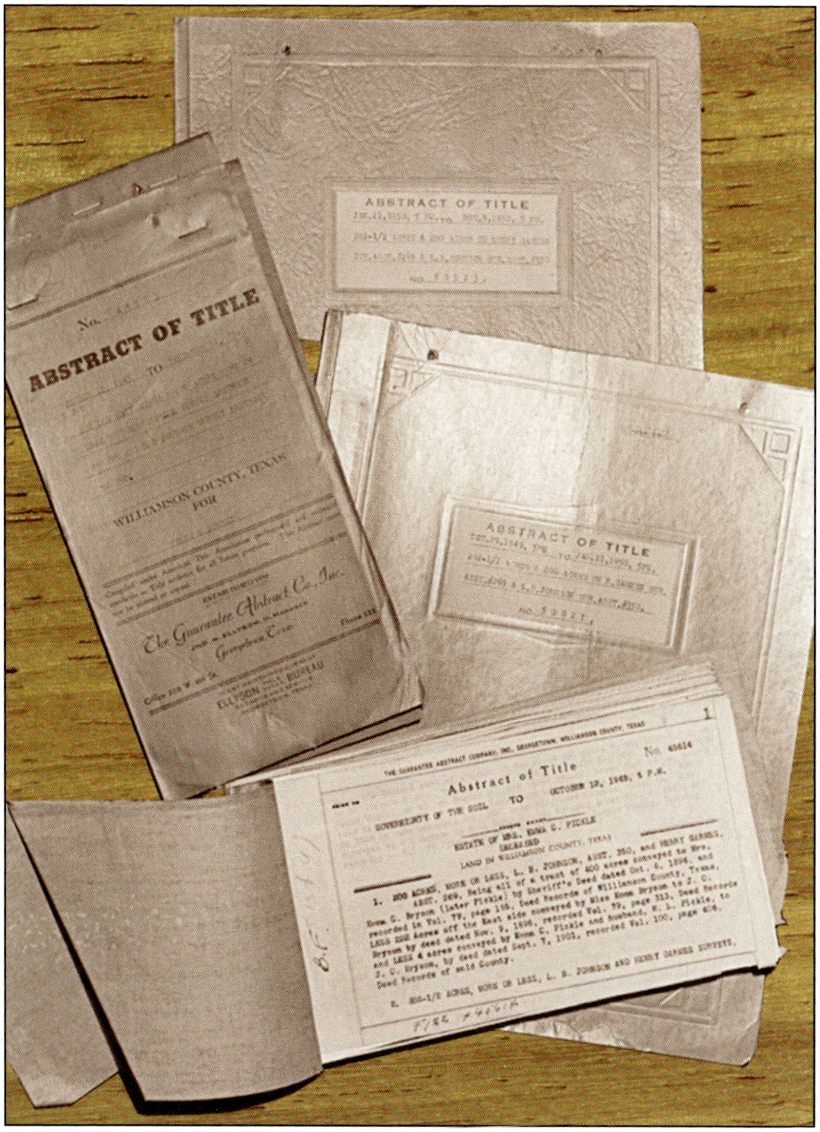

Figure 4.1. An abstract of title traces the history of ownership of a property.

State and Federal Agencies

Information about state-owned lands can be obtained from the state agencies listed in Chapter 2. (See table 2.1.) Records relating to lands owned by the U.S. government are on file in Washington, D.C., in state land offices of the Bureau of Land Management (BLM) and of the Bureau of Ocean Energy Management (BOEM). A landman is well-advised to check the records in these state offices, even if the company employs a Washington attorney to look over the records in the national BLM office. The Washington files might not contain all the information needed for leasing.

Abstract or Title Companies

An abstract of title is a full collection of documents pertaining to a land's title.

Where the landman begins a search for the owners of privately held property depends upon his or her experience and resources. Some years ago, the search would very probably have begun with a visit to an abstract company. Such companies, also known as *abstract plants*, were primarily in the business of preparing and selling abstracts of title. They kept indexes and records, which they sometimes allowed landmen to examine free. These indexes were a very helpful place to begin a check of the records; from them, the landman could learn the book and page numbers required to find the relevant instruments in the county records. Today, however, a landman would be lucky to be given free access to those types of records by a private company. There are a number of reasons for the change.

First, many abstract companies, especially in larger cities and towns, have been replaced by or transformed into title companies. Their business has shifted from selling abstracts to insuring property titles. In most states, these insured titles do not involve oil and gas properties; rather, they are sought by lenders, builders, and private sellers of residential and commercial real estate. While the title companies still keep active abstract departments—staffed by researchers, examiners, and abstractors—they are mindful of increased costs. Even plants that still specialize in oil and gas work resist the idea of giving away information. One abstractor added that, "Our files are hard to use without special instructions. We don't want people misplacing or misfiling our materials." A veteran landman agreed that carelessness in the use of abstractors' files has damaged the old rapport. He also pointed out that privileges like the free examination of indexes have been taken for granted and, in some cases, abused: "If friendly abstract plants are rare these days, landmen have brought the situation on themselves."

A takeoff is a list of all the recorded documents pertaining to a land's title.

Friendly or hostile, most abstract companies will, of course, do work for a fee. A complete abstract that includes all the documents related to a tract's ownership because the original land grant or patent can be extremely expensive to prepare: Some abstracts cost thousands of dollars. The preparation can also be time-consuming. A landman might need information in a hurry and has no wish to pay more for it than is necessary, so he or she often dispenses with a complete abstract in the early stages of the inquiry. In the place of a complete abstract, the landman might order a *takeoff*, a list of all documents filed of record pertaining to a given tract. The takeoff costs far less than a complete abstract, or *base abstract*, and often includes a brief summary or description of the listed documents. Alternatively, the landman might pay a fee to look at the indexes of a plant that allows it. With luck, a friendly plant might make its files available without a charge. Abstract plants vary, of course, and their records are not always complete, reliable, or easy to access. A truly reliable abstract plant can be a real boon—and the preferred starting place—for a landman. An unknown or less reliable one might seem a less-attractive place to begin than the county courthouse.

County Clerk Offices

Each state has its own system for recording legal instruments—a system that depends, in part, on how the land in that state was measured and patented. Recorded instruments are kept in county courthouses; the county clerk (or, in Louisiana, the clerk of court for the parish) can help an inquirer use the courthouse indexes to find legal documents (fig. 4.2). These indexes might be arranged by the names of *grantors* and grantees, by tract (with the instruments relevant to each tract listed chronologically), or by some combination method. In some counties, computers are used to facilitate searches. After locating the instruments pertinent to a title chain in the county indexes, the landman must look at the pages in the books that record the information. This information will include the record owners, any prior mineral reservations or mineral deeds, any existing leases or liens on the surface or mineral estates, and any court proceedings—probates, foreclosures, judgments, and so forth—that might affect title. Records of such proceedings can usually be found in the county clerk's office. Records of tax payments will be filed in the county assessor's office; a check of these records will yield the names and current addresses of people who pay taxes on the tracts in question.

In a conveyance of real property, the grantor transfers the title to the grantee.

Courtesy of J. G. Domke

Figure 4.2. A landman searching for records at the county clerk's office

Landowners

A final and often very helpful source of information is the actual landowner, particularly if he or she lives on the land (fig. 4.3). Some companies, when they are considering tracts to lease, routinely ask their landmen to give landowners printed ownership questionnaires and to obtain as much detail about the land's legal history as possible. Because mineral interest can be very complicated—involving the business (and sometimes the marital) transactions of dozens of owners—detailed knowledge is essential. A landowner who can produce deeds, wills, mortgages, leases, tax records, and so on can be a great help in determining who (if anyone) shares in the ownership of the mineral interests and must therefore be contacted to lease. Resident owners are also more likely to produce partial or even complete abstracts of title when queried about their land's history. Base abstracts are often lent to landmen on the understanding that any supplements ordered to bring the abstract up to date will be given to the landowner when the company has finished with them.

Courtesy of Five State Land Services, Inc.

Figure 4.3. A landman should consider approaching the landowner for information about a land's legal history.

PRELIMINARY NEGOTIATIONS

The landman and landowner carry out the last step in preparing the lease: negotiating the lease instrument. (For a summary of preparations for leasing, see table 4.1.) Landman and landowner do not always negotiate a lease while leaning comfortably on a gate or drinking a cup of coffee. Many leases are negotiated by telephone or letter, and even those that are negotiated in face-to-face encounters are often sold or traded by the acquiring company.

However, when a lease is acquired, its terms are negotiated. Each party wants to make the best deal possible and negotiates with certain questions and constraints in mind. The landman will be mindful of the company's resources and policies and sensitive to the local situation and the going price in the area. The landowner, on the other hand, will be concerned with making an informed evaluation of the landman's offer. The landowner will wonder about additional matters like tract size and spacing—and just how becoming a lessor can affect his or her tax returns.

Table 4.1
Summary of Preparations for Leasing

Step in Preparations	Person(s) Involved
Prelimary Explorations	
Geological scouting and data collection	Geologists and geophysicists
Search for tracts available for leasing	Landmen and lease brokers
Prelimary Title Checks	Landmen and lease brokers
Preliminary Negotiations	Landmen and lessors

Concerns of the Landman

Company Size, Policy, and Financial Resources

A landman's instructions, when he or she is authorized to buy leases, will include the maximum bonus, rental, and royalty that can be paid to landowners, and any permissible variations on the company's standard lease form. (Such variations are discussed in Chapters 5 and 6.) The landman's instructions also authorize him or her to offer a minimum primary term–the initial duration of time within which a well must be drilled to keep the lease in effect so that a secondary (productive) term can be entered into. Clearly, the leasing policies of the buying company will help to set these maximum prices as well as the lower limit on the primary lease term offered. Smaller companies, which usually have more limited financial resources, often have more cautious buying policies. Those companies tend to look for low-risk buys, aiming at steady development and a reliable cash flow. There are high-risk, high-return companies, of course, even among the independents;

Concerns of the landman:

- Bonus, rental, and royalty
- Length of the primary term

small companies of this sort are usually working with promotional money from investors. Larger companies, especially those with diversified interests, can afford to take more and bigger risks. A large company will also find that its land costs—the bonuses, rentals, and royalties it pays landowners—make up a smaller part of its total outlay than is true of a small, independent operator. When a large company can comfortably afford to meet a shrewd landowners' demand for, say, ⅕ royalty instead of ⅛, the small operator might be financially unable to buy a lease on such terms unless the bonus consideration is reduced accordingly.

The length of the lease's primary term might also be more critical to a small company. If the money to drill must be raised through joint ventures that take several years to arrange, a longer primary term is clearly desirable. On the other hand, if a long primary term means an increase in the bonus payment, a short-term lease might have its attractions, considering that a small company's ability to move quickly can give it a competitive edge over larger companies. Large companies commonly bargain for—and can pay larger bonuses to acquire—primary terms of considerable length. From the company's point of view, there is a decided advantage to having ample time in which to finish exploration, make drilling decisions, and raise the capital for test wells and possible completions. The landowner, however, might not see a long primary term as advantageous.

No matter what the size and resources of the company are, its exploration and leasing policies for a particular area will rarely be spelled out anywhere in detail. Silence is protective, and companies naturally wish to withhold from rivals the details of their plans and procedures. If the company landman is utilizing lease brokers to contact and negotiate leases, he or she is prudent to withhold the company's exploration plans from the brokers. If brokers don't know about the company's commitments, drilling objectives, and well locations, they cannot accidentally reveal them; nor do they need to pretend to be unaware of them.

Area Considerations

Bonus, rental, and royalty figures vary widely from state to state. Even within a given state, variations might be considerable: A specific area or even a specific tract might earn offers near the top of the scale, while a neighboring tract or area is leased for a much lower figure. Bonuses, for example, have been as high as $25,000 per acre in very productive parts of shale plays. However, in a state with limited production, a bonus of $5 to $10 per acre has been common; a rental of $1 per acre per year and a primary term of 5 or 10 years will satisfy some landowners.

Between these extremes, historically dependable producing areas can earn bonuses of $4,000 or more per acre; rentals run at $1 or $2 per year, and 3-year primary terms tend to be the rule. With respect to royalties, historically nonproducing areas still commonly receive ⅛ of total production, but 3/16 is becoming the new standard in several states. A 1/6 royalty would be moderately low these days for a promising tract; moving up the scale, some Louisiana and South Texas landowners ask for 1/3 to 1/4. Needless to say, a landman will not make an initial offer that tops the scale of permissible prices or royalties. He or she will try to save the company money, and to that end, might suggest a 5-year lease at the rate of 1/8 royalty and $1 per year in rent. It is up to the landowner, then, to decide whether these figures are acceptable or whether careful bargaining is likely to bring better terms.

Concerns of the Landowner

Concerns of the landowner:

- Bonus, rental, and royalty
- Tract size and spacing

Evaluation of Offers

To evaluate the terms first offered, a landowner will often ask for time to think it over. "Thinking it over" generally means making telephone calls to neighboring owners, bankers, attorneys, accountants, or local lease brokers (if the landowner happens to know any) in order to satisfy the vague idea that he or she might be able to strike a better deal. A landowner who has leased before or who is simply a shrewd manager of the property might already have a good idea of the going rate in the area, having followed newspaper accounts of any drilling or exploration in the neighborhood, investigated state and federal lease sale prices, and joined local associations or even subscribed to information services.

In addition to checking on prices, the landowner will have formed a notion of what constitutes an acceptable primary lease term. If the prospects for production look uncertain or risky, it might be in his or her best interest to grant the lessee as long a primary term as the company proposes. This concession would be especially tempting if it meant a larger bonus. On the other hand, many landowners hold out for short primary terms. A short term can mean prompt development of the property or the opportunity to lease again in a year or two—and to garner fresh bonuses and rentals.

Tract Size and Spacing

Spacing is a measure of how far apart a well is from other wells and how far it is from property lines.

Density is a measure of how many acres are assigned to a well.

The spacing of oil and gas wells is a measure of how far apart in feet wells must be from each other and how far from property or lease lines. Their *density* is defined as how many acres must be assigned to each well. These two properties are determined by the oil and gas regulatory agencies of the various states. These agencies decide how a given pool or reservoir can best be developed while avoiding waste, ensuring efficient production, and protecting the owners' correlative rights. A landowner preparing to lease a property should obtain a copy of the spacing and density regulations that apply to the area, keeping in mind the possibility that exceptions might be warranted in that particular case. He or she might be able to argue successfully for an exception to the rules if the results minimize waste or prevent confiscation of property (by preventing the drainage of hydrocarbons across property lines, for example).

The owner should know, too, that a given oil or gas field might be subject to special rules; the relevant state agency will be glad to provide information on specific areas and fields. Regulatory agencies for top producing states can be found in table 4.2.

Table 4.2

State Regulatory Agencies for the Top Ten Oil-Producing States

1. Texas
   Texas Railroad Commission
   Austin, TX
   www.rrc.state.tx.us

2. Alaska
   Alaska Oil and Gas Conservation Commission
   Anchorage, AK
   doa.alaska.gov/ogc

3. California
   Department of Conservation
   Division of Oil, Gas, and Geothermal Resources
   Sacramento, CA
   www.conservation.ca.gov/dog

4. North Dakota
   Industrial Commission
   Oil and Gas Division
   Bismarck, ND
   www.dmr.nd.gov/oilgas

5. Oklahoma
   Corporation Commission
   Division of Oil and Gas
   Oklahoma City, OK
   www.occeweb.com/og/oghome.htm

6. Louisiana
   Department of Natural Resources
   Office of Conservation
   Baton Rouge, LA
   dnr.louisiana.gov

7. New Mexico
   Energy, Minerals and Natural Resources Department
   Oil Conservation Division
   Santa Fe, NM
   www.emnrd.state.nm.us/ocd

8. Wyoming
   Oil and Gas Conservation Commission
   Casper, WY
   wogcc.state.wy.us

9. Kansas
   Corporation Commission
   Topeka, KS
   www.kcc.state.ks.us/conservation

10. Colorado
    Oil and Gas Conservation Commission
    Denver, CO
    cogcc.state.co.us

Data for the top ten oil-producing states are for the years 2009 to 2011. Source: U.S. Energy Information Administration (IEA), "Crude Oil Production." http://www.eia.gov/dnav/pet/pet_crd_crpdn_adc_mbbl_a.htm. Last viewed June 13, 2012.

Once a landowner knows the well density permitted in a given field, he or she might wish to lease in tracts of that size. For example, if a regulatory agency requires 80 acres per well, an owner might decide not to grant a 160-acre lease but instead to lease in 80-acre tracts. If the lessee can be persuaded to accept these terms, the landowner can be protected from the possibility that the lessee might tie up all 160 acres by drilling and producing only one well on the tract. Leasing in smaller units can leave more land free to be leased later or to be re-leased when a lease expires. A well drilled on one 80-acre tract cannot hold the land in the adjacent 80 acres. The size limits that might benefit an owner vary, of course, from field to field and state to state. Deep wells require far more *acreage* than shallow wells do. For example, the Texas Railroad Commission requires that 640 acres be allocated to deep gas wells, where it might only require 40 acres for oilwells.

A landowner who knows the requirements for well spacing and density might chose to lease in smaller tracts in order to have more than one lease on the land.

From the oil company's point of view, such attempts on the part of the landowner to limit lease size or control spacing are undesirable. Hard bargaining might be necessary before these matters are agreed upon. Some companies have even declared their unwillingness to negotiate with an owner who limits lease size. While a shrewd landowner is rarely so inflexible in his or her demands as to lose the opportunity to lease, he or she might indeed prefer to hold out for a company or operator that is willing to meet some or all of those requirements.

SUMMARY

- A certain amount of preliminary work must be done for the companies that wish to develop in order to determine whether a property is a good prospect.
- Company geologists and geophysicists conduct research using publicly available sources such as maps and well-log data. In addition, companies can acquire proprietary data, such as data from seismic studies. A company might also enter into a seismic option agreement with a landowner, which would allow it to study production potential prior to acquiring a lease. Technology has allowed exploration to become very sophisticated, but there are still elements of guesswork and (therefore) risk involved.
- Once company geologists have identified a potential prospect, a landman conducts research to determine who owns mineral rights to the land and whether the mineral estate is available for lease. If it is, the landman will probably initiate offers and negotiate leases. The landman may also be called on to negotiate with surface owners over property damage.
- Lease brokers work as landmen but on a freelance basis, rather than for an individual company. Because they tend to operate in a particular area all the time, they can offer knowledge of the area and contacts. They report to a company landman about title checks and lease negotiations and often require authorization before they can change the terms of a contract.

- There are several title checks carried out when land is leased for exploration and development. The landman or a lease broker performs a preliminary title check before the lease is signed to determine the names and addresses of the current mineral owners and whether the mineral interest is already leased. The landman will make other determinations during this initial title check, such as who owns rights to the surface and whether the title is encumbered. The documents of record will be listed in a runsheet for later reference when a full examination of title is conducted after the lease is signed.
- Traditionally, records of tract ownership have been compiled in reports called "abstracts of title." An abstract company will put together such a report, but it will probably be very expensive. A landman conducting a title search will more likely have to rely on public records (available online or at a county clerk's office, for example), the records of an abstract company, or the records of the landowner.
- When the landman and the mineral owners enter into negotiations, the landman will be authorized by the company to pay a maximum bonus, rental, and royalty to the landowners. He or she will also have instructions on what kinds of variations are allowed on the company's standard lease form and the minimum length of the primary term.
- Companies do not publish information on the financial terms they offer, even for their own lease brokers, and lease terms vary widely from area to area. So the landowner must look to other sources of information—testimony from other landowners and local lease brokers, newspaper articles, and Web sites, for example—to determine what terms can reasonably be expected.
- A landowner who is ready to negotiate a lease should be informed of the spacing and density regulations that apply to the property. A well-informed owner of a 160-acre tract might discover, for instance, that the state regulatory agency requires only 80 acres of space per well and decide to lease only half of the tract so that the rest remains to be leased to another company.

In this chapter:

- Form leases
- Elements of the lease
- Preamble: the basics of the lease
- Provisions: the various "clauses" of the lease
- Signature block: execution of the lease
- Acknowledgment: verification to make the lease recordable

5 Elements of the Lease

LEASE FORMS

While many standard lease forms varying by state or geographic region are still used today in negotiating a lease (table 5.1), most sophisticated lessors hire attorneys to prepare *addendums* to attach to these standard lease forms or draft a lease form to meet their demands. Regardless of the form, each oil and gas lease contains several basic elements. These include a description of the land, a conveyance of specified rights, consideration for the rights conveyed, and an obligation to drill and to pay a percentage of the production to the landowner.

An addendum is an addition to a completed document. It may correct the document, offer clarification, or add terms to it.

Table 5.1
Types of Standard Lease Forms

Leases from state and federal agencies	
Leases from private companies	• Producers 88 leases • Revised Producers 88 leases
Leases from individuals and associations	• Landowner's leases • Attorney's leases

State and Federal Forms

The forms used by the federal government and by state governments for the lease of their lands are clearly standardized. Many forms are available online. While such forms might vary as to the kinds of property to be leased, a prospective lessee has only to query the proper office to get samples and instructions on how to proceed. In contrast, the lease forms used by private companies vary far more widely. There are literally hundreds of different forms in use, and more are being drawn up all the time.

Forms Published by Private Companies

Leases from private companies requested by name:

- Producers 88
- Bath forms

The Producers 88

Traditionally, many of the lease forms used by the industry have been titled *Producers 88* or Standard Form 88, Producers Special. The "88" title is often joined with a term such as "Revised" or "Pooling." When an operator, landman, or royalty owner mentions a "standard lease," the phrase usually refers to some form of the Producers 88. (Figure 5.1 is an example of a Producers 88 lease form.) As a result of alterations to individual leases, the standard title now runs across the top of hundreds of very different forms, all of them considerably changed from the original Producers Special. That original form was published by an Oklahoma printing company, which simply indicated the number of the form it was currently printing at the top of the document. Historically, the number 88 has, so far as anyone can tell, no more significance than that. The oil and gas lease printed was called a "producer's form" because the printer wanted to create a form acceptable to a number of oil producers in its own state of Oklahoma and nearby states. Because the printing company had the reputation of not changing its forms without changing titles as well, Oklahoma landowners felt that they could rely on the Producers 88 as a standard oil and gas lease. The form quickly became so popular that many landowners refused to sign leases that did not bear the familiar title. (In Louisiana, the closest thing to a standard lease form is probably one of the Bath forms printed by the M. L. Bath Company of Shreveport.)

Revised Versions of the 88

The original 88 form was, of course, drawn up to meet the needs of those who would be obtaining leases. Today, many oil and gas companies have their own 88 forms, and careful attention is given to drafting the clauses in these updated versions of the Producers Special. A number of printing companies also produce 88 forms and revise them regularly to keep them consistent with court decisions on leasing. Indications of such revisions generally appear on the form, often in the upper left-hand corner. For example, a form might be titled Producers 88 (12, 82) Revised.

NOTICE OF CONFIDENTIALITY RIGHTS: IF YOU ARE A NATURAL PERSON, YOU MAY REMOVE OR STRIKE ANY OR ALL OF THE FOLLOWING INFORMATION FROM ANY INSTRUMENT THAT TRANSFERS AN INTEREST IN REAL PROPERTY BEFORE IT IS FILED FOR RECORD IN THE PUBLIC RECORDS: YOUR SOCIAL SECURITY NUMBER OR YOUR DRIVER'S LICENSE NUMBER.

Producers 88 (4/76) Revised Paid Up
With 640 Acres Pooling Provision

©POUND PRINTING COMPANY • www.poundprintingcompany.com
P.O. Box 683046, Houston, Texas 77268-3046 • (713) 552-9797

OIL, GAS AND MINERAL LEASE

THIS AGREEMENT made this day of , , between

Lessor (whether one or more), whose address is: ,

and ,
Lessee, WITNESSETH:

1. Lessor in consideration of Dollars ($), in hand paid, of the royalties herein provided, and of the agreements of Lessee herein contained, hereby grants, leases and lets exclusively unto Lessee for the purpose of investigating, exploring, prospecting, drilling and mining for and producing oil, gas and all other minerals, conducting exploration, geologic and geophysical surveys by seismograph, core test, gravity and magnetic methods, injecting gas, water and other fluids, and air into subsurface strata, laying pipe lines, building roads, tanks, power stations, telephone lines and other structures thereon and on, over and across lands owned or claimed by Lessor adjacent and contiguous thereto, to produce, save, take care of, treat, transport and own said products, and housing its employees, the following described land in County, Texas, to-wit:

This lease also covers and includes all land owned or claimed by Lessor adjacent or contiguous to the land particularly described above, whether the same be in said survey or surveys or in adjacent surveys, although not included within the boundaries of the land particularly described above.

2. This is a paid up lease and subject to the other provisions herein contained, this lease shall be for a term of years from this date (called "primary term") and as long thereafter as oil, gas or other mineral is produced from said land or land with which said land is pooled hereunder.

3. As royalty, Lessee covenants and agrees: **(a)** To deliver to the credit of Lessor, in the pipelines to which Lessee may connect its wells, the equal one-eighth part of all oil produced and saved by Lessee from said land, or from time to time, at the option of Lessee, to pay Lessor the average posted market price of such one-eighth part of such oil at the wells as of the day it is run to the pipe line or storage tanks, Lessor's interest, in either case, to bear one-eighth of the cost of treating oil to render it marketable pipe line oil; **(b)** to pay Lessor for gas and casinghead gas produced from said land (1) when sold by Lessee, one-eighth of the amount realized by Lessee, computed at the mouth of the well, or **(2)** when used by Lessee off said land or in the manufacture of gasoline or other products, one-eighth of the amount realized from the sale of gasoline or other products extracted therefrom and one-eighth of the amount realized from the sale of residue gas after deducting the amount used for plant fuel and/or compression, **(c)** To pay Lessor on all other minerals mined and marketed or utilized by Lessee from said land, one-tenth either in kind or value at the well or mine at Lessee's election, except that on sulphur mined and marketed the royalty shall be one dollar ($1.00) per long ton. If, at the expiration of the primary term or at any time or times thereafter, there is any well on said land or on lands with which said land or any portion thereof has been pooled, capable of producing oil or gas, and all such wells are shut-in, this lease shall, nevertheless, continue in force as though operations were being conducted on said land for so long as said wells are shut-in, and thereafter this lease may be continued in force as if no shut-in had occurred. Lessee covenants and agrees to use reasonable diligence to produce, utilize, or market the minerals capable of being produced from said wells, but in the exercise of such diligence, Lessee shall not be obligated to install or furnish facilities other than well facilities and ordinary lease facilities of flow lines, separator, and lease tank, and shall not be required to settle labor trouble or to market gas upon terms unacceptable to Lessee. If, at any time or times after the expiration of the primary term, all such wells are shut-in for a period of ninety consecutive days, and during such time there are no operations on said land, then at or before the expiration of said ninety day period, Lessee shall pay or tender, by check or draft of Lessee, as royalty, a sum equal to one dollar ($1.00) for each acre of land then covered hereby. Lessee shall make like payments or tenders at or before the end of each anniversary of the expiration of said ninety day period if upon such anniversary this lease is being continued in force solely by reason of the provisions of this paragraph. Each such payment or tender shall be made to the parties who at the time of payment would be entitled to receive the royalties which would be paid under this lease if the wells were producing, and may be deposited in the

Bank at , or its successors, which shall continue as the depositories, regardless of changes in the ownership of shut-in royalty. If at any time that Lessee pays or tenders shut-in royalty, two or more parties are, or claim to be, entitled to receive same, Lessee may, in lieu of any other method of payment herein provided, pay or tender shut-in royalty, in the manner above specified, either jointly to such parties or separately to each in accordance with their respective ownerships thereof, as Lessee may elect. Any payment hereunder may be made by check or draft of Lessee deposited in the mail or delivered to the party entitled to receive payment or to a depository bank provided for above on or before the last date for payment. Nothing herein shall impair Lessee's right to release as provided in paragraph 5 hereof. In the event of assignment of this lease in whole or in part, liability for payment hereunder shall rest exclusively on the then owners of this lease, severally as to acreage owned by each.

4. Lessee, at its option, is hereby given the right and power to pool or combine the acreage covered by this lease or any portion thereof as to oil and gas, or either of them, with any other land covered by this lease, and/or with any other land, lease or leases in the immediate vicinity thereof to the extent hereinafter stipulated, when in Lessee's judgment it is necessary or advisable to do so in order properly to explore, or to develop and operate said leased premises in compliance with the spacing rules of the Railroad Commission of Texas, or other lawful authority, or when to do so would, in the judgment of Lessee, promote the conservation of oil and gas in and under and that may be produced from said premises. Units pooled for oil hereunder shall not substantially exceed 40 acres each in area, and units pooled for gas hereunder shall not substantially exceed in area 640 acres each plus a tolerance of ten percent (10%) thereof, provided that should governmental authority having jurisdiction prescribe or permit the creation of units larger than those specified, for the drilling or operation of a well at a regular location or for obtaining maximum allowable from any well to be drilled, drilling or already drilled, units thereafter created may conform substantially in size with those prescribed or permitted by governmental regulations. Lessee under the provisions hereof may pool or combine acreage covered by this lease or any portion thereof as above provided as to oil in any one or more strata and as to gas in any one or more strata. The units formed by pooling as to any stratum or strata need not conform in size or area with the unit or units into which the lease is pooled or combined as to any other stratum or strata, and oil units need not conform as to area with gas units. The pooling in one or more instances shall not exhaust the rights of the Lessee hereunder to pool this lease or portions thereof into other units. Lessee shall file for record in the appropriate records of the county in which the leased premises are situated an instrument describing and designating the pooled acreage as a pooled unit; and upon such recordation the unit shall be effective as to all parties hereto, their heirs, successors, and assigns, irrespective of whether or not the unit is likewise effective as to all other owners of surface, mineral, royalty, or other rights in land included in such unit. Lessee may at its election exercise its pooling option before or after commencing operations for or completing an oil or gas well on the leased premises, and the pooled unit may include, but it is not required to include, land or leases upon which a well capable of producing oil or gas in paying quantities has theretofore been completed or upon which operations for the drilling of a well for oil or gas have theretofore been commenced. In the event of operations for drilling on or production of oil or gas from any part of a pooled unit which includes all or a portion of the land covered by this lease, regardless of whether such operations for drilling were commenced or such production was secured before or after the execution of this instrument or the instrument designating the pooled unit, such operations shall be considered as operations for drilling on or production of oil or gas from land covered by this lease whether or not the well or wells be located on the premises covered by this lease and in such event operations for drilling shall be deemed to have been commenced on said land within the meaning of paragraph 5 of this lease; and the entire acreage constituting such unit or units, as to oil and gas, or either of them, as herein provided, shall be treated for all purposes, except the payment of royalties on production from the pooled unit, as if the same were included in this lease. For the purpose of computing the royalties to which owners of royalties and payments out of production and each of them shall be entitled on production of oil and gas, or either of them, from the pooled unit, there shall be allocated to the land covered by this lease and included in said unit (or to each separate tract within the unit if this lease covers separate tracts within the unit) a pro rata portion of the oil and gas, or either of them, produced from the pooled unit after deducting that used for operations on the pooled unit. Such allocation shall be on an acreage basis - that is to say, there shall be allocated to the acreage covered by this lease and included in the pooled unit (or to each separate tract within the unit if this lease covers separate tracts within the unit) that pro rata portion of the oil and gas, or either

Figure 5.1. A Producers 88 lease form

of them, produced from the pooled unit which the number of surface acres covered by this lease (or in each such separate tract) and included in the pooled unit bears to the total number of surface acres included in the pooled unit. Royalties hereunder shall be computed on the portion of such production, whether it be oil and gas, or either of them, so allocated to the land covered by this lease and included in the unit just as though such production were from such land. The production from an oil well will be considered as production from the lease or oil pooled unit from which it is producing and not as production from a gas pooled unit; and production from a gas well will be considered as production from the lease or gas pooled unit from which it is producing and not from an oil pooled unit. The formation of any unit hereunder shall not have the effect of changing the ownership of any shut-in production royalty which may become payable under this lease. If this lease now or hereafter covers separate tracts, no pooling or unitization of royalty interest as between any such separate tracts is intended or shall be implied or result merely from the inclusion of such separate tracts within this lease but Lessee shall nevertheless have the right to pool as provided above with consequent allocation of production as above provided. As used in this paragraph 4, the words "separate tract" mean any tract with royalty ownership differing, now or hereafter, either as to parties or amounts, from that as to any other part of the leased premises.

5. If at the expiration of the primary term, oil, gas, or other mineral is not being produced on said land, or from the land pooled therewith, but Lessee is then engaged in drilling or reworking operations thereon, or shall have completed a dry hole thereon within 60 days prior to the end of the primary term, the lease shall remain in force so long as operations on said well or for drilling or reworking of any additional well are prosecuted with no cessation of more than 60 consecutive days, and if they result in the production of oil, gas or other mineral, so long thereafter as oil, gas, or other mineral is produced from said land, or from land pooled therewith. If, after the expiration of the primary term of this lease and after oil, gas, or other mineral is produced from said land, or from land pooled therewith, the production thereof should cease from any cause, this lease shall not terminate if Lessee commences operations for drilling or reworking within 60 days after the cessation of such production, but shall remain in force and effect so long as such operations are prosecuted with no cessation of more than 60 consecutive days, and if they result in the production of oil, gas, or other mineral, so long thereafter as oil, gas, or other mineral is produced from said land, or from land pooled therewith. Any pooled unit designated by Lessee in accordance with the terms hereof, may be dissolved by Lessee by instrument filed for record in the appropriate records of the county in which the leased premises are situated at any time after the completion of a dry hole or the cessation of production on said unit. In the event a well or wells producing oil or gas in paying quantities should be brought in on adjacent land and within 330 feet of and draining the leased premises, or land pooled therewith, Lessee agrees to drill such offset well or wells as a reasonably prudent operator would drill under the same or similar circumstances. Lessee may at any time execute and deliver to Lessor or place of record a release or releases covering any portion or portions of the above described premises and thereby surrender this lease as to such portion or portions and be relieved of all obligations as to the acreage surrendered.

6. Lessee shall have the right at any time during or after the expiration of this lease to remove all property and fixtures placed by Lessee on said land, including the right to draw and remove all casing. When required by Lessor, Lessee will bury all pipe lines below ordinary plow depth, and no well shall be drilled within two hundred (200) feet of any residence or barn now on said land without Lessor's consent.

7. The rights of either party hereunder may be assigned in whole or in part, and the provisions hereof shall extend to their heirs, successors and assigns; but no change or division in ownership of the land, or royalties, however accomplished, shall operate to enlarge the obligations or diminish the rights of Lessee; and no change or division in such ownership shall be binding on Lessee until thirty (30) days after Lessee shall have been furnished by registered U.S. mail at Lessee's principal place of business with a certified copy of recorded instrument or instruments evidencing same. In the event of assignment hereof in whole or in part, liability for breach of any obligation hereunder shall rest exclusively upon the owner of this lease or of a portion thereof who commits such breach. If six or more parties become entitled to royalty hereunder, Lessee may withhold payment thereof unless and until furnished with a recordable instrument executed by all such parties designating an agent to receive payment for all.

8. The breach by Lessee of any obligation arising hereunder shall not work a forfeiture or termination of this lease nor cause a termination or reversion of the estate created hereby nor be grounds for cancellation hereof in whole or in part. No obligation reasonably to develop the leased premises shall arise during the primary term. Should oil, gas or other mineral in paying quantities be discovered on said premises, then after the expiration of the primary term, Lessee shall develop the acreage retained hereunder as a reasonably prudent operator, but in discharging this obligation it shall in no event be required to drill more than one well per forty (40) acres of the area retained hereunder and capable of producing oil in paying quantities and one well per 640 acres plus an acreage tolerance not to exceed 10% of 640 acres of the area retained hereunder and capable of producing gas or other mineral in paying quantities. If after the expiration of the primary term, Lessor considers that operations are not at any time being conducted in compliance with this lease, Lessor shall notify Lessee in writing of the facts relied upon as constituting a breach hereof, and Lessee, if in default, shall have sixty days after receipt of such notice in which to commence the compliance with the obligations imposed by virtue of this instrument.

9. Lessor hereby warrants and agrees to defend the title to said land and agrees that Lessee at its option may discharge any tax, mortgage or other lien upon said land, either in whole or in part, and in event Lessee does so, it shall be subrogated to such lien with right to enforce same and apply royalties accruing hereunder toward satisfying same. Without impairment of Lessee's rights under the warranty in event of failure of title, it is agreed that if this lease covers a less interest in the oil, gas, sulphur, or other minerals in all or any part of said land than the entire and undivided fee simple estate (whether Lessor's interest is herein specified or not), or no interest therein, then the royalties, and other monies accruing from any part as to which this lease covers less than such full interest, shall be paid only in the proportion which the interest therein, if any, covered by this lease, bears to the whole and undivided fee simple estate therein. All royalty interest covered by this lease (whether or not owned by Lessor) shall be paid out of the royalty herein provided. Should any one or more of the parties named above as Lessors fail to execute this lease, it shall nevertheless be binding upon the party or parties executing the same.

10. Should Lessee be prevented from complying with any express or implied covenant of this lease, from conducting drilling or reworking operations thereon or from producing any oil, gas or other minerals therefrom by reason of scarcity of or inability to obtain or to use equipment or material, or by operation of force majeure, and Federal or state law or any order, rule or regulation of governmental authority, then while so prevented, Lessee's obligation to comply with such covenant shall be suspended, and Lessee shall not be liable in damages for failure to comply therewith; and this lease shall be extended while and so long as Lessee is prevented by any such cause from conducting drilling or reworking operations on or from producing oil or gas from the leased premises; and the time while Lessee is so prevented shall not be counted against Lessee, anything in this lease to the contrary notwithstanding.

IN WITNESS WHEREOF, this instrument is executed on the date first above written.

LESSOR	SS. OR TAX I.D. NO.	LESSOR	SS. OR TAX I.D. NO.

ACKNOWLEDGMENT

STATE OF
COUNTY OF

This instrument was acknowledged before me on the day of , by

Notary Public, State of Texas
Notary's name (printed):
Notary's commission expires:

ACKNOWLEDGMENT

STATE OF
COUNTY OF

This instrument was acknowledged before me on the day of , by

Notary Public, State of Texas
Notary's name (printed):
Notary's commission expires:

Producers 88 (4/76) Revised Paid Up
With 640 Acres Pooling Provision

Figure 5.1, cont. A Producers 88 lease form

The so-called "standard form," then, appears in so many variations that it is no standard at all. The courts have long recognized this fact, though some landowners and even some attorneys have not. In *Fagg v. Texas Co.* (Tex. Comm'n App. 1933), the court decided that language referring to "an 88 form lease" was too vague to be useful, given the number of different 88 forms on the market. "As we see it, the reference to an 88 Form lease is as incapable of definite application as if the term 'oil and gas lease form' had been used instead." Currently, Producers 88 forms are available on CD-ROM and online. Because there are many different versions, the buyer must exercise some care to be sure of getting the precise form desired.

Forms Prepared for Individuals and Associations

Landowner's Forms

A number of local and regional associations formed to advance the interests of surface and mineral owners print lease forms that they recommend their members use. These forms vary a great deal, and a lease suitable for one region might be unacceptable to landmen and oil companies in another area. In general, forms printed for landowners or even specifically requested by them will be very carefully scrutinized by potential lessees.

Attorney's Forms

Many oil and gas attorneys who regularly represent landowners not only draft leases but also have their own printed lease forms. And many of these printed forms are titled Producers Special 88—out of convention, as the forms are not likely to favor the producer. They are often modeled on state lease forms that, quite naturally, favor the lessor. In Texas, for example, the forms that can be obtained from the General Land Office for the leasing of mineral-classified lands are sometimes used as examples by attorneys drawing up their own forms.

The urge to produce a neatly printed form seems almost universal in the industry. Best of all, from the clerical and administrative points of view, are standard, familiar forms that present none of the unusual features of a special lease. The landowner, of course, might take a different view of the matter, reading the fine print with care and holding out for special provisions that tailor the lease to his or her needs.

ELEMENTS OF THE LEASE

The parts of a standard oil and gas lease appear in table 5.2. Some of the clauses listed, though common, apply only to gas wells. Virtually all the clauses are negotiable, as more and more landowners are discovering. Certainly, all leases need care and thought in the drafting. While it might not seem that matters as apparently simple as the title of the lease or the names of the parties could give rise to dispute, even these elements should be as clear as possible. Otherwise, a judge might someday be forced to rule on the intended meaning of an ambiguous choice of words.

Title

Lessor and lessee can avoid disagreements by naming the specific substances covered by the lease rather than simply calling them "minerals."

The sample Producers 88 lease in figure 5.1 includes the word "mineral" in its title and refers to "other minerals" in the body of the lease. Because some older leases have been used as precedent to justify the mining of coal, iron, uranium, clays, and other substances (though the lessor might have intended only the removal of oil or natural gas), courts have tended to rule very carefully on what can be called a mineral. Lessor and lessee should avoid ambiguities by naming the specific substances that the lease is to cover. In fact, in the Commonwealth of Pennsylvania, the words "oil" and "gas" must specifically be mentioned in the conveyance for the rights to explore, drill, and produce those minerals.

In addition to limiting the lease title to "Oil and Gas," some attorneys add a provision that specifies that the oil and gas in question are those "derived from petroleum substances only" or "derived from petroleum or associated hydrocarbons." If by-products such as sulfur or helium are expected in any quantity, such products are usually named in the lease; separate royalties might be arranged for one or more of them. In any case, unintended substances like lignite or uranium should not slip into a lease by a vague catchall phrase such as "other minerals."

Date

Dates recorded on a lease:

- Effective date
- Date of execution
- Date of acknowledgment
- Date of recordation

An undated lease is not void but generally takes effect when it is executed or delivered to the lessee. Any lease should be dated, however, and its dating might prove important if there is any dispute later about which of two documents is the earlier one. The controlling date for any lease is the one written in the instrument as the lease effective date; it is not the date on which the instrument was executed, notarized, or *recorded* (entered into public records).

Parties

A lease must name all the parties involved in the agreement. The party granting the lease, or grantor, is referred to in the body of the lease as the lessor, even if it consists of several people who all sign. The grantee, or person receiving the right to search for and produce oil or gas, is subsequently referred to as the lessee. In some states, lessors' addresses, as well as their names, must appear on the lease. Some states (Louisiana, for example) also require an indication of the parties' marital status.

Table 5.2
Parts of a Standard Oil and Gas Lease

Preamble
- Title of the agreement
- Effective date of the agreement
- Names of the parties
- Consideration promised
- Description of the land to be leased

Provisions
- Granting clause
- Mother Hubbard clause
- Habendum clause
- Royalty clause
- Shut-in royalty clause
- Drilling and delay rental clause
- Dry hole clause
- Cessation of production clause
- Continuous drilling clause
- Pooling and unitization clause
- Surrender clause
- Damage clause
- Assignment clause
- Warranty clause
- Proportionate reduction clause
- Force majeure clause
- Legal effect clause

Signature Block
- Signature of at least the lessor
- Possible signature of the lessee
- Date(s) of execution of the agreement

Acknowledgment
- Declaration of the identity of the signers and of the purpose of signing
- Signatures of the lessor, lessee, and notary
- Seal of the notary and date of signing

When possible, cotenants (co-owners) are named as lessors in one lease. The awkward alternative is to have each owner execute a separate lease that covers only his or her undivided interest. Lessees also try to provide for the possible failure of one or more of the named lessors to execute the lease. In such a case, the lease is generally enforceable between the lessee and any lessors who do sign.

Consideration

Consideration is something promised to induce the other party to contract, and it is necessary to make a contract legally binding.

Consideration is the benefit required to make a contract valid; it is the inducement to contract that makes the agreement legally binding, or enforceable by law. Even in states that do not view oil and gas leases as contracts but as, for example, conveyances of an interest in land, consideration is still required. This benefit to the lessor can be broken down into payments in cash and *payments in kind.*

The lease bonus is the upfront cash payment to lease the lands for oil and gas exploration and development and is typically paid at lease signing or shortly thereafter. These payments can vary from $10 per acre to as much as $25,000 per acre. (The higher figure was paid during the height of the shale boom in Louisiana.)

Royalties are payments made by the lessee to the lessor based on a percentage of the total production—traditionally ⅛, or 12.5%, but sometimes higher, if the lessor is in a position to negotiate for more. Royalties can take the form of payments in kind—that is, the landowner's share of the oil or gas actually produced. That type of payment is rare, though; usually, royalties are paid in the form of cash sums.

Types of consideration under a lease:

- Payments in cash
- Payments in kind

If the lessee anticipates not being able to drill a well or finish drilling a well by the end of the primary period, the lease contract might offer the lessee the option of making *delay rentals* to extend the lease. Delay rental payments are usually a small sum of money paid on a per-acre basis to keep the lease in force while delaying the drilling of a well.

In an oil and gas lease, royalties and rentals have their own separate clauses, and the lease bonus is mentioned in the *granting clause.* (For an explanation of granting clauses, see the passage that follows.) In government leases, the amount of the bonus commonly appears in full. In private leases, the bonus consideration is often set out as a nominal amount—$10 or so, as the parties to the lease often like to keep the amount paid confidential. The real bonus (a greater sum of money) is paid by *draft* or check. In Louisiana, "serious consideration" is necessary to complete the transfer; elsewhere, nominal amounts will generally suffice to support all the terms and provisions spelled out in a lease.

Granting Clause

The granting clause, an important part of the lease, specifies the rights and interests granted by the lessor to the lessee (figs. 5.2, 5.3). Certain words are used to establish a *leasehold,* or the property created and held by a lease. These words include ones such as "grant," "devise," and "let." In return for consideration (the bonus), a lessee usually obtains the "exclusive" rights to search, drill for, and produce oil and gas. While such rights could, in theory, be nonexclusive, most lessees would consider a competitive cotenant arrangement undesirable and should make sure that the word exclusive is contained in the granting clause of a lease form prepared by the lessor.

The kinds of operations that can be carried out in the course of exploration, drilling, and production should be clearly described. Many leases, however, use rather broad terms for these operations. As a result of such vagueness, the courts have defined a number of activities implied by an oil

OIL, GAS AND MINERAL LEASE

THIS AGREEMENT made this __________ day of ______________________________, 20_________, between

____

Lessor (whether one or more), whose address is: ____

____

and ____

Lessee, (whether one or more), whose address is: ____

____

WITNESSETH:

1. Lessor, in consideration of ____ Dollars ($ ___________), in hand paid, of the royalties herein provided, and of the agreements of Lessee herein contained, hereby grants, leases and lets exclusively unto Lessee for the purpose of investigating, exploring, prospecting, drilling and mining for and producing oil, gas and all other minerals, conducting exploration, geologic and geophysical surveys by seismograph, core test, gravity and magnetic methods, injecting gas, water and other fluids, and air into subsurface strata, laying pipelines, building roads, tanks, power stations, telephone lines and other structures thereon and on, over and across lands owned or claimed by Lessor adjacent and contiguous thereto, to produce, save, take care of, treat, transport and own said products, and housing its employees, the following described land in __________________________________ County, Texas, to-wit:

This lease also covers and includes all land owned or claimed by Lessor adjacent or contiguous to the land particularly described above, whether the same be in said survey or surveys or in adjacent surveys, although not included within the boundaries of the land particularly described above. For all purposes of this lease, said land is estimated to comprise ________________________ acres, whether it actually comprises more or less.

***Figure 5.2.** A typical lease begins with a title that names the subject of the agreement and a statement of the effective date, the names of the parties, and the consideration promised. In this example, the consideration is stated in the granting clause. (Usually, the bonus stated in the lease is $10.00 rather than the actual bonus, which is kept confidential.)*

and gas lease, whether these are spelled out in the granting clause or not. In Texas, for example, these implied rights include permission to enter and exit from the property, to set up equipment, to drill, and to use improved recovery techniques and saltwater injection. Use of the land's surface, though, has given rise to so much litigation that both lessor and lessee should not rely on implication. The extent of surface use—for roads, pipelines, tanks, power stations, employee housing, and so on—should be specified.

1. Lessor, in consideration of four thousand seven hundred and fifty Dollars ($ 4,750), in hand paid, of the royalties herein provided, and of the agreements of Lessee herein contained, hereby grants, leases and lets exclusively unto Lessee for the purpose of investigating, exploring, prospecting, drilling and mining for and producing oil, gas and all other minerals, conducting exploration, geologic and geophysical surveys by seismograph, core test, gravity and magnetic methods, injecting gas, water and other fluids, and air into subsurface strata, laying pipelines, building roads, tanks, power stations, telephone lines and other structures thereon and on, over and across lands owned or claimed by Lessor adjacent and contiguous thereto, to produce, save, take care of, treat, transport and own said products, and housing its employees, the following described land in Lee County, Texas, to-wit:

Granting Clause

> 50 acres, more or less, out of the James Joseph 1/3 League, Abstract 175, known as Lot No. 6, in the subdivision of N. F. Newhouse Estate, in Lee County, Texas, being particularly described by metes and bounds in the Deed from John Silver to Mark A. Brown, Jr., et ux dated June 25, 1985, of record in Vol. 162, Pg. 209, Deed Records of Lee County, Texas to which said Deed and its record reference is hereby made for all pertinent purposes; SAVE AND EXCEPT 0.219 of an acre described in the Deed from C. B. Frieberg to the State of Texas, dated October 17, 1965, of record in Vol. 104, Pg. 68, Lee County Deed Records; and being the same property described in the Deed from Mark A. Brown, Jr., et ux to Robert E. Layman, et ux, dated March 1, 1979, of record in Vol. 194, Pg. 131 Lee County Deed Records.

Land Description

This lease also covers and includes all land owned or claimed by Lessor adjacent or contiguous to the land particularly described above, whether the same be in said survey or surveys or in adjacent surveys, although not included within the boundaries of the land particularly described above. For all purposes of this lease, said land is estimated to comprise fifty (50) acres, whether it actually comprises more or less.

Mother Hubbard Clause

Figure 5.3. A granting clause, a land description, and a Mother Hubbard clause

The granting clause is also the place for clarity about which minerals are covered by the lease. In addition to oil and natural gas, other related substances found in the oil and gas stream (such as distillate, condensate, casinghead gas, helium, and sulfur) need to be mentioned. If the lessor is concerned about having his or her land restored after production has ceased, a stipulation may be added requiring the lessee to leave the property as it was found, or as nearly so as possible. Finally, the granting clause is usually the section of the lease that describes the land.

Description

A legal description of the leased premises following one of the methods discussed in Chapter 3 is a necessary element in an oil and gas lease (fig. 5.3). If the lessor owns the entire undivided interest in the land being leased, the description should be perfectly straightforward. If the lessor owns only a part interest in the mineral estate, certain points need to be considered. If, for example, the description makes use of an earlier instrument, like a deed, it might include the fractional interest conveyed in that earlier instrument. But the landowner might now own or intend to lease a different fractional interest. Reliance on instruments such as deeds should be discriminating.

The purely descriptive parts of earlier documents should be used, and the question of whether to specify the fractional interest owned by the lessor should be decided separately.

If a lesser interest clause is included in a lease, there may be contention over the warranty clause or a description specifying only a partial interest in the land.

Many leases are taken as quickly as possible after a check of the county records, so a lessee is often in the position of not knowing whether a lessor does in fact own all or only a portion of the mineral rights. This uncertainty (left unclarified until the title examination) has led to the use of *lesser interest* or *proportionate reduction clauses* that allow lessees to reduce rents and royalties proportionately if it turns out that the lessor owns less than all of the minerals. From the lessee's point of view, it is desirable that no confusion arise to limit this right to reduce rents and royalties. When a lease does contain a lesser interest clause, the landman will usually urge that the land description omit any reference to a fractional undivided interest. Leases that contain both a lesser interest clause and a description specifying a partial interest have led to litigation, sometimes ending in decisions in favor of the lessor. From the landowner's point of view, a lesser interest clause (though fair in and by itself) seems inconsistent with another commonly included clause that warrants title. Attorneys who represent landowners will very frequently argue for the removal of *warranty clauses*. This done, there is little to object to in a lesser interest clause that allows an oil company to pay in proportion to actual ownership. Finally, landowners might wish to follow the land description with a *depth limitation*, thereby leasing their minerals to specified depths from the drill pad. Strata below these depths are not covered by the terms of the lease. It is generally desirable to measure depth limits in feet, yards, or metres rather than by reference to named producing strata, though either method can have unusual or unwanted results when drilling reveals more about the geology underlying the land. Measurement in standard units is, in some cases, so difficult that the safer, less ambiguous reference would be to the "base of (a known formation)."

Mother Hubbard Clause

The *Mother Hubbard clause*, also referred to as a *coverall clause*, sometimes follows the land description (fig. 5.3). Its intention is to perfect that description by including in the lease any small or oddly shaped bits of land owned by the lessor and "contiguous with," "adjoining," or "adjacent to" the described tract. Such bits and pieces can be left out of surveys and boundary descriptions and can be very common in states such as Pennsylvania. A Mother Hubbard clause scoops up "lands adjoining the herein described land up to the boundaries of the abutting landowners" and includes them in the lease. The difficulty arises when such a clause seems to make the lease apply to lands that the landowner did not actually intend to lease. An overbroad clause can be strictly interpreted by the courts, and in fact, litigation has put various Mother Hubbard clauses to the test. To avoid such problems, many attorneys suggest omitting the clause or at least carefully limiting its applicability—for example, to 5% or 10% of the amount of land in the legal description.

Habendum Clause

The habendum clause establishes the primary term as a period of development and the secondary term as a period of production.

The *habendum clause* is sometimes called the *term clause* and fixes the duration of the lessee's interest (fig. 5.4), just as the granting clause fixes the nature of that interest. The primary term—generally used as an exploration period—is usually given in years; during this term, the lessee is obliged to begin or complete a well (as specified in the lease) or pay delay rentals that usually begin on the next anniversary date of the instrument. Lessees are often interested in a lease that is paid in full, or a *"paid-up" lease,* as this type allows them to avoid paying rentals every year. The *secondary term* is conditional and depends upon the production of oil, gas, or other minerals. Even when it is not stated in the lease, courts have generally held that production in *paying quantities* or in *commercial quantities* is required to hold the lease in effect during this secondary term. The courts have variously interpreted "paying" production to mean profitable or such as would encourage a reasonable and prudent operator to continue even in the absence of cash profit. Because standard habendum clauses sometimes limit a secondary term to a well capable of producing—or capable of producing in paying quantities—a lessee might want to establish other ways to extend the lease into a secondary term. The lessee may, for example, incorporate an option to extend the lease for a specified time or, if a dry hole is drilled during the primary term, an option to maintain the lease by operations to drill a new well within a specified time period.

> TO HAVE AND TO HOLD the same for a term of five (5) years from and after the date hereof and so long thereafter as Lessee shall conduct development (including, without limitation, drilling, redrilling, repairing and reworking) or producing operations on the leased land or lands pooled therewith without cessation for more than 180 consecutive days, or be excused therefrom as hereinafter provided.

Figure 5.4. A habendum clause fixes the primary term of the lease.

Royalty Clause

In an arm's length transaction, a lessee would sell a royalty owner's minerals to an independent buyer (rather than an affiliate).

As previously stated, royalty is the percentage of production paid to the landowner. Oil royalties may be paid in kind; the lessor may, if he or she chooses, receive oil from the lessee and market it. Most lessors prefer, however, to receive the posted market price of the oil in money.

Gas royalties are normally paid in money. Establishing the value of the gas, however, has led to much confusion, disagreement, and even litigation. Landowners who want the "market value at the mouth of the well," meaning whatever price the market will bear prior to any cost reduction for treating or transporting the gas, have been urging their interpretation of this phrase on producers hard-pressed by the rapid rise in gas prices. Such producers might be caught in long-term contracts with pipeline companies. In that situation, if the phrase is interpreted favorably for the landowners, the producers are required to pay royalties calculated on current (higher) market values while receiving payment from gas purchasers at previous (lower) prices.

An alternative to this problematic way of determining the value of gas for royalty payments is for the landowner to take gas royalties in kind and arrange to market the gas him- or herself. Some Louisiana owners, for example, do their own marketing if the producer is unable or unwilling to. If the owner prefers not to market the gas, it is possible to specify in the royalty clause that he or she will join the lessee in any marketing contract undertaken as an *arm's length transaction*. These types of transactions take place between parties that agree to act independently and without a relationship with one another so that neither party can influence the other unfairly. A variation on these kinds of agreements would include the possibility that the lessee purchase the lessor's gas at an arm's length price, or at a price that two unrelated parties would agree to. In any case, the landowner should not receive a royalty based on a lower price than that received by the lessee. Such is the intended meaning of the phrase "market value at the mouth of the well" in leases.

The royalty clause (fig. 5.5) is the place to specify any separate royalties for substances produced as by-products of the oil and gas stream—sulfur, for instance. It is also the place to mention the free use of gas by the landowner. Many landowners wish to include this money-saving provision, but they should consider the risks involved and be willing to stipulate that their use of gas from the producer's wells is at their own risk and expense. Finally, landowners concerned about prompt receipt of royalties sometimes place a royalty due date in the lease. Failure to make timely payment might involve the addition of interest charges or the termination of the lease by the lessee after written notice and a period of time.

9. ROYALTY SHARE. The term "royalty share" as used herein means one-eighth (1/8).

10. OIL ROYALTY. Lessee shall pay Lessor as royalty on oil the value of the royalty share of the proceeds received from the sale of all oil produced and removed from or allocated to the leased land, after making the customary adjustments for temperature, water and basic sediment at the posted available market price at the well for oil of like gravity and quality on the day the oil is so removed. Lessee may deduct therefrom a reasonable charge for dehydration, processing, cleaning and treating such oil and a reasonable charge for transportation to and from the treating plant. Nothing herein contained shall be construed as obligating Lessee to treat oil.

11. GAS ROYALTY. Lessee shall pay Lessor as royalty on natural gas the royalty share of a value, which shall be the sum of the following:

a) The net proceeds received by Lessee from the sale of gas produced from wells into or allocated to the leased land (whether such gas is sold by Lessee in its natural state or as residual dry gas after extracting gasoline and other content therefrom). Gas treated at a gasoline extraction plant not owned or operated by Lessee and for which Lessee received a royalty from the operator of such plant shall be deemed sold in its natural state for an amount equal to the market value of the royalty received by Lessee. Except as otherwise provided herein, gas used or consumed by Lessee in operations other than under this lease or leases pooled therewith shall be deemed sold for the market value thereof. The value of gas and products extracted therefrom, used or consumed in the operation of a gasoline extraction plant (to the extent that it is so used for processing gas from or allocated to the leased land), or in operations on the leased land or lands pooled therewith, or in repressuring any oil-bearing formation from which a well or wells on the leased land or lands pooled therewith is producing, shall not be included. The cost of processing, treating, compressing, handling and transporting gas in connection with the sale thereof shall be deducted in determining net proceeds of sale.

b) The market value at the extraction plant of all gasoline and other liquid hydrocarbons, extracted and saved from natural gas from or allocated to the leased land as a result of processing such gas at a plant owned or operated by Lessee, less the cost of such processing, which cost for the purposes hereof will be deemed to be sixty percent (60%) of said last-mentioned market value.

c) The market value, at the plant where extracted, of all gasoline and other liquid hydrocarbons received by Lessee as a result of the processing of natural gas from or allocated to the leased land at a plant not owned or operated by Lessee (if such processing is not on a royalty basis) less the cost to Lessee of such processing.

d) During such limes that a market at the well for the gas produced from said leased land or lands pooled therewith does not exist, Lessee may suspend the operation of any such gas well or wells; provided however, that if, at the expiration of any calendar year, Lessor shall not have received as royalty from the proceeds of the sale of any such gas an amount equal to or in excess of One Dollar ($1.00) per acre for the total acreage then held subject to this lease, Lessee shall on or before the last day of January next succeeding pay Lessor an amount equal to the difference between the total amount of all such royalties paid to Lessor during such calendar year from the proceeds of the sale of such gas and the said amount of One Dollar ($1.00) per acre for such total acreage so held, provided that any and all sums so paid by Lessee to Lessor in excess of the actual amount of royalties paid by Lessee to Lessor from the proceeds of the sale of such gas shall be considered as advance royalties to be repaid to Lessee from any royalties which shall thereafter become payable to Lessor hereunder, and Lessee is authorized to deduct the same from royalties thereafter due and payable.

Nothing herein contained shall obligate Lessee to treat or process natural gas, nor shall Lessee be obligated to save, sell or otherwise dispose of natural gas or residual dry gas, as the case may be, unless there is a market therefor at the well or processing plant at a price and under conditions which Lessee believes to be for the best interest of both parties hereto, or to pay royalty on any gas which is not sold.

12. OTHER ROYALTY. Lessee shall pay Lessor as royalty the market value of the mineral produced from or allocated to the leased land, in the condition as produced, of the royalty share of any substances covered by this lease, other than oil and gas and the products thereof, which Lessee may elect to produce and save or market or utilize from the leased land.

COURTESY OF L. RAE CONNET

Figure 5.5. A royalty clause states the percentage of production to be received by the lessor.

Shut-In Royalty Clause

Shut-in payments—payments made in lieu of royalty payments for gas wells shut in by the producer—must be paid to royalty owners, including the lessor if he or she owns a royalty interest. The purpose of this provision is to allow a lessee to hold the lease on a nonproducing well until a market is found or until a transmitting pipeline becomes available. Producing wells are sometimes shut in for workover (fig. 5.6), either because of a cutback in production by the pipeline company, or, in new frontier areas, because a pipeline has not been built yet. Today, landowners are likely to limit shut-in royalties to definite terms of two, three, or five years and to negotiate for higher shut-in royalties. They often believe that higher royalties will spur producers to find markets or give up their leases. Shut-in royalties of whatever size are intended to apply to wells that can produce in commercial amounts; the lease should mention this condition.

Figure 5.6. A producing well being shut in with a workover rig

Drilling and Delay Rental Clause

A paid-up lease is one that is paid up through the primary term so that no delay rentals will be due.

As mentioned previously, many standard lease forms today do not provide for the payment of delay rentals; rather, the lessor receives a higher bonus up front. This kind of lease is called a "paid-up lease." However, in some geographic regions, the delay rental clause is still popular (fig. 5.7). Also known as the "unless" clause, the drilling and delay rental provision has replaced the old "drill or pay" notion. Drill or pay was a means of forestalling conflict over the question of how quickly leased land should be developed. In the early days of the industry, landowners' only consideration came from royalties; they wanted their property made productive as rapidly as possible. On the other hand, oil companies had begun to acquire leases to have petroleum reserves and had their own timetables for development of those reserves. Eventually, this source of conflict was partially settled by lease provisions that gave the lessee three choices: to drill, to pay rentals to defer drilling, or to terminate the lease. These days, a lease usually expires one year from the anniversary date on the instrument unless the operator begins operations for drilling or makes timely payment of delay rental.

A number of states, Texas among them, are strict about nonpayment or untimely payment of delay rentals. A check or draft posted in good time but lost in the mail might be viewed with leniency, but other excuses might do nothing to save the lease. Lessors sometimes wonder, when they do not receive a rental check, just what constitutes the "commencement" of drilling. To avoid dispute about this issue, the required operations are frequently specified in the lease.

6.

(a) If operations for drilling are not commenced on said land or on acreage pooled therewith as above provided on or before one year from this date, the lease shall then terminate as to both parties, unless or before such anniversary date Lessee shall pay or tender (or shall make a bona fide attempt to pay or tender, as hereinafter stated) to Lessor or to the credit of Lessor in Monroe State Bank at Lexington, Texas (which bank and its successors are Lessor's agent and shall continue as the depository for all rentals payable hereunder regardless of change in ownership of said land or the rentals), the sum of five hundred Dollars ($500.00) (herein called rentals), which shall cover the privilege of deferring commencement of drilling operations for a period of twelve (12) months. In like manner and upon like payments or tenders annually, the commencement of drilling operations may be further deferred for successive periods of twelve (12) months each during the primary term. The payment or tender of rental under this paragraph and of royalty under paragraph 3 on any gas well from which gas is not being sold or used may be made by the check or draft of Lessee mailed or delivered to the parties entitled thereto or to said bank on or before the date of payment. If such bank (or any successor bank) should fail, liquidate or be succeeded by another bank, or for any reason fail or refuse to accept rental, Lessee shall not be held in default for failure to make such payment or tender of rental until thirty (30) days after Lessor shall deliver to Lessee a proper recordable instrument naming another bank as agent to receive such payments or tenders. If Lessee shall, on or before any anniversary date, make a bona fide attempt to pay or deposit rental to a Lessor entitled thereto according to Lessee's records or to a Lessor, who, prior to such attempted payment or deposit, has given Lessee notice, in accordance with subsequent provisions of this lease, of his/her right to receive rental, and if such payment or deposit shall be ineffective or erroneous in any regard, Lessee shall be unconditionally obligated to pay to such Lessor the rental properly payable for the rental period involved, and this lease shall not terminate but shall be maintained in the same manner as if such erroneous or ineffective rental payment of deposit had been properly made, provided that the erroneous or ineffective rental payment or deposit be corrected within 30 days after receipt by Lessee of written notice from such Lessor of such error accompanied by such instruments as are necessary to enable Lessee to make proper payment. The down cash payment is consideration for this lease according to its terms and shall not be allocated as a mere rental for a period. Lessee may at any time or times execute and deliver to Lessor or to the depository above named or place of record a release or releases of this lease as to all or any part of the above-described premises, or of any mineral or horizon under all or any part thereof, and thereby be relieved of all obligations as to the released land or interest. If this lease is released as to all minerals and horizon under a portion of the land covered by this lease, the rentals and other payments computed in accordance therewith shall thereupon be reduced in the proportion that the number of surface acres within such released portion bears to the total number of surface acres which was covered by this lease immediately prior to such release.

(b) Lessor hereby designates Monroe State Bank at Lexington, Texas, and its successors as Lessor's agent to serve as the depository for any payment due with respect to any shut-in gas well. Payment of shut-in gas royalty may be made in the manner provided in paragraph 6(a) hereof for the payment or tender of rentals, including all terms with respect to the deposit of same in the designated depository bank, notwithstanding paragraph 6(a) being otherwise stricken or inoperative due to this lease having a primary term not exceeding one year, if such be the case.

Figure 5.7. A delay rental clause allows extension or termination of the lease if a well is not drilled during the primary term. The rental is paid on an annual basis, usually beginning on the effective date of the lease.

Dry Hole, Cessation of Production, and Continuous Drilling Clauses

The *dry hole clause* allows an operator to keep the lease in the event that the hole is dry. The operator is allowed a specified period of time, which can range from 60 days to a year, within which to begin drilling a second well or resume payment of delay rentals. Similarly, if production stops for some reason, the *cessation of production clause* allows the lessee a specified length of time to begin new operations. These operations might include workover on a sluggish well to make it produce in paying quantities. Usually, the clause calls for restored production, commencement of a new well, or a return to delay rentals.

A *continuous drilling clause*, or *development clause*, aims to keep drilling operations going steadily after the primary term has expired. Designated intervals—of 180 days, for example—between completion and new drilling require the operator to develop leased land up to its allowable density. Some landowners leave the rate of development up to the lessee. Others are particular about the designated time limits; failure to comply with these intervals commonly releases the undeveloped portions of the leased land.

Pooling and Unitization Clause

The terms "pooling" and "*unitization*" are often used interchangeably, but they refer to different undertakings. When a lessee pools leased land, small or irregular tracts are combined into a unit big enough to meet state spacing regulations for drilling. The pooled unit size required or permitted will vary from one state to another and sometimes from one field to another. For example, a lessee might need units of 40 acres to drill oilwells and units of 640 acres to drill deep gas wells. A clause in the lease that permits the lessee to merge separately acquired tracts and treat them as a single unit is advantageous in several ways. Such a clause (fig. 5.8) allows the lessee to develop the tracts more efficiently and more economically without drilling *offset wells*. In some cases, pooling allows the lessee to pay fewer delay rentals, as well, because a producing well anywhere on the pooled acreage will mean the beginning of royalty payments to all the landowners and the end of rentals to all. Unless the landowners have specified otherwise, a well anywhere on the unit will also hold the leases on each pooled tract through the primary and secondary terms. Royalty is almost invariably shared on the basis of percentage of surface acres in the pool.

28. POOLING. Lessee shall have the right at its option, at any time and from time to time, either before or after the discovery of oil, gas or other substances into the leased land, to combine and pool all or any part of the leased land or interest therein and/or as to any one or more of the formations thereunder and the minerals produced therefrom into one or more operating units with any other land, formation or interest therein (whether held by Lessee or others and whether or not the surface of such other land may be used for oil or gas development purposes). Each operating unit may be of such size and shape as Lessee may desire, provided that no such unit created hereunder for oil or gas development purposes shall exceed the number of acres permitted to be included in a drilling unit according to the provisions of paragraph 6 hereof, plus a tolerance of ten percent (10%). If any of the land to be pooled has not been divided into sections by the United States Government, then Lessee shall project sections thereon, following as nearly as practicable the usual Government system, and such projected sections shall be deemed "sections" for the purpose of this provision.

Each operating unit created hereunder shall be created by and shall become effective upon the execution by Lessee of a Declaration of Pooling setting forth the exterior boundaries of the unit so created and describing the lands, formations or interests pooled thereunder. An operating unit may be on a well only or certain wells-only basis and may overlap with the boundaries of one or more other operating units. Any units which overlap with the boundaries of another unit shall be modified to apply only to a specific well or to specific wells or to differing formations. Lessee may, at any time after creation of such unit, enlarge, reduce or otherwise modify such unit by executing a Supplemental Declaration of Pooling, but no retroactive adjustment of royalties shall be made. Promptly after execution of each Declaration of Pooling and each Supplemental Declaration of Pooling, Lessee shall give written notice thereof to Lessor, but the giving of such written notice shall not be required to make any such Declaration of Pooling or Supplemental Declaration of Pooling effective.

Any operating unit may include land upon which a well has theretofore been completed or upon which operations for drilling have theretofore been commenced, and within the meaning of the requirements of this lease any such well or operations shall be considered as having been commenced immediately after the effective date of such pooling. Production, drilling or reworking operations anywhere on any operating unit created hereunder shall be treated as production, drilling or reworking operations into the leased land. There shall be allocated to the leased land the proportion of the pooled production from any such operating unit (whether or not such production is from the leased land) that the number of surface acres covered by this lease and included in such unit bears to the total number of surface acres in such unit; royalties shall be paid hereunder only upon that portion of such production so allocated, and as to pooled production from land in such unit, such royalties shall be in lieu of any other royalties.

If taxes of any kind are levied or assessed which are based upon the quantity of pooled substances underlying or produced from any such operating unit, then the share of such taxes to be borne by Lessor as provided in this lease shall be in proportion to the share of production from such unit allocated to the leased land.

Lessee may at any time quitclaim to the persons entitled thereto all or any part of the land in any such operating unit, and no owner of land in such unit not owning any interest in quitclaimed land, except by virtue of such pooling, shall have any interest in such quitclaimed land after the quitclaim is delivered or recorded. Allocation of production as aforesaid from any such operating unit, whether to the leased land or in like manner to other lands therein, shall continue notwithstanding any quitclaim or other termination, either in whole or in part, of this or any other lease covering lands in such unit until such time as the owner of such land shall (or shall give others the right to) drill for or produce any of the pooled substances from any part of such lands, whereupon all such lands formerly included in such unit and as to which the lease covering the same shall have been terminated, shall be excluded in determining the production to be allocated to the respective lands in such unit and in prorating taxes; and in the event of the failure of Lessor's or any other owner's title as to any portion of the land included in any such operating unit, such portion of such land shall

COURTESY OF L. RAE CONNET

Figure 5.8. A pooling and unitization clause allows the lessee to combine tracts with others in a pool or a unit for the purpose of drilling.

likewise be excluded from such unit, provided that Lessee shall not be held to account for any production allocated to any lands excluded from any such operating unit unless and until Lessee has actual knowledge of the aforesaid circumstances requiring such exclusion.

Lessee may, at any time either before or after the commencement of the drilling of a well on lands included in any such operating unit, wholly dissolve such unit by executing a Declaration of Dissolution. Promptly after execution of such Declaration of Dissolution, Lessee shall give written notice thereof to Lessor. Upon the dissolution of any such operating unit, whether or not this lease or any other lease involved herein remains in effect, all rights of Lessor hereunder to royalty on pooled substances produced which were so pooled (other than the leased land) shall cease and terminate; but such dissolution shall not otherwise affect or impair any of Lessee's rights or obligations under this lease, including its right to create a new operating unit or units out of the lands previously pooled pursuant to this paragraph, or constitute a surrender of any part of or any interest in the leasehold estate created hereby. The sale, conveyance or other transfer of, or of any interest in, any portion or portions of the leased land which are, at the time of transfer, subject to an operating unit shall (unless the instrument effecting such transfer expressly provides otherwise) be deemed to include and shall operate as a transfer and assignment of all of the transferor's interest, rights and benefits under this lease (including the right to royalty on allocated production from the lands subject to any such unit) insofar as such interest, rights and benefits pertain to or are allocable hereunder to the portion or portions of the leased land or interest therein so transferred.

29. UNITIZATION. In addition to the rights granted Lessee in paragraph 28 hereof, Lessee is hereby given the right to make this lease and Lessor's rights therein and the leased land, or any part hereof, subject to any unit agreement or any plan or agreement which be subscribed to or entered into by Lessee and approved by any governmental authority, having for its purpose orderly and efficient development and operation of one or more oil or gas producing zones underlying the leased land and other lands within the field or productive area in which the leased land is situated, the prevention of waste and damage to subsurface reservoirs, or the promotion of conservation of the oil, gas and mineral deposits underlying said area by any method now known or which may hereafter be discovered, including, without limitation, secondary or tertiary operations which employ repressurization, the injection of water, steam, foam or other substances designed to enhance the ultimate recovery of oil, gas or mineral reserves. Lessee has the right to unilaterally enlarge or decrease the unit or to change the unit boundaries before or after production has been obtained. The development and operation of the leases and properties included within the productive area designated in said agreement or plan in accordance with the terms and conditions thereof shall constitute full performance of all obligations and conditions imposed upon Lessee by this lease for the development and operation of the leased land; and provided further, that the royalties herein reserved shall thereafter be calculated on the proportion of the production of oil, gas, hydrocarbons, minerals and associated substances produced from all the leases and properties unitized within said area, allocated under said agreement or plan to said lands and shall be in lieu of royalties on production from the leased land. If there shall be production in paying quantities on any of the leases or tracts covered by said unit agreement or plan, this lease shall continue in force so long as such production continues. Upon the termination of any such unit agreement or plan, this lease shall not terminate on account of lack of development and/or on said leased lands if Lessee shall commence operations and thereafter prosecute such drilling operations with reasonable diligence on the leased lands or lands pooled therewith. If requested, Lessor shall formally express Lessor's consent to any such unit agreement or plan adopted by Lessee by executing the same or a consent thereto upon request of Lessee, but such formal consent is not required to give such unit agreement or plan effect.

Courtesy of L. Rae Connet

Figure 5.8, cont. A pooling and unitization clause allows the lessee to combine tracts with others in a pool or a unit for the purpose of drilling.

The practice of pooling lands of a size greater than 640 acres is more common today in the unconventional plays due to the drilling of horizontal wells. While standard lease forms often do not address the larger pooled units, many lessees are replacing the standard pooling language in lease forms to allow themselves to drill and pool a greater amount of oil and gas interests. Some states regulate the size of the units, while other states, new to the unconventional plays, have yet to address this issue. However large a lessee wishes to make a unit, it is important to anticipate regulation and state carefully that the unit will comply with any unit size permitted by a governing authority, rather than any unit size required by a governmental authority, as a governing authority might only require a 640-acre unit but might permit a much larger one. It is also important to address whether a pooled unit can be revised either through decreasing or increasing the size of the unit because at the time the well is drilled, an operator might not know how much acreage will be necessary in a pooled unit to drain the reservoir.

Pooling combines tracts to form one unit for drilling.

Like pooling, unitization involves combining tracts, but generally on a larger scale. Whole reservoirs, or large sections of them, are often unitized to make secondary or tertiary recovery operations possible. The principle is the same, and the advantages to the operator very similar. Landowners might also benefit from these arrangements. They should negotiate the relevant clauses with care, though, because the legal effects are quite complex. For example, royalty owners must share production with other parties in the unit. Shares are often calculated on the percentage of reservoir each owner has contributed to the unit. If engineering and geological studies show the reservoir to be unequally distributed underneath the tracts of land, one owner might have a lower or a higher percentage of royalty than others with tracts of the same size. (A unitization requires ratification by a substantial majority of the owners involved precisely because shares might not be proportionate to the number of acres contributed. Pooling, however, generally requires no consent from the landowners but does require the consent of the *nonparticipating royalty owners.*)

Unitization combines tracts on a larger scale to exploit an entire reservoir or a large part of a reservoir.

A pool or unitization can also affect the habendum clause in each owner's lease. To keep a well anywhere on the unit from holding all the leased land, owners sometimes require the insertion of a *Pugh clause* (discussed in the next chapter). Such a clause provides for the release of nonproducing acres and strata (layers of earth) at a specified date or in the absence of specified development.

Surrender Clause

A *surrender clause*, or *release clause*, spells out the procedure for a lessee's voluntary surrender of all or part of its leased interests. The lessee can also terminate the lease by failing to comply with the lease's conditions, but such failure is presumably involuntary. It is always prudent to require a written notice of surrender from the lessee; this notice can be recorded and will provide the landowner with a clear title if the property is to be leased again.

Damage Clause

Many operators voluntarily pay for damage to the surface. However, most leases do include a clause that specifies that the lessee will be liable to the surface owner for damage to all growing crops and other items listed (fig. 5.9). Some *damage clauses* leave out the reference to growing crops. Some add improvements to the site, along with any special considerations such as timber or pasture that need protection. The damage clause should be particularly tailored to the requirements of the individual landowner. Damage clauses should also be limited when the oil and gas owner is not the same as the surface owner.

Courtesy of Enid News & Eagle. Photo by Billy Hefton

Figure 5.9. A damage clause addresses how the lessee will compensate the surface owner for such things as losses resulting from accidents. This photo shows the fire that followed an explosion at a drilling rig in Oklahoma.

Assignment Clause

In a release of an oil and gas lease, the lessee or the assignee gives up its rights and interests under the lease.

Leases can be freely assigned by lessor or lessee. Ordinarily, neither must have the other's permission to sell, trade, or otherwise transfer a lease to someone else. From the lessee's point of view, especially, this assignable character of a lease can be quite an asset; leases frequently change hands a number of times before and sometimes after production begins. It is a good idea, therefore, to require that both parties give notice of such transfers. The landowner will need to know the names and addresses of all the assignees that the original lessee has dealt with, if only to be sure about who has a right to be on the property. Should delay rental payments ever stop (suggesting that the lessee has simply dropped the lease), the landowner will also want to know whom to contact to get a *release*. Lessees who assign only a part of their interest are, of course, obliged to arrange for the timely payment of delay rentals (dividing these, perhaps, between themselves and their *assignees*) to keep the lease in force.

The lessee should be promptly informed of any assignments by the landowner so that rentals and royalties will be paid to the proper persons. The lessee must also change the lease records to reflect changes in ownership. An *assignment clause* (fig. 5.10) usually specifies that such changes are not binding on a lessee until it has received formal notice. In general, assignments that change or divide leased interests must not increase the obligations or decrease the rights of the lessee .

27. ASSIGNMENT. If this lease shall be assigned as to a particular part or parts of the leased land, such division of the leasehold estate shall constitute and create separate and distinct holdings under the lease of and according to the several portions of the leased land as thus divided, and the holder or owner of each such portion of the leased land shall be required to comply with and perform Lessee's obligations under this lease for, and only to the extent of, his/her portion of the leased land, provided that nothing herein shall be construed to enlarge or multiply the drilling or rental obligations, and provided further that the commencement of the operations and the prosecution thereof, as provided in paragraphs 1, 5, and 6 hereof, either by the Lessee or any assignee hereunder, shall protect the lease as a whole. No change in the ownership of land or minerals covered by this lease, and no assignment or transfer by operation of law or otherwise of rents or royalties shall be binding on Lessee until it has been furnished with a certified copy of the instrument of transfer, together with proper evidence that there has been compliance with the laws of the State of California with respect to the transfer or assignment of any royalty or mineral interest.

Courtesy of L. Rae Connet

Figure 5.10. An assignment clause allows the lessee to assign the lease rights to another party and specifies how notice of assignment should be given.

Warranty and Proportionate Reduction Clauses

Types of warranty clauses:
- General
- Special

As mentioned in the discussion of the land description, many landowners and their attorneys believe that the warranty and the proportionate reduction clauses contradict each other. The first seems to guarantee clear title, while the second provides for the possibility that an owner owns less than the land description claims. Although few owners dispute the justice of a proportionate reduction in rentals and royalties if their interests turn out to be smaller than at first thought, a number of owners refuse to provide title guarantees at all and insist that warranty clauses be removed. If the lessor wants to strike the *general warranty clause*, then the lessee should request a *special warranty clause* where the lessor warrants title by and through that lessee. Other portions of this clause are less likely to cause objections. These generally include the lessee's rights in the event that the lessor defaults on obligations such as taxes and mortgages.

Force Majeure Clause

The *force majeure clause* usually contains a reminder that the lease is subject to state and federal laws (fig. 5.11). It also excuses the lessee from the timely performance of obligations if certain kinds of events beyond the lessee's control should occur. Examples are acts of war or rebellion, fire, flood, and other disasters referred to as "acts of God." Forms of government interference that cannot be blamed on the lessee should also be taken into consideration and mentioned, such as inability to obtain permits for drilling or hydraulic fracturing. Courts have often strictly construed force majeure clauses, and it is important for the lessee to specifically mention what kinds of events are covered in this clause: for example, ice storms, strikes, lack of demand in the market, lack of equipment, or lack of skilled personnel—conditions commonly encountered in new frontier areas.

Figure 5.11. A force majeure clause keeps the lease in force even though delays specified in the lease prevent the lessee from meeting its obligations.

12. When drilling, production or other operations on said land or land pooled with such land, or any part thereof are prevented, delayed or interrupted by lack of water, labor or materials, or by fire, storm, flood, war, rebellion, insurrection, sabotage, riot, strike, difference with workers, or failure of carriers to transport or furnish facilities for transportation, or as a result of some law, order, rule, regulation or necessity of governmental authority, either State or Federal, or as a result of the filing of a suit in which Lessee's title may be affected, or as a result of any cause whatsoever beyond the reasonable control of Lessee, the lease shall nevertheless continue in full force and effect. If any such prevention, delay or interruption should commence during the primary term hereof, the time of such prevention, delay or interruption shall not be counted against Lessee and the running of the primary term shall be suspended during such time; if any such prevention, delay or interruption should commence after the primary term hereof, Lessee shall have a period of ninety (90) days after the termination of such period of prevention, delay or interruption within which to commence or resume drilling, production or other operations hereunder, and this lease shall remain in force during such ninety (90) day period and thereafter in accordance with the other provisions of this lease. Lessee shall not be liable for breach of any express or implied covenants of this lease when drilling, production or other operations are so prevented, delayed or interrupted.

Legal Effect Clause and Lessor's Signature

The *legal effect clause* binds the parties and declares the lease effective for the lessor when he or she signs the instrument. Lessors' signatures are dated and, depending upon the state in which the lease is executed, must follow certain conventions. More will be said about the execution of leases in the next chapter. Here it can be pointed out that a lessor needs to sign in the same way he or she did when acquiring the land. If maiden names, nicknames, initials, and so forth appear on earlier instruments such as deeds, then these same forms should be used—with any additions or alternatives—on the lease. Representatives of other persons should clearly specify the legal capacity in which they are signing, along with their own names and the names of those they represent.

The signature of at least the lessor is required for the transfer of interests and rights to be binding.

Acknowledgment

In principle, the purpose of the acknowledgment is to verify the identities of those signing the lease and that the signers executed the lease for the reasons stated in the instrument. In practice, the purpose of the acknowledgment is to make a lease recordable; a lease will not be entered into public records without a proper acknowledgment. The acknowledgment on a lease consists of a declaration on the part of the officer making it (usually a *notary*) that the signers either proved their identity or are known to him or her and that they made an oath that they signed the instrument for the consideration named in it. For more information on acknowledgments, see Chapter 6.

SUMMARY

- While oil and gas leases might contain some specific provisions prepared by an attorney of the landowner or an attorney of an oil and gas company, they all tend to contain the following basic elements: the names of the lessor and lessee, a description of the land, a conveyance of specified rights, consideration for the rights conveyed, and an obligation to drill and to pay a percentage of the production to the landowner.
- Because leases tend to consist of the same elements, they can also be made on forms. Traditionally, forms have been printed on paper and filled in (on blanks) or modified with strike-outs or addendums. Today, the online environment provides a multitude of customizable electronic forms. Some specialized lease forms are modeled on the laws and regulations of a particular region or state.
- State and federal agencies require lease applications to be made on their own forms. Many of those forms are available online.
- Forms are also published for profit by private companies. Producers 88 is a conventional name given to form leases. These "standard" leases are, in fact, so different in their provisions that they are not standard at all. Anyone signing such a lease would be advised to read it carefully to be certain that it expresses the intent of the parties signing.

- There are other types of form leases, including forms designed to advance the interests of landowners by regional associations and by oil and gas attorneys.
- A lease is made up of four main parts—the preamble, provisions, signature block, and acknowledgment.
- The preamble consists of basic information that identifies what the lease is. It consists of the title of the lease, names of parties to the agreement, effective date, and consideration promised.
- To be valid, any oil and gas lease must include a legal description of the land or a reference to a previous document with such a description. The land description might appear in the preamble or in the granting clause.
- The provisions of a lease specify the rights and obligations of the parties under the agreement—the right of the lessor to royalties and the obligation of the lessee to compensate the lessor in the event of damage to the surface, for example.
- The signature block is where the lessor signs the lease. The lessee might also sign the lease. Any party signing the lease should also include a date of execution.
- An acknowledgment is added to a lease to make it recordable. Only when an officer such as a notary has verified the identities of the signing parties and that they signed the instrument for the reasons stated in it will the lease be filed in public records.

In this chapter:

- Special provisions added to leases
- Acceptable variations in the execution of a lease
- Importance of proper acknowledgment and recording of a lease
- Method of payment of bonuses: bank drafts
- Procedures for recording a lease
- Ratification of a lease

6 Execution of the Lease

FINAL NEGOTIATIONS

Many lease forms are completed and signed without additions or amendments. Often, though, the lessor will bargain to include some changes that make the lease provisions more detailed and specific. For example, the pipelines and flow lines needed for oil or gas production are ordinarily buried in the ground rather than set above the surface. Many leases describe the depth at which such lines will be buried (upon the lessor's request for their burial) as "below plow depth." Landowners sometimes wish to amend such phrases to make them more specific. They ask that the depth be specified as 36 inches or some other measurement that suits their particular circumstances. They may also request that the topsoil be replaced after the lines are buried.

Whether such changes are acceptable to the lessee will depend, in part, on the lessee's bargaining position. If the property to be leased is highly promising, the lessee might be willing to make a number of concessions in the form of amendments and special clauses; a lessee who is wildcatting in unproved country is likely to refuse such requests. The desirability of the property is not the only factor, of course, in any final bargaining that might occur before a lease is signed. Company policy and resources have their effect, as does the eagerness of the landowner to lease.

Special Terms and Provisions

Assuming that the landowner is not too eager to lease, here are some, though by no means all, of the special provisions that he or she might ask for in a lease:

- Plat/aerial photo approval for equipment placement
- Free gas and a special price for gas
- A Pugh clause, or *Freestone rider*
- Requirements to drill an offset well or, alternatively, to make compensatory royalty payments
- A market value clause
- Protection of water resources and domestic animals
- Requirements to restore the site and to comply with regulations in plugging and abandoning

Plat Map Approval and Equipment Placement

Landowners concerned about protecting valuable surface features such as pastures and springs might ask for the right to approve or at least be consulted on the placement of equipment, storage facilities, pipelines, and roads. They might also wish to specify a maximum width for access roads. A plat map or aerial photographs can show precisely which parts of the property are to be protected (fig. 6.1). Even leases that do not include such protective clauses for special features of the land often do stipulate that wells may not be drilled within a given distance—usually 200 feet—of buildings like houses and barns. In other cases, ongoing surface activities such as irrigation might need special mention so that drilling and production equipment, storage tanks, and so forth do not interfere with the landowner's use of the property. Finally, some landowners who are concerned that oil or gas production will turn their premises into a disaster area ask for limited beautification efforts such as the painting of tanks and the filling in of slush pits.

COURTESY OF GEOSOUTHERN ENERGY CORPORATION

Figure 6.1. An aerial photo of a ranch. A photo such as this one could be marked to indicate areas to be protected from operations.

Free Gas and Gas Purchase

In some parts of the country, such as Kansas and Oklahoma, owners frequently bargain for free gas from gas-producing wells. That gas is generally used in the owner's home. Owners might also want the right to buy gas at the wellhead price to use in their farming operations. Similar arrangements are, however, uncommon in other parts of the country.

A Pugh clause releases property not used by the lessee for production within a set period of time.

Pugh Clauses

The point of a Pugh clause, or Freestone rider, is to release property that is not being used by the lessee for production within a specified period—at the end of the primary term, for example. A horizontal clause releases nonproducing acres; a vertical clause releases depths below the zone that is producing. The concern behind such a clause is the landowner's fear that the entire tract, possibly a large one with potential for significant production, could be held for years by marginal production from a shallow well. The clause itself can be drafted in a variety of ways, but it generally aims to release unproductive or untested zones and lease acreage outside a producing pooled unit if drilling or exploration does not take place by the end of the specified time.

Types of Pugh clauses:
- Horizontal
- Vertical

Offset Wells

When a producing well is located within a certain distance of the lease line on a neighboring tract, the lease might require the drilling of an offset well to protect the leased lands from drainage. In some states, the lessee has an implied obligation to protect the leased premises from being drained. However, adding a provision to that effect in the lease gives the lessor more protection. An additional provision that can be negotiated into the lease form gives the lessee the option of making a monthly payment to the lessor, usually called a *compensatory royalty payment,* in lieu of paying to drill an offset well.

Market Value Clause

This provision guarantees that the lessor is paid the current market value for oil or gas produced within a specified geographic area—not the price received by the operator.

Water and Animals

Laws concerning water rights are complex and vary by state. In some states, water is owned by either the surface owner or the mineral owner, depending on the depth of the water-bearing zone. In others, water is owned by the state. The biggest concern to property owners is that their drinking or agricultural water rights are not interfered with. The biggest concern to states and conservationists is that the freshwater supply be protected from chemicals. Many landowners are now adding language to the lease that requires the lessor to test their water wells prior to commencing drilling operations on their land and then retest after the well is completed.

Landowners are also seeking to protect their water supplies with lease language that requires the lessee to remove from the property any fluids used for drilling or completing a well (such as frac fluids).

Landowners might look to protect their property in other ways, as well. If the leased property has game animals or stocked ponds and streams, the lessor might contractually restrict the lessee from hunting and fishing. The lessor might additionally restrict drilling and other operations from being conducted during various hunting seasons. Domestic animals might also be protected by provisions requiring that cattle guards be installed, fences maintained, gates kept closed and locked, and other similar precautions observed (fig. 6.2).

Figure 6.2. There can be lease provisions that protect domestic animals or compensate the owner in the event that animals are harmed by operations carried out on the land.

Site Reclamation and Well Plugging

When exploration or production comes to an end, a lease generally requires that the well site be restored—as nearly as possible—to its original condition. A lease also generally requires that wells be plugged and abandoned according to state regulations.

EXECUTION AND ACKNOWLEDGMENT

Variations in Proper Execution

A properly executed oil and gas lease is a written instrument signed by the mineral owner (lessor). States differ somewhat in their special requirements for leases executed by married persons, the blind, the illiterate, corporate officers, and so on. The signature of the lessor should conform to that used on any earlier document by which the land was acquired, such as a deed. Nicknames, initials, and name changes can usually be handled by signing with both names. For example, a man might sign a lease "Robert Hatchet, also known as R. L. Hatchet," or "Robert L. Hatchet, also known as Bobby Hatchet." A woman whose name has changed since she acquired her property might sign as "Nancy Todd Cooper, a married woman, formerly known as Nancy Todd, a single woman."

In a lease, a caption next to a name indicates the capacity in which the person is signing the document as representative for another person.

People who sign as representatives must include a *caption* that indicates the capacity in which they sign and (in most cases) the party for whom they sign. Normally, these names will appear twice—once in the caption and once with the signature itself. For example, an attorney signing for a client would use a form like the following one:

Robert L. Hatchet, appearing herein
through Avery Smith, his Agent and
Attorney-in-Fact, under Power of
Attorney dated ____________ ,
and recorded in Book ________
Page ________ of the records of
______________ County,
State of ______________

ROBERT L. HATCHET

By ______________________
Avery Smith, Agent and
Attorney-in-Fact

An attorney-in-fact is a person acting under a power of attorney.

When the person signing acts as the representative of someone in a special category, that fact is usually indicated:

Wilfred Smith, Guardian of the
Estate of Susan Cooper, a Minor

____
Wilfred Smith, Guardian
of the Estate of Susan Cooper,
a Minor

Or

Rafael Ramos, Executor of the Estate
of Josefina Ramos, Deceased

____
Rafael Ramos, Executor
of the Estate of
Josefina Ramos, Deceased

The Importance of Proper Acknowledgment

The execution of an instrument refers chiefly to its signing. The acknowledgment serves to prove proper execution. An officer who provides an acknowledgment is, in effect, pledging—with a written certificate and an official signature—that the lessor signed his or her lease without being coerced. The notary also assures the identity of the signing party. Anyone who examines an executed and acknowledged lease can be reasonably confident that the instrument was not obtained under duress or signed with a false name. The officer frequently sought for acknowledgments is the nearest notary public, but some states allow justices of the peace, mayors, clerks of court, and other officers to serve in this capacity. While not all states require acknowledgment for an oil and gas lease to be valid between the parties, prudence suggests that leases be recorded—and to record an instrument in the county records, one needs to have it acknowledged.

RECORDING OF THE EXECUTED LEASE

Both lessor and lessee have a strong interest in seeing their lease recorded, or officially entered into the relevant county records. All inquirers, whether competitors of the leasing parties, creditors, or merely the curious, can then see that a valid lease exists for that particular tract of land. Title cannot be challenged and defeated by, for example, a creditor of the lessee or a mortgage holder of the lessor on the grounds of an unrecorded transaction. Recording should always be carried out as promptly as possible. Not only should the oil and gas lease itself be recorded, but attendant instruments, such as assignments, releases, deeds, ratifications, and judgments should, as well. Ordinarily, the recording of a lease is handled by the lessee or a representative of the lessee. Quite commonly, too, the recording procedure follows the issuing and honoring of a draft for payment of the lease bonus, as described below.

Memorandum of Lease

Sometimes, the parties to an oil and gas lease would like for some of the terms of the agreement to remain confidential—for instance, the sums offered as royalty and bonus. In that case, a *memorandum (memo) of oil and gas lease* can be recorded in the place of the lease itself. A memorandum is a shortened form that only provides details such as names of the parties and a description of the land. Since it refers to the original lease by reference, it "stands in" for it and serves as notice in the public records, but it has the advantage of keeping out of public records the specific and material terms of the lease. (For an example of a lease memo, see figure D.1 in the appendices.)

Bonus Drafts

At the time of signing, the landman might give to the lessor a draft, or written order on a bank, authorizing the bonus payment. When the landowner presents this draft and the signed lease at his or her own bank, both lease and draft will be sent on to the lessee's bank. How promptly the landowner gets the payment depends on the nature of the draft. A *sight draft* must be picked up at the lessee's bank on the day that it arrives. A five-day draft allows the lessee to wait for five days. The landman picking up the draft at the bank is responsible for making certain the lease was properly executed and acknowledged.

Recording Procedures

The various states handle the recording of legal instruments in slightly different ways. Usually, when a lease is sent from the lessee's office to the appropriate county recorder or clerk of court, the original instrument is returned with recording information noted on it (fig. 6.3). Some states will keep the original and return a second original or certified copy on request.

Generally, a lease is sent or delivered to the courthouse immediately following execution and payment of a bonus. There are some exceptions to this rule of thumb. If, for example, leasing activity on private lands needs to be kept secret to minimize competition, the acquiring oil and gas company might choose to file all leases simultaneously after the leasing is complete. This would eliminate the chance of competitors identifying the lands as they are being leased because the leases are on file immediately after execution.

Recording is entering a document into public records.

Recordation is the act of recording.

FILED AND RECORDED
OFFICIAL PUBLIC RECORDS
Diane Gonzales, County Clerk
Atascosa County Texas
March 27, 2012 03:51:29 PM
FEE: $20.00
RATIFY
130009

Source: Atascosa County Clerk

Figure 6.3. A recordation stamp

RATIFICATION

A ratification is an agreement that confirms a lease already executed—often by someone else. Such an agreement can be formalized as a written instrument and titled, for example, Ratification of Oil and Gas Lease. (A sample ratification of an oil and gas lease appears as figure 6.4.) A ratification can be executed at almost any time after the original lease has been signed. Co-owners of interest in the property are historically known to ratify leases when they agree to the same terms. However, attorneys might request ratification from ex-spouses, new spouses, or others who might eventually have a claim to a mineral interest in a leased property.

SUMMARY

- A lessor might negotiate for special provisions to be added to a lease. Whether the lessee will accept those provisions will probably depend on the relative bargaining position of the two parties, which is determined by such factors as whether the leasehold is perceived as a promising prospect or an unproven risk.
- Among the provisions that lessors commonly negotiate is one specifying locations where equipment can be placed on the property. The lessor might also seek a provision to protect domestic animals or the water supply in areas of a leasehold.
- In some states, it is common for the mineral rights owner to negotiate for free gas from the well. A landowner concerned that the mineral assets might be drained away by a well on a neighboring tract might ask for a clause that would require the lessee to drill an offset well. Lessors who ask for Pugh clauses are seeking to release acres or strata unused by the lessee so that they might be leased to another party.
- State statutes address what legal obligations exist for plugging and abandoning a well. It is in the interest of the lessor that there be provisions in the lease that specifically state the obligations of the lessee in that process and of the lessee to restore the site as nearly as possible to its original condition.
- States vary to some degree in their requirements for the execution of an oil and gas lease. However, some generalizations can be made about what constitutes proper execution. For example, the lease is a written instrument signed by the lessor, preferably with the same name that the lessor has used on any previous conveyances for the land.
- While, in some cases, a lease does not have to be recorded to be a binding agreement between the parties, it is advisable to do so, as recording is considered to provide notice to all inquirers, including creditors and competitors of the leasing parties. And notice of the agreement can provide certain benefits—protection against certain kinds of claims to title, for instance. For a lease to be recorded, it must be properly acknowledged by an officer such as a notary public.

NOTICE OF CONFIDENTIALITY RIGHTS: If you are a natural person, you may remove or strike any of the following information from this instrument before it is filed for record in public records: your social security number or your driver's license number.

RATIFICATION OF OIL, GAS AND MINERAL LEASE

STATE OF TEXAS §
COUNTY OF ATASCOSA §

KNOW ALL MEN BY THESE PRESENTS:

WHEREAS NELDA B. HAZE, as Lessor, executed an Oil, Gas and Mineral Lease in favor of Black Gold Oil & Gas, L.L.P. as Lessee, which said Oil, Gas and Mineral Lease covers land situated in that County and State, described as follows:

> 72 acres, more or less, out of the Southern Texas RR Survey No. 1253, A-502, Atascosa, County, Texas, and being more particularly described in a Warranty Deed from Nelda B. Haze, a single woman, to Leonard Lemoine, a married man, dated December 5, 2011, and recorded in Document #118569, Official Public Records, Atascosa County, Texas.

NOW THEREFORE, for valuable consideration, the receipt and sufficiency of which is acknowledged, the undersigned, as Lessor, does hereby adopt, ratify and confirm said Lease and all of its terms and provisions, and lets the land covered by the Lease to the Lessee named above, subject to and in accordance with all of the terms and provisions of the Lease. The undersigned hereby further declares that said Lease in all of its terms and provisions is a valid and subsisting Oil, Gas and Mineral Lease and that said Lease is binding on the undersigned and the undersigned's successors and assigns.

IN WITNESS WHEREOF, this ratification is executed on the 13th day of March, 2012

Nelda B. Haze
Nelda B. Haze, Lessor

ACKNOWLEDGMENT

STATE OF TEXAS §
COUNTY OF ATASCOSA §

This instrument was acknowledged before me on this 13th day of March, 2012 by Nelda B. Haze, Lessor.

Leroy McAvoy
(Signature of Notary Public)

Leroy McAvoy
(Printed Name of Notary)

My commission expires: 06/01/2013

SOURCE: ADAPTED FROM A RATIFICATION OF OIL, GAS, AND MINERAL LEASE FROM THE ATASCOSA COUNTY CLERK

Figure 6.4. A sample ratification of an oil and gas lease. (The names that appear in the document are fictitious.)

- If the parties to a lease do not want the financial terms to be in public records, they can record a memorandum of oil and gas lease, which will serve as notice but avoid revealing all the terms of the agreement.
- When the lease is executed, the landman might give the lessor a draft from a bank for the bonus payment.
- When a lease has already been executed and the signature of a co-owner of an interest in the property is still required, a ratification will often be drawn up. This type of instrument confirms the agreement of the co-owner to the lease.

In this chapter:

- Examination of title in preparation for drilling
- Title opinions
- Methods of curing title
- Procedures for obtaining a permit to drill
- Examination of title to accompany division orders
- Preparation of division orders

7 Preparations for Drilling, Producing, and Selling

Once a landowner has signed a lease and received a bonus, his or her paperwork is, for the moment, complete. The landowner might monitor the situation, update files, or negotiate leases on other properties, but without access to venture capital, there isn't much that he or she can contribute to the drilling of a well. This is not the case for the landman, whose work has often just begun. Depending on the landman's experience and the needs of the company or client, he or she might be called upon to arrange—in the most precise terms—the financing of exploration and drilling. The trades, joint ventures, and operating agreements that might be required to drill and then develop property are a complex subject in their own right and will be considered together in Chapter 8. This chapter will assume that the money to drill has been found. It will look at the other preliminary steps the landman might take part in, particularly the examining and curing of titles to leased properties.

EXAMINING TITLES

Though a preliminary check of the records is one of the landman's responsibilities, the examination of title is a job that will be carried out by the company's legal department or a title attorney hired by the company. The landman must, however, often work with the title examiner and remember the importance to the oil company or operator of good title—that is, title that can be legally defended. Sometimes, the landman is an attorney with the specialized knowledge needed to examine titles; more often, he or she must turn to a qualified specialist for assistance in completing that task.

Title Examiners

Marketable title is not perfect title; rather, it is title that can be successfully defended.

Attorneys who examine titles to oil and gas properties might be employed by petroleum companies, but more often than not, they are in private practice. Their responsibilities call for methodical, painstaking work, and on their decisions rest further important decisions—to proceed with drilling, for example, or to begin royalty payments. A title examiner hopes for a perfect, unclouded title but nearly always finds an imperfect one.

What would constitute a perfect title to land? Presumably, a set of recorded instruments that show an unbroken *chain of title* stretching all the way from the original land patent or land grant to the present owner's deed. Conveyances, leases, severances—all transactions involving the ownership of the land, particularly the oil and gas rights—would be on record and their wording would be crystal clear. There would be neither gaps nor ambiguities. The present owner's claim to the property would be invulnerable to claims by possible heirs, creditors, or others. In such a case, the examiner could write a *title opinion* that would send the client out fearlessly to drill and develop. Unfortunately, most often, perfect title does not exist and the best a landman can hope for is *marketable title.*

Title Opinions

A division order is a document that directs a purchaser of oil or gas to pay interest owners.

In the absence of such perfect chains of title, legal opinions about a title might be written at almost every stage of an oil or gas operation. Some companies order opinions before paying bonuses, before paying delay rentals, before drilling, and before executing *division orders.* In a particular situation, a number of supplementary opinions might be necessary and prudent—say, where a number of owners are involved and the various interests are complicated. The speed with which a company wishes to act can affect the number of opinions it orders, as can its general policy on title opinions. Some companies are more conservative than others, and what seems necessary to one might be judged hypercautious by another. Quite commonly, though, title opinions are needed at two different stages in an operation. The first document is called a *drill site opinion*; it is ordered when a drill site has been selected, and it can sometimes eliminate the need for producing new opinions later. When it does, the second document can simply be a copy of the first. That document is the *division order opinion*; it is ordered when division orders are to be drawn up.

However, when more information is required to pay all owners their proper shares of production, an examiner will draw up a separate division order opinion to clarify the question of who gets what. (Drill site opinions often do not show all royalty owners and what percentages they own.)

Companies differ on the forms they use for title opinions. Figure 7.1 shows a composite form that serves as an example. The sources of information available to a title examiner also vary. Depending on which sources are used, a title opinion is referred to as *abstract-based* or *stand-up*.

DESCRIPTION OF LAND:

ABSTRACTS AND OTHER INSTRUMENTS EXAMINED:

RECORD TITLE:

- Surface Ownership:
- Royalty Ownership:
- Mineral Interests under Lease:
- Mineral Interests Unleased:
- Easements and Encumbrances:

BASIC LEASE:

- Date of Lease:
- Date Recorded:
- Lessor:
- Lessee:
- Description of Land:
- Interest Conveyed:
- Primary Term:
- Royalties:
- Delay Rentals (Amount and to Whom Payable):
- Extended Term:
- Depository Bank:
- Drilling Obligations:
- Pooling Clause:
- Shut-In Clause:
- Unusual Clauses and Provisions:

ASSIGNMENTS OR SUBLEASES:

STATUS OF TAXES:

SEVERANCE FROM SOVEREIGNTY:

COMMENTS, OBJECTIONS, AND REQUIREMENTS:

Figure 7.1. A sample form for a title opinion

Types of title opinions:

- Abstract-based opinions
- Stand-up opinions

Abstract-Based Opinions

Title opinions often depend upon abstracts, and if a landman has not ordered an abstract at the time of the preliminary check, it might need to be done when a drill site is selected. An experienced landman, accustomed to working with title examiners, can sometimes judge how complete the required abstract needs to be and can give detailed instructions to the abstractor, noting what can safely be left out and what should be included. An experienced professional will also have collected other things the examiner might ask for—maps, rental and tax receipts, releases, *affidavits*, and so on. Again, thoroughness in the preliminary check can save time and money later on. The landman, for example, who has acquired a landowner's base abstract (or a copy of it) and ordered supplements to bring it up to date can turn these papers over to the examiner with minimal delay. In some situations, a takeoff—a list and brief description of the documents relevant to the title of a particular piece of property—ordered from an abstract office at a cost much below that of a complete abstract, might be adequate for the examiner's purposes.

Stand-Up Opinions

Before a lease is signed, the landman usually prepares a runsheet that briefly describes all the relevant documents in a tract's history of ownership (fig. 7.2). A landman's runsheet is much like an abstractor's takeoff. In the absence of an abstract, such a list can be a valuable starting point for the title examiner. If the examiner takes a runsheet to the county courthouse, carefully looks over all the documents that the list mentions, decides whether or not additional facts are needed, and then writes an opinion, he or she has produced what is known as a stand-up title opinion.

Stand-up opinions save the time and expense of abstract preparation. They might also seem preferable to dealing with unknown abstract plants. Here again, particular situations create particular needs. Some companies and some examiners depend heavily on runsheets prepared by experienced, reliable lease brokers or landmen. Others find abstracts well worth the investment of money and time. Whatever the examiner's sources and procedures, he or she is unlikely to find a perfect title and very likely to conclude that additional information is needed to *cure* a defective one.

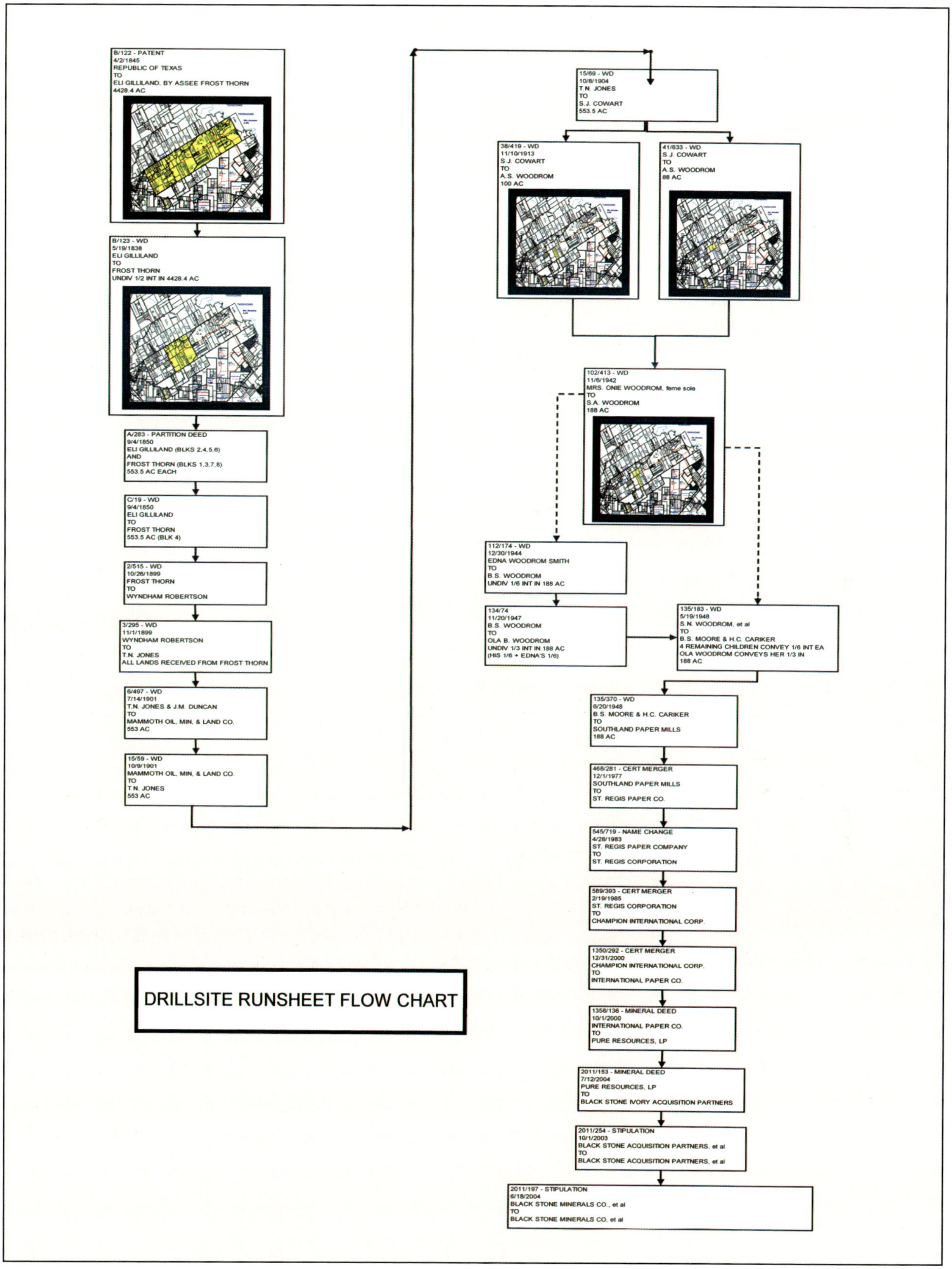

Figure 7.2. A runsheet mapping the ownership of mineral rights

Courtesy of Ted W. Walters & Associates, L.L.P.

CURING TITLES

A "cloud on title" is a defect in a title.

To "cure title" is to remedy defects in a title by affirming ownership.

When there are gaps in the chain of title or other defects that leave a *cloud* on the present owner's claim, the examiner often asks the landman to secure additional facts. The landman takes the examiner's requirements and goes in search of the requested information. These additional facts, properly attested to, are needed to cure the title—that is, to remedy defects and omissions that could make the present owner's claim to the property questionable. By satisfying the examiner, the landman hopes to rule out or at least minimize the risk of adverse claims to the property and make the lease title marketable. The company or client can then drill and develop the land. To meet the requirements, disinterested witnesses familiar with the facts must affirm them before a notary public; an owner or occupant of the land who makes an affirmation may be accused of being self-serving. Witnesses who swear to the written, notarized affirmations of fact known as affidavits might also be needed to testify in court.

Affidavits

The person who makes an affidavit is called the *affiant.* As an affiant might be called to testify in court, the landman looks for a reliable witness who will be likely to be available at a later date. The forms for affidavits and acknowledgments differ somewhat from state to state, so the landman must take care to see that the appropriate forms are used. Some of the most common types of affidavits used in curing titles are described in the passages that follow.

- *Affidavit of death and heirship*
- *Affidavit of identity*
- *Affidavit of nonproduction*
- *Affidavit of use, occupancy, and possession*
- *Affidavit of adverse possession*

Death and Heirship

An affidavit of death and heirship serves to affirm certain facts that would otherwise be established by a probate proceeding. An affiant might affirm, for example, that Leon Stubbs, the owner of a parcel of land, has indeed died and that Nadine Lamotte is legal heir. In such a situation, a disinterested witness with no financial or even emotional stake in the facts would be very helpful. Nadine Lamotte could not be viewed as a disinterested person.

Identity

An affidavit of identity simply establishes the fact that, in a given instance, a difference in name does not mean a difference in person. For example, a woman who once went by Bunny Smith may now go by her married name, Bunny Jones. Witnesses could swear that the "Bunny Smith" whose name appears on a property deed dated 1989 is in truth the same woman as the "Bunny Jones" who signed a lease on that property last week. It is usually not difficult to find witnesses for this type of affidavit, since any number of disinterested people know these types of facts and can attest to them.

Nonproduction

In a case of nonproduction at a well, the facts to be established concern nonproduction under an old lease. Ordinarily, the landman should obtain a release of the lease for the property, but a number of circumstances might make it difficult or even impossible to acquire a release from the lessee. In some cases, a lessee has died or closed down the business and moved away. In others, the lease has gotten old and been forgotten until the possibility of a new lease was presented to the landowner. In such a case, an affidavit of nonproduction executed by the lessor or the lessor's depository bank can testify to the facts required to terminate the lease. If the land is not under production and delay rentals are not being paid, then the land can be leased again. Where old leases are concerned, the lessor might be the only person in command of all the relevant facts and might serve as the affiant without much likelihood of a challenge.

Use, Occupancy, and Possession

An affidavit of use, occupancy, and possession can be very important for curing an old defect in title. An example of such a defect might be a gap in the chain of title caused by a courthouse fire that destroyed certain recorded instruments. The affidavit itself does not cure the defect; no affidavit does that. However, it can point to the existence of appropriate facts that support the present occupant's claim. For maximum effectiveness, the affidavit should be signed by at least two disinterested persons. (Separate instruments called *corroborating affidavits* are sometimes more convenient for the affiants in these cases.) The affiants must provide evidence for, not merely opinions or conclusions about, the present owner's possession of the property. Their evidence should cover as many years as they can accurately remember. For example, if a Clement Jones claims to have been in possession of a parcel of land for a certain number of years, his neighbor's statement that merely confirms what he has said would be insufficient to support his claim. If, on the other hand, the affiant can swear that Mr. Jones has lived on the property since December 1980 (a specific time), she is helping to establish relevant facts. Other helpful affirmations might specify what the occupant has done on the land, such as raising crops, grazing cattle, or building a house and living in it. Details such as these can do much to confirm a claim of ownership, despite the gap in the chain of title.

Adverse Possession

With an affidavit of adverse possession, the occupant of land asserts a claim to it against someone who holds title. The possessor says, in effect, that the occupancy and use of the land—carried out openly, continuously, and visibly—gives him or her a better claim than the record owner can assert. State statutes regulating claims made by adverse possession vary, particularly in regard to the time required to make possession effective. A possession of 5 years might carry certain requirements, one of 10 years certain other requirements, and one of 15 or 25 years a third set of requirements.

Adverse possession is a means of acquiring title to land formally owned by another, usually by occupying the land for an uninterrupted period of time.

A landman preparing or having an attorney prepare this kind of affidavit must be thoroughly familiar with relevant state statutes and must plan to supply the facts of possession in even greater detail than would be needed for an affidavit of use, occupancy, and possession. Proof of tax payments will often be particularly important.

The statutory language describing adverse possession can make the relations between a person holding legal title and a person claiming possession sound more belligerent than they are. Such statutes tend to use terms such as "notorious" and "hostile," which have special legal meanings. An affidavit of adverse possession might reflect real antagonisms or only confusion in the history of possession and ownership. Claims of adverse possession are fairly common in parts of central and East Texas, where early Spanish land grants were made. Succeeding governments and jurisdictions have left a number of titles in disarray. Occupants given the chance to lease their property and profit from its development might need to clarify their situation by means of affidavits, even though no rival claimant is glaring at them across the fence.

Other Kinds of Documents

The other kinds of documents that might be needed to cure defects in title are diverse. The following list includes some of the documents that are typically used.

- Tax receipts or certificates
- Rental receipts
- Mortgage instruments (including *deeds of trust*)
- *Subordinations*
- Releases
- *Quitclaim deeds*
- *Disclaimers*
- Ratifications

Tax and Rental Receipts

It has been mentioned that, in a claim of adverse possession, proof of tax payments by the occupant can be very important. Tax receipts or a tax certificate bearing the occupant's name should be turned over to the examiner along with the necessary affidavits. Rental receipts could be useful in certain instances—if, say, a landowner is establishing proof of untimely or terminated rental payments to free the land from an old lease.

Mortgage Instruments and Subordinations

The landman or examiner might also discover the existence of an old mortgage or deed of trust for the property. (A deed of trust, not to be confused with a simple deed, is an instrument that creates a special kind of mortgage used in certain states.) If the mortgage is no longer in effect, it can be released and the release recorded. If a deed of trust is still in effect, the holder of such an instrument (the creditor) has rights superior to any subsequent parties with an interest in the property. Without the creditor's consent, neither the landowner nor the current lessee can develop the land without taking undue risk. To avoid litigation, the landman needs to get a subordination from the mortgage or lien holder. An agreement of this type resolves the priority of rights and subordinates the earlier instrument to the oil and gas lease so that a foreclosure would not render the lease void. Mortgages or liens obtained after the execution of an oil and gas lease are already subordinate; the lessee does not need special instruments to protect the lease from those types of claims.

A deed of trust is not a simple deed; rather, it is an instrument used to create a special kind of mortgage.

Releases, Quitclaims, and Disclaimers

A landman who finds an old lease on record and suspects that it has expired can ask the lessee for a release. Most lessees honor such requests as a matter of course. When the lease has changed hands, the approval of the assigning party is also sometimes needed to obtain a release. A landman may also encounter a situation where someone with a possible claim to land is simply not interested in it. In that case, he or she might be able to obtain a quitclaim deed from the claimant. In a quitclaim deed, a person waives rather than asserts a claim to land; a quitclaim relinquishes any rights or interests a person might have in a property. Similarly to quitclaims, disclaimers, which are often signed by surface tenants, waive a claim on the part of a signer to the title; they state that the tenant merely uses the surface rather than owns the land.

In a quitclaim deed, a person waives any possible interest he or she could have in a property.

Ratifications

Finally, ratifications might be judged necessary or prudent supplements to a lease when a title is being cured. If, for instance, the title examination has turned up an unexpected mineral owner, the newcomer might be willing to ratify the existing lease. Ratifying an existing lease can often be easier than executing a new lease.

PERMITTING AND DRILLING

An encumbrance is a claim by another to title that reduces the value of the title or prevents it from being transferred.

When the examiner agrees that the title to a chosen drill site has been cured and that no outstanding claims or *encumbrances* impair it, the company or operator is almost ready to drill. In many states, the next step is to obtain a *well permit* from the agency that enforces the state conservation laws. The permit serves to ensure that the well site conforms to spacing regulations and other state requirements or that the site merits the granting of an exception to such rules. Generally, large companies have a regulatory department that handles the permitting of the wells with state agencies. The regulatory department works alongside the land department to ensure that the names of the mineral or surface owners are included on the well permits.

The permit form generally shows information such as the proposed depth of the well, the name of the operator, and so on. When an application conforms to rules, agency approval for a well site is ordinarily a routine matter. To avoid difficulties, applicants must be familiar with the rules and avoid the temptation to bend the rules to fit their situation.

With the necessary permit acquired, the title cured, and the landowner or occupant notified, drilling can begin. With luck and hard work, the operator might have a producing well in short order. At that point, it will be time to draw up a division order title opinion. This opinion will make it possible to draft and execute accurate division orders, thereby assuring payment to the various interest owners.

EXECUTING DIVISION ORDERS

Working interest is a share of production revenues. It includes an obligation to pay for development and operations.

A division order is an instrument confirming the interest each party has in the well and is generally signed by the *working interest* owners and the royalty owners (fig. 7.3). Therefore, it names all the parties to be paid—mineral owners, royalty owners, working interest owners, and so on—and converts their fractional shares into decimal figures. Payments for the oil or gas sold are then calculated on the basis of each owner's interest. (To learn more about oil and gas interests, see Appendix K.) Division orders commonly serve additional purposes, as they can give the purchaser certain rights in determining how the oil or gas is handled, what accounting procedures are used, and how market values are reckoned. In many states, landowners are not required to sign the division orders, and in most states, division orders cannot alter the terms of the oil and gas lease.

Black Gold

OIL AND GAS

Division Order

Return to: Black Gold Oil & Gas, L.L.P.
2100 South Freeway
Lafayette, LA 70507

Date: January 2. 2013
Effective: Date of First Production

Property Name: High Island 410A
Operator: Black Gold Oil & Gas, L.L.P
County/Parish and State: Offshore Gulf of Mexico

OWNER NAME	INTEREST
G. Dan Pickett	0.1462333

Production: ☐ Oil ☐ Gas ☐ Condensate ☑ All

The undersigned certifies the ownership of his/her decimal interest in production or proceeds as described above payable by Black Gold Oil & Gas, L.L.P.

The undersigned shall notify Black Gold of any change in ownership, decimal interest, or payment address. Any such changes shall be effective the first day of the month after receipt of notice.

Black Gold is authorized to withhold payment pending the resolution of a title dispute or adverse claim to interest in production claimed by the undersigned. The undersigned agrees to indemnify and reimburse the payor for any amount attributable to an interest to which the undersigned is not entitled. Black Gold may accrue proceeds until the amount totals $25.00 or pay semi-annually, whichever occurs first or is required by applicable statutes.

This division order does not amend any lease or operating agreement between the undersigned and the lessee or the operator or any other contracts for the purchase of oil or gas.

In addition to the conditions of this division order, the undersigned and Black Gold may have certain statutory rights under the laws of the state where the property is located.

OWNER: ______________________

BY: ______________________

ADDRESS: ______________________

____

____

TIN/S.S. NUMBER: ______________________

PHONE NUMBER: ______________________

Federal Law requires you to furnish your Social Security or Taxpayer Identification Number. Failure to comply will result in 31% withholding that will not be refundable by Black Gold.

Figure 7.3. A sample division order

In a division order, a revocation provision allows all parties to revoke, or cancel, the agreement.

Who issues division orders and sees to the disbursement of sale proceeds? Originally, the purchaser did these things. Division orders were developed in the early days of the oil industry to accomplish two chief aims: to distribute proceeds from the sale of oil to the various owners and to protect the purchaser from claims (by these same owners) that their payments were incorrect. For oil production, the purchaser might still handle division orders and payments. Before preparing the orders, it might conduct an investigation to be sure that the sellers have good title to the product being sold. (In this case, the purchaser often asks the operator to furnish abstracts for its own attorney to examine.) It will then have the orders drawn up and sent out for execution by the operator, the royalty owners, and anyone else shown to have an interest in the production. It takes responsibility for paying the owners. This purchaser might be a pipeline company, an agency affiliated with such a company, or someone else who has access to a pipeline. Whoever the purchaser is, there will usually be protective language in the division orders to guard against claims made by owners not listed in those orders. If the listed owners warrant (or guarantee) their interests, they have little ground for later complaints that their percentages are incorrect. Division orders are, however, revocable: By canceling a division order, an owner can correct a mistake to increase a share of future production. Past production is usually protected from such claims.

For gas production, the title to all gas goes to the lessee when the gas is produced. When the gas is sold, the lessee or the lessee's representative has the responsibility of accounting to the royalty owners and handling the division orders. Because division orders have been the subject of much litigation over the years, whoever sends a division order out for execution might find an experienced royalty owner striking through language that does not pertain to the division of interest. Ratification language might be struck out, for example, or any sentences that seem to extend or alter provisions of the lease. Owners are increasingly wary of court decisions such as that of *Exxon Corp. v. Middleton* (Tex. Civ. App. 1981), which found that the signing of division orders established a binding agreement to accept each payment as a final settlement of the royalty due. In that case, larger payments were owed under the terms of the lease. As no law requires a royalty owner to sign a division order to get paid, some owners simply refuse to sign. Signing is an accepted industry practice, however, and one that has been honored by the courts in Texas and Louisiana. Failure to sign can result in delaying the disbursement of an owner's share of the proceeds. Consequently, most owners will be satisfied by the inclusion of a *revocation provision* that allows the division order to be canceled by either party upon 30 days' written notice.

SUMMARY

- After a lease has been executed, the lessee begins a more serious assessment of what kind of title it has to the leasehold and seeks to cure any defects that might exist in the title.
- During examination of title, there are often discoveries of gaps in the chain of title, ambiguities in the terms of the instruments, encumbrances, or adverse claims, so the lessee hopes to establish marketable rather than perfect title.
- Examination of title can occur at several stages of an oil and gas operation, but most often, title opinions will be needed at two stages. The drill site opinion is drawn up when a drill site has been selected, and the division order opinion is drawn up when it is time to issue division orders.
- While the landman's runsheet from the preliminary title check before the lease is taken might be used as a starting point, a company title examiner must conduct a more thorough search to complete a drill site opinion.
- When a title examiner makes use of a runsheet as an inventory of documents to examine in public records and makes a report based on that inquiry, the report is called a "stand-up opinion." When an examiner bases a report on a collection of documents from an abstract company (an abstract of title), the report is called an "abstract-based opinion." Because a company must pay a substantial fee for an abstract of title, it is considerably less expensive for a company to produce a stand-up opinion.
- When there is a cloud on the lessor's claim to title, a landman will assist a company's title examiner in finding documents that can cure the title, or remedy defects and gaps in the chain. These documents do not correct the defects; rather, they provide evidence for the lessee's claim.
- The methods used to cure title will vary according to what kinds of defects are found. For example, an affidavit might testify that the mineral owner who executed the lease is the grantee on a deed conveying the property even though the names in the two documents are not the same. A quitclaim, which is a release of claim to a property, might eliminate the possibility that an adverse claim to the title can be asserted by another party.
- Once a lessee is satisfied that it holds a marketable title to the property, the company's regulatory department will seek a well permit from the appropriate state agency to begin drilling.

- When drilling has taken place and a well has proved productive, division orders will be issued as part of the process of paying the mineral owners, royalty owners, and working interest owners. To produce accurate division orders naming the percent of production each party will receive, another title opinion might be drafted. Here, the title examiner confirms, for example, that the operator has good title to the product (and can therefore sell it) because it has marketable title to the leasehold.

8

Agreements to Explore and Develop

In this chapter:

- Reasons companies seek partnerships to explore and develop
- Support agreements: dry-hole and bottomhole contribution agreements
- Farmout agreements
- Joint operating agreements
- Forms of agreements between companies
- Special provisions in joint operating agreements

After oil and gas leases have been acquired, companies commonly seek partnerships with other companies for the joint exploration of their leased lands or for support of their exploration efforts. At first glance, some might wonder why a company would spend months or even years acquiring leases and developing a prospect, and then consider sharing its efforts with another company when the other company is considered a competitor. Actually, in many cases, it is the right business decision. For instance, Company A might seek to reduce its risk and exposed drilling dollars by entering into a *joint operating agreement* (*JOA*) with Company B, by which Company B pays a disproportionately higher percentage of well costs to casing point. After that, if the logs look good and the well is completed, Company B's interest might decrease, while Company A's interest might increase. Or perhaps Company B also has leases in the area and offers to give Company A money towards the drilling of Company A's well in exchange for data from *well logs*.

In the early days of the industry, when drilling was unrestricted, each company preferred to explore and develop its own leases. Fierce competition led to the rapid development of many oilfields, but it also resulted in too many wells being drilled into the same formation, which damaged structures and reduced total production volumes. For example, if ten wells are drilled into a formation that could have produced the same volumes with three wells, then seven wells were unnecessarily drilled. The adoption of conservation laws changed the industry and resulted in necessary cooperation between companies. Increased drilling costs have also encouraged cooperation and partnerships. Competition certainly remains, and no one would wish to eliminate it. But today, most companies prefer to share with other companies some of the risks involved in exploration and development. Historically, the company landman has been responsible for the drafting and negotiating of agreements bringing about cooperation. Some agreements are basic; more often, agreements are complicated, requiring legal, accounting, and tax support.

With new technologies associated with horizontal drilling and hydraulic fracturing that allow the exploitation of shale plays, more international companies are now seeking opportunities to invest in a company's wells, or its "prospects," as they are called—not only for the financial rewards, but also for knowledge that can be used to drill wells and develop similar play types in their own countries. These arrangements are complex, and often there is more than one agreement that will need to be executed between the parties. The following types of agreements can be used individually or together in these complex transactions. (Table 8.1 provides a summary of the different types of agreements discussed in this chapter.)

Table 8.1
Types of Exploration and Development Agreements

Support Agreements	One company contributes money to another company's drilling operation in return for information gained from the drilling.
Dry-hole contribution agreements	One company makes payments to another in exchange for drilling information in the event that the well is a dry hole. If the well is productive, the first company makes no payments and still receives the information.
Bottomhole contribution agreements	One company makes payments to another in exchange for drilling information only if the second company is able to drill to a certain depth.
Farmout Agreements	The owner of a lease (*farmor*) assigns the leasehold interest or some part of it to a third party (*farmee*) who agrees to drill a well within the primary term of the lease. The farmee (rather than the farmor) incurs the drilling costs as a condition of the agreement.
Joint Operating Agreements	Two or more co-owners of the operating rights in a tract of land join together to share the costs of exploration and possible development.

SUPPORT AGREEMENTS

A company might wish to drill a well on its own leases and request money or acreage support from another company owning offsetting leases. These agreements are known as *support agreements* when money is provided, or as *farmout agreements* when acreage is contributed. By contributing money or acreage (acres of land), a company can gain valuable well information without incurring the expense of drilling a well. For several reasons, companies might desire to share in the risk, expense, and possible reward of drilling a well. In that case, they might enter into a joint operating agreement.

In a support agreement, a company promises money to support another.

The following scenario is useful to understand support agreements. Company A leased a prospect, but while checking courthouse records, it learned that Company B has leased lands that offset its prospect. Company B's prospect will be de-risked if Company A drills its prospect first because both drilling targets are located in the same formation; in other words, the risk of exploration by Company B will be lower if it knows the results of exploration already carried out by Company A in the formation.

In this situation, well information from Company A would be valuable to Company B. Company A would have reasons of its own to consider entering into a support agreement with Company B. First, as much as Company A might attempt to keep its drilling and completion information confidential, Company B could gather information on its operations by scouting the drill site. For instance, Company B's scouts might observe completion equipment (such as hydraulic fracturing trucks) at the drill site—equipment that is only used when drilling has resulted in a discovery. Second, with the cost of drilling easily exceeding millions of dollars, Company A might consider swapping well information with Company B in exchange for dollars to support drilling the well. Types of support agreements include *dry-hole contribution agreements* and *bottomhole contribution agreements.*

In a farmout agreement, a company promises land to support another.

Dry-Hole Contribution Agreements

Types of support agreements:

- Dry-hole contribution
- Bottomhole contribution

Under this type of agreement (table 8.2), in exchange for receiving drilling information, Company B could propose to pay a certain price per foot drilled by Company A in the event that the well is a dry hole. In the case of a 10,000-foot well that cost Company A $1,000,000 to drill, a dry-hole contribution of $10 per foot on the part of Company B would result in Company A's receiving $100,000 if the well were plugged and abandoned as a dry hole. If the well were successful, Company A would receive no monetary contribution toward the drilling of the well; however, Company B would still receive the well information. In this scenario, Company A would reduce the total cost of drilling by $100,000 in the event it drilled a dry hole, and Company B could possibly save itself $900,000 in costs by knowing that drilling a similar well on Company B leases would probably result in a dry hole.

Table 8.2

Advantages of a Dry-Hole Contribution Agreement for Both Parties

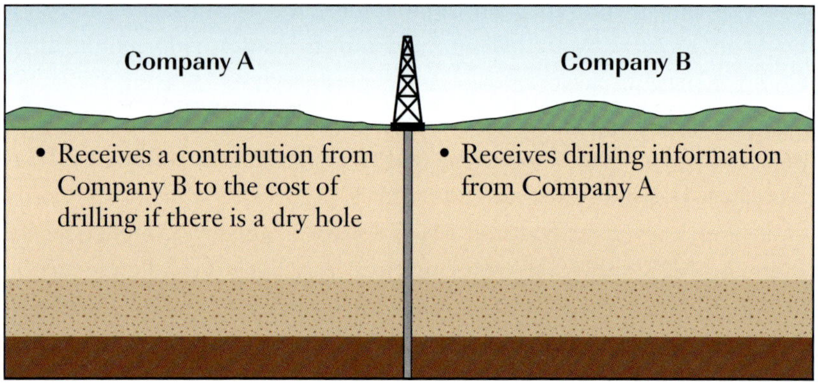

Bottomhole Contribution Agreements

Under this type of agreement (table 8.3), similar to a dry-hole contribution agreement, Company B could offer to pay a certain price per foot drilled in exchange for well information from Company A. However, Company B would only pay the contribution to Company A in the event the well were drilled to a specific depth. For example, if Company B acquired its leases to explore a formation thought to be found at a depth between 9,500 and 9,700 feet, well information from Company A would be of very little value to Company B if, for any reason, Company A's well were not drilled and logged to at least a depth of 9,700 feet. If Company A were unable to drill and log its well at a depth agreed to in the bottomhole contribution agreement, Company A would receive no monetary contribution for drilling that specific well. The agreement might provide for Company A to have the opportunity to receive monetary support in the event that it drilled a substitute well that reached the specified depth.

Table 8.3

Advantages of a Bottomhole Contribution Agreement for Both Parties

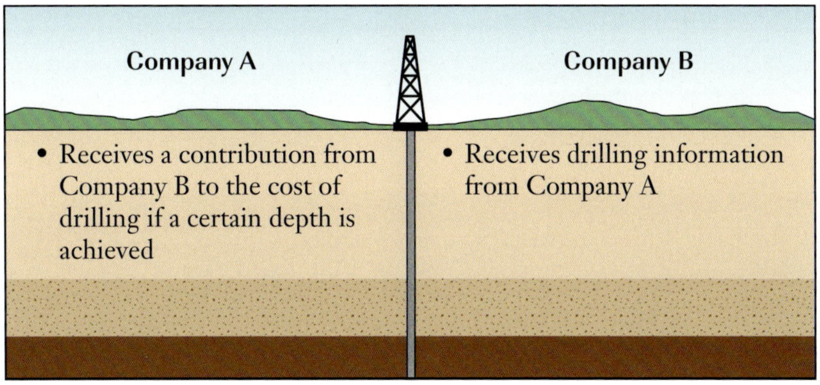

FARMOUT AGREEMENTS

In another common scenario, Company A is examining title in the county courthouse to determine if there is acreage available to lease when it determines the prospect has already been leased by Company B.

In most cases, Company B either (1) acquired the leases many years ago, drilled shallow wells, and all the leases are currently held by production, or (2) identified the same geological feature and recently acquired the leases to drill a well similar to the one that Company A wishes to drill. The only option would now be for Company A to request a farmout, or an agreement by which Company A is allowed to explore and, if successful, earn an assignment of the leasehold from Company B (table 8.4). Company B, owning the leases, would be referred to as the "farmor" and Company A as the "farmee."

Table 8.4

Advantages of a Farmout Agreement for Both Parties

Company A (Farmee)	Company B (Farmor)
• Pays 100% of the costs to drill and complete; receives all production until payout.	• Pays no cost to drill and complete.
• Carries operation costs alone only until payout; afterwards, Company B shares costs.	• Receives payment of overriding royalty, which can be converted to a working interest after payout.
• Is assigned an interest in the farmout lands if the initial well is successful.	• Does not pay lessor; Company A pays royalties.

An overriding royalty is an interest in production revenues free of the costs of operations and production (except taxes).

The farmout request would include the offer from Company A to drill a well on the leases owned by Company B. This well, called the *initial well*, would be drilled to a specified depth and formation as agreed to between the companies. Company A would be responsible for paying 100% of the cost of drilling. If, after reaching total depth and logging the well, it is determined that the well will not be successful, Company A would also be responsible for all costs associated with plugging and abandoning the well. In the case of a dry hole, the farmout agreement would terminate unless it contained a provision allowing the farmee to drill a substitute well.

If the initial well—or a substitute well—were completed as a producer, Company A would pay royalties to lessors under the leases owned by Company B. In addition, Company A would pay Company B an *overriding royalty*, an interest in the proceeds of the sale of the oil or gas free of all costs of development and production, until Company A received (from production) an amount equal to the cost of drilling, completing, and operating. This cost recovery is also referred to as "payout." After payout of the well, the farmout agreement might provide that Company B could convert its overriding royalty to a working interest, an interest in the lease (a percentage of production) accompanied by the right to explore and develop. In exchange for that percentage of production, the owner of working interest is required to share in the costs of exploration and production. Under the agreement between Companies A and B, for example, the overriding royalty retained by Company B could equal the difference between 25% and lease burdens. If the lease burdens (royalty to lessor) equaled 20%, then Company B's overriding royalty would equal 5% until payout. If the farmout agreement provided for Company B to have the option to convert its overriding royalty to a 25% working interest at payout, then at payout, Company A would own a 75% working interest, Company B would own a 25% working interest, and both companies would share proportionately the 20% royalty to be paid to the lessor. (For more information on working and overriding royalty interests, see Appendix K.)

The farmout agreement between Companies A and B would contain a joint operating agreement attached as an exhibit. The JOA would become operative once the well paid out and Company B elected to convert its overriding royalty to a working interest. In this case, under the joint operating agreement, the co-owners of the operating rights would agree to share operating costs of further exploration and development. Additionally, with the successful completion of the initial well, Company A would earn an assignment from Company B of an interest in the farmout lands. Many farmout agreements provide that, in the event that the farmee drills a successful well, the farmee will earn an assignment covering rights from the surface down to a depth of 100 feet below the total depth drilled in the successful well. If the leases were currently held by production from wells producing at a shallower depth, those currently producing depths would be excluded from the assignment. If the farmout agreement covered an area large enough for multiple wells, the farmee might have the opportunity to continuously drill wells to the stratigraphic equivalent of the initial well to earn an assignment of additional lands.

LETTER AGREEMENTS AND FORMAL CONTRACTS

Liquidated damages are money compensation agreed-upon in advance in a contract for the event of a loss.

Farmout agreement forms are available from online vendors. However, larger companies generally prefer to use their own internally generated and approved forms for farmout agreements. It is a common industry practice for two companies to enter into a *letter agreement* even before executing a formal contract.

A letter agreement allows two companies to quickly reach an understanding of the major deal terms and is usually subject to a formal agreement encompassing those deal terms as well as other provisions that are customary industry practice. In many instances, the letter agreement is negotiated between the landmen representing each company. Upon execution of the letter agreement, each company gets its legal department involved. Such an agreement could be two pages in length, whereas a formal contract with exhibits might be fifty pages. A letter agreement covering major deal terms might read as follows:

> Upon execution of this letter agreement, Company A agrees to commence drilling operations at a mutually agreeable location on the lease owned by Company B covering Section 4 of Township 12 North, Range 15 East, DeSoto Parish, Louisiana. Said well is to be drilled to a depth of 9,500 feet or a depth in the opinion of Company A which is sufficient to test the Hosston formation. Upon successful completion of the initial well, Company A will earn an assignment of said lease from the surface down to 100 feet below total depth drilled. In said assignment, Company B will retain a 5% overriding royalty, which may be converted to a 25% working interest at payout. In the event Company B elects to convert its overriding royalty to a working interest, the interests of both parties will be subject to the terms of a mutually agreeable operating agreement.

Provisions to be included in the formal contracts that are not discussed in letter agreements could include:

- *Liquidated damages* if the farmee fails to drill the initial well
- Force majeure provisions that could allow for delays in drilling
- *Liability* for operations and environmental matters
- Compliance with state and federal regulations
- The name of the party responsible for paying royalties, rentals, and taxes
- Tax partnership provisions
- Marketing arrangements for production
- *Area of mutual interest* (*AMI*) provisions (discussed in a later section of this chapter)

Other provisions could state that:

- The farmor will not warrant title to the leases.
- The farmor has the right to take over the initial well if the farmee proposes to plug and abandon.
- The farmee is to provide drilling and well information to the farmor.

JOINT OPERATING AGREEMENTS

A third scenario describes yet another common situation. Company A is leasing land on its prospect and, while running records in the county courthouse, learns that Company B has already acquired leases covering 50% of Company A's prospect.

In this case, if the regulatory agency requires 640 acres to be leased and allocated to a well and Company B has already leased 320 acres within Company A's prospect, then both companies will need to work together to get a well drilled. Historically, the Company A landman would contact the Company B landman and recommend a meeting to discuss the possibility of jointly drilling a well.

A drilling and spacing unit is a unit of land where drilling can occur. Its minimum size is determined by statute or by regulations.

When two or more companies join together to share the costs of exploration and possible development, they commonly do so by entering into a joint operating agreement. These companies might individually own oil and gas leases covering a 100% interest in the minerals in tracts within an area or leases covering a portion of the minerals in the same tracts. In either case, before a well is ever drilled, these companies will execute a JOA. The JOA will identify the leases being contributed by each company and accurately describe the area to be governed by the JOA, which is called the *contract area*, or *prospect area.* The agreement will also designate which company will be the operator of the joint account and establish guidelines for all operations proposed and conducted within the contract area.

The contract area governed by the JOA might cover an area as small as a one-well *drilling and spacing unit* (a *DSU*, as prescribed by the regulatory agency) or it could cover thousands of acres. Companies that mutually agree to enter into a JOA will often want to share geological and geophysical data, conduct joint technical meetings, and plan to expand their development area in the event that the first well they jointly drill proves up additional prospect areas and drilling opportunities.

Model Forms

As joint operating agreements began to cover more complicated exploration scenarios, they became more complex and took longer to negotiate. With every company having its own internally approved form, reaching a mutually acceptable agreement with another company became a very lengthy process. The situation was remedied in 1956, when a group of landmen and attorneys in the industry gathered to develop a model form of agreement. Their efforts resulted in the AAPL Form 610 Model Form Operating Agreement–1956. This form has been modified by the AAPL as recently as 1989. The AAPL Form 610–1989 Model Form Operating Agreement still does not fit every exploration scenario, but it does reduce the time required to negotiate and obtain various approvals from the many different departments within each company.

Other specialized forms exist: For instance, the Rocky Mountain area has forms that allow for the probable presence of federal leases. Canada has its own form (CAPL 99, discussed in Appendix J), and the AAPL has developed two different model forms for offshore operations: 2002 710 AAPL Joint Operating Agreement (Shelf) and 2007 810 AAPL Joint Operating Agreement (Deepwater) (fig. 8.1).

Figure 8.1. The AAPL joint operating agreements for offshore operations are available through the Web site for the OCS Advisory Board (www.ocsadvisoryboard.org).

Special Provisions

The Model Form Operating Agreement includes provisions that the industry would consider as standard for joint operations. In many cases, the majority of time spent negotiating operating agreements is spent on the following special provisions:

- *Authorizations for expenditure* (*AFE*s)
- Area of mutual interest
- Accounting procedure

Proposals, Authorization for Expenditure, and Responses

An authorization for expenditure is an operator's estimate of costs to be approved before work can be undertaken.

Before the operator can incur expenses on behalf of the joint account that exceed the limitation of expenditures, it must provide non-operators with a detailed estimate of the costs to be incurred. This detailed estimate is an authorization for expenditure. For instance, if the operator wishes to drill a well within the contract area, a well proposal including an AFE must be made in writing to the non-operators. Non-operators will then generally have a response period of 30 days in which to elect to participate in the proposed operation. Non-operators can also elect not to participate, or "go non-consent." In the case of an election not to participate, the operator or other participating parties can absorb the working interest of the non-consenting party and move forward with the drilling of the proposed well. The JOA provides that the participating parties who absorbed the interest of the non-consenting parties can, in the event the well is successful, recover 100% of their portion of the non-consenting parties' share of costs incurred in drilling, completing, and equipping the well. It also provides that they can recover a percentage—usually a 300% non-consent penalty—before a non-consenting party will be considered a participating party owning its original working interest share in the well drilled as proposed.

If the limitation of expenditure provision of the JOA is $50,000, then the operator will be required to prepare an AFE for all expenditures estimated to be more than $50,000. This limitation of expenditure provision and response deadline will not be operative in emergency situations within the contract area.

With regard to approved operations, the operator may pay expenses and bill non-operators for their proportionate shares. The operator also has the right to estimate expenses for the succeeding 30 days and require participating parties to pay their proportionate shares in advance of incurring expenses.

The JOA will allow any party to propose an operation. However, it might provide that, for a proposed operation to move forward, it must receive a certain threshold of approval from the working interest owners. For instance, in a case where each of four companies owns a 25% working interest, the JOA might stipulate that for an operation to move forward, there must be approval by three or more parties owning a minimum combined total of 75% interest. Therefore, in this case, if two parties do not approve the proposed operation, it will not be initiated.

An area of mutual interest provision defines the geographic area to be shared by parties to a JOA and sets out their respective rights.

Area of Mutual Interest

An area of mutual interest provision is necessary when there are lands within the contract area that might either (1) be unleased, or (2) become available for leasing during the term of the JOA. For example, if the companies that are parties to the JOA agree to share seismic and other technical information over the contract area, they want to be assured that the information they are sharing will be utilized for the benefit of the JOA partners. So if a company owning a 25% interest in the JOA acquired a lease within the contract area, that company would be required to offer the other parties to the JOA the opportunity to acquire their proportionate shares of the lease. This provision does not restrict competition. In fact, it incentivizes companies to share seismic, geological, and well information with other working interest owners, knowing that all parties will have the opportunity to share equally in any interest acquired by another party to the JOA within the contract area.

Accounting Procedure

The accounting procedure attached to a JOA specifies the methods to be used by the operator in charging and accounting for all the expenses of operating the joint property. The procedure is therefore crucial to the daily use of the joint account. Over the years, this procedure has been standardized by the work of various groups, such as the *Council of Petroleum Accountants Societies, Inc.* (*COPAS*). The COPAS-North America accounting procedure is available with options that address specific problems encountered in the United States and Canada.

SUMMARY

- While companies competing for business usually do not collaborate on their ventures, oil and gas companies might seek partnerships with each other to jointly explore leased lands for a number of reasons. One reason is that there are only so many wells that can be drilled into a formation without violating government regulations or damaging the geological structure.
- There are additional reasons for such partnerships. Under an agreement, a company might offer confidential information from drilling operations conducted on its leasehold in exchange for money or acreage from another company owning offsetting leases. With the contribution of the other company to the cost of exploratory drilling, the drilling company reduces the risk it runs in investing in its prospect. The competitor company benefits from information about the formation that might be relevant to its own nearby prospects.
- When a company enters into a support agreement, it promises to contribute money in exchange for drilling information. If the company only agrees to pay in the event that the lessee drills a dry hole, it has entered into a dry-hole contribution agreement; if it agrees to pay in the event that the lessee drills to a certain depth, it has entered into a bottomhole contribution agreement.
- When a company enters into a farmout agreement, it promises to assign leased land to another in exchange for obligations to carry out operations on the leasehold and pay royalties. The potential for a large share of production motivates the company assigned the leasehold; the potential for overriding royalties without the risk and expense of operations motivates the company that originally took the lease.
- Farmout agreements can take many forms. Sometimes, the parties use a letter agreement to reach an understanding about the terms before executing a formal contract.
- When companies enter into a joint operating agreement, they promise to share the costs of exploration and possible development. There can be different reasons for companies to carry out joint operations. For instance, two companies with leases on small tracts of land adjacent to each other might enter into a JOA to meet the acreage requirement for a drilling and spacing unit.
- Model forms can be used for joint operating agreements, but often, the parties to a JOA might want to add special provisions that detail how the operator obtains authorization for expenditure, how the parties will share in the acquisition of leases that become available during the term of the contract (areas of mutual interest), and accounting procedures to be used by the operator.
- The agreements that companies enter into for joint exploration and development are complex, and often more than one type of agreement—support, farmout, or joint operating—will be used in such an arrangement.

9 Pooling, Unitization, and Release of Oil and Gas Leases

In this chapter:

- Definitions of pooling and unitization
- Reasons for pooling and unitization
- Voluntary and involuntary pooling and unitization
- Legal processes for forming pooled units and unitized fields
- Instruments for lease terminations
- Awareness of changing regulations in leases on public lands

Oil and gas leases normally include a clause empowering the lessee to pool or unitize the lease with other leased tracts to comply with state well-spacing regulations and to conduct operations more efficiently. (See the section on pooling and unitization clauses in Chapter 5.) "Pooling" is the term usually applied to combining small tracts into a unit large enough to satisfy spacing requirements. The immediate aim of pooling is the formation of a drilling unit. Another term used in reference to the formation of a drilling unit, "unitization," generally refers to field-wide or reservoir-wide operations that are planned and carried out as if all the tracts in a field were held under a single lease. Geologic structures know nothing of property lines, and the optimum use for some technologies of reservoir exploration and stimulation is on a large scale, so unitization can be crucial to long-term success. The final aim of both pooling and unitization is successful, efficient production. Operators hope to extract oil and gas with a minimum of waste and in amounts that will earn steady profits.

Pooling and unitization can be advantageous to some mineral, royalty, and overriding royalty owners, as well as to lessees, while at the same time, disadvantageous to others. For example, in Texas, a geologic structure with gas potential might require a 640-acre unit. If all the leased tracts over the structure were 40 acres in size, 16 of these 40-acre tracts would need to be pooled together to form a 640-acre unit. The mineral owner of a drill-site tract might expect to receive royalties from all the gas produced by the well and be disappointed to discover that her royalties are based on her acreage contribution to the pool—just like the other tract owners' royalties are. As a result of pooling the 16 tracts, the owner of each tract would receive royalties based on a proportionate share 1⁄16 interest. By the same token, the owner of a tract in the pooled unit that has no production potential might be happy to receive the same proportionate share of allocated production, as a producing well would not have otherwise been drilled on his tract.

POOLING

Voluntary Pooling

Prorationing limits production over a period of time. It is enforced by government agencies.

Pooling is a result of state conservation laws passed during the 1930s and 1940s. Before the days of effective regulations for well spacing and density, unrestrained drilling sometimes led to situations like that in the East Texas field, where wells were drilled so close together that the legs of the derricks overlapped. Restraints were imposed not only on drilling practices but also on the amount of oil actually produced; by the mid-1930s, overproduction had threatened to swamp the market and had driven the price of oil down to 10 cents per barrel. Two kinds of statutes were passed in a number of states to help conserve resources and to match supply with demand: *Prorationing* limited the amount of oil that a well was allowed to produce, and spacing rules established the amount of acreage that could be efficiently drained by a single well. Statutes such as these were encouraged by the Interstate Oil Compact Commission, a coordinating body formed by the oil-producing states in 1935.

Prorationing, along with well spacing and density rules, created the concept of the drilling and spacing unit (DSU, also known as a *proration unit*). A typical size requirement for an oil proration unit was—and still is—40 acres. But a leased tract is not always of the size desired to form a proration unit. Sometimes, a DSU has to be made up by pooling tracts (fig. 9.1). When tracts owned by different lessors—and perhaps leased by different lessees—are pooled by mutual agreement, the result is *voluntary pooling*.

Pooling arrangements are usually made by landmen, and the timing of these arrangements varies with the particular situation. Companies usually prefer to pool after they have done most of the developmental drilling in a field where they hold leases. That is, they try to form enough proration units without pooling to gain an accurate idea of where their productive and nonproductive acreage lies. With that knowledge, they can pool where necessary to achieve the most efficient use of their leases. This goal is not always attainable, however. To give only one example, it might be necessary to pool before drilling if a company holds a lease without a pooling clause. (Older fields in which leases were acquired a number of years ago can present this problem.)

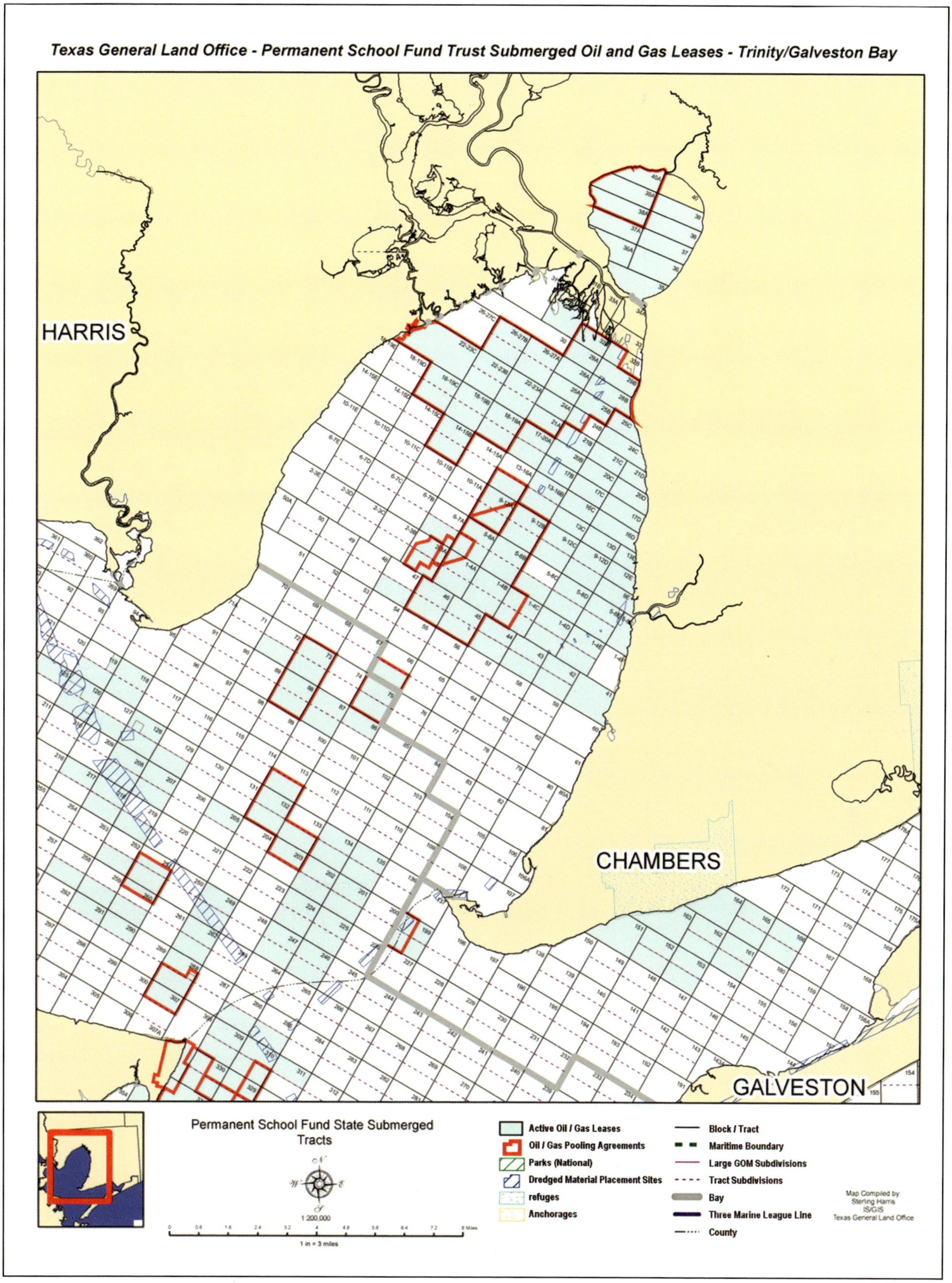

COURTESY OF TEXAS GENERAL LAND OFFICE

Figure 9.1. The areas outlined in red on the map represent tracts that have been pooled to form drilling and spacing units.

Types of pooling:
- Voluntary
- Involuntary, or forced

In such a case, the company might prefer to pool first on the supposition that the drill site owners will be reluctant to pool (and share royalties) after a well has demonstrated its productiveness.

In addition to the timing, the instruments used in creating a pooled unit vary with the situation. In a simple case, one lessee will hold leases with pooling clauses on several neighboring tracts. To pool these tracts, the lessee need only comply with the formalities set out in the pooling clauses and secure ratification from *nonexecutive royalty owners* or nonparticipating royalty owners—that is, from those who own a royalty interest but do not have the authority to execute a lease (and are therefore said to have nonexecutive rights). The formalities might include filing a declaration of intent to pool with the state regulatory agency and taking care to follow the state's unit size and spacing rules. The name given to a unit varies across the states. In Texas, for example, a pooled unit formed in this way is called a "designated unit."

In a somewhat more complicated situation, the exercise of a pooling authority by a lessee might involve other working interest owners and their royalty owners in the formation of a drilling unit. If they, and any *unleased owners* affected, consent to the proposed pooling, they will generally execute an instrument to that effect. Generally, such an instrument is acknowledged and recorded in the public records.

Where no pooling authority exists, as in the hypothetical older oilfield, securing signatures from the affected owners (on what is often called a *pooling agreement*) will allow a pooled unit to be formed. The agreement is usually recorded. Finally, whenever more than one working interest owner is party to a pooling arrangement, the working interest owners will generally conduct joint operations within the pooled unit under the terms of a mutually agreeable joint operating agreement (JOA). The details of pooling vary, but the crucial point is simply this: Whether or not a lease grants the authority to pool, pooled units can be formed with the approval of mineral, royalty, and overriding royalty owners, and of lessees. If any of the leases within a pooled unit are subject to overriding royalty interests, it is important for the lessee of such a lease to secure consent or ratification from the owner of the overriding royalty interest to the pooling agreement.

Though pooling can benefit lessors as well as lessees, everyone concerned should be aware of the changes that pooling can bring. For example, unless leases contain Pugh clauses, or Freestone riders, all the lands covered by the leases will be held by the pooled unit, including lands outside the pooled area as well as lands inside it. Royalties will be shared by the interest owners, usually on the basis of acreage contributed to the pool unit. Finally, a well drilled anywhere on the pooled lands will hold all the leases without further payment of delay rentals unless the leases provide for some other arrangement.

Involuntary Pooling

Most of the major producing states have some kind of *statutory pooling* or forced pooling laws to meet those situations in which lessees cannot reach an agreement to form a drilling unit by pooling. In some states—Oklahoma and Louisiana, for instance—forced pooling is fairly common. In others, state regulatory boards are more reluctant to compel owners to join in a pooling arrangement. In Louisiana, for example, Louisiana Revised Statute 30:10 allows an operator to propose the drilling of a well by sending mineral owners a proposal and well-cost estimate. Owners have 30 days in which to participate. Failure to participate still allows the operator to proceed with drilling. The operator can recover expenditures incurred in drilling and operating a well from notified owners who elect not to participate in the well (meaning those who elect not to bear any costs associated with operations), either as payments from the non-participating owners or as payments from those owners' allocated shares of production from the well. Under the same statute, these operations can be conducted without need for a mutually agreeable joint operating agreement.

However involuntary or mandatory pooling works in each state, certain features of the process are much the same across the United States. The underlying theme in this process is that companies wishing to undertake the cost of drilling have regulatory support for getting their well drilled when they are unable to secure support and agreement from other lessees or unleased mineral interest owners within the boundaries of the unit.

UNITIZATION

Unitization is usually a much larger undertaking than pooling is. (Table 9.1 provides a comparison of pooling and unitization.) The amount of land involved is far more extensive and the number of interest owners correspondingly higher. However, unitizing a field can have advantages that support the increased complexities. These advantages include the elimination of wasteful practices, the maintenance of reservoir pressure to maximize production,

Table 9.1
Comparison of Pooling and Unitization

	Size of Unit	Agreements Required	Participation Can Be Voluntary	Participation Can Be Forced
Pooling	Large enough to form a drilling and spacing unit, with only one well	• Pooling agreement • Joint operating agreement	Yes	Yes
Unitization	Large enough to exploit an entire field, possibly with more than one well	• Unit agreement • Unit operating agreement	Yes	Yes

and the performance of secondary recovery operations (again to maximize production). Considering that primary production might extract only 15% to 25% of the oil in place, and that improved recovery methods such as water flooding and gas injection might bring that figure up to 80%, such methods can clearly have benefits. They are extremely costly, though, and hardly feasible except on a field-wide or reservoir-wide scale.

Private Lands

Unitization for the purpose of conducting secondary recovery operations is usually suggested by the largest owner in a field, and only after a cost-benefit analysis. Achieving a unitized field depends on persuading large numbers of people that unitization will serve their interests. At each stage of the planning, those who propose a unitization need sound arguments and convincing evidence.

After the proposing company's geologists and engineers have finished their studies and a firm decision to unitize has been made, the next step is often a preliminary meeting with other working interest owners. At that meeting, the proposal to unitize can be explained and the economics of the situation outlined for the group. If the group agrees that unitization is feasible and desirable, committees can be formed to work on the many details that will need attention. A land committee, for example, might be selected to contact the royalty owners, who are usually numerous. Another committee might be put in charge of drafting the *unit agreement* and *unit operating agreement.* A third might collect information to help decide on the basis for participation in the unit, and so on.

As just noted, two types of agreements can be used to cover the provisions of a unitization. The unit agreement pools the interests of the parties and acts as a grant by the royalty owners to the working interest owners of the tracts so that the tracts can be developed as a unit. The unit operating agreement is signed by the working interest owners only. It establishes a committee (with a voting procedure) to oversee unit operations and decide on the sharing of costs. There is some inevitable overlap between these two instruments, but there are advantages to using both of them. For example, the use of the two agreements allows for royalty owners to have a shorter document to sign and one that clearly does not involve them in any of the working interest owners' obligations.

Once the agreements have been drafted, the landmen working on the unit's land committee can secure signatures from royalty owners. Many signatures for this purpose can be obtained by mail. In other instances—with local owners, civic groups, and local school boards, for example—meetings can be helpful and might be required. A unit representative who meets face-to-face with royalty owners will do best, of course, if he or she has prepared a careful presentation, is ready to answer questions, and can explain how the proposed unit will affect the interests of the people concerned.

Sometimes the royalty owners will form their own association or committee, complete with an attorney and technical advisor. Negotiating with such a group can be time-consuming but usually results in securing a significant number of approvals.

Types of unitization:
- Voluntary
- Compulsory

Finally, the unit will generally need approval from the state regulatory agency. With voluntary unitization, agency approval might be optional. In that case, it is normally obtained anyway to avoid the possibility of violating antitrust laws. When the unit is not formed voluntarily, agency approval and an agency order will be needed. The process required to obtain an agency order usually involves notice, a hearing, expert testimony, an offer of fair and reasonable terms, and the agreement of some specified percentage ownership of lessees and royalty owners. When a number of owners contest approval of the unitization, a common result is a modified plan. In states with statutes authorizing *compulsory unitization*, an agency order might complete the formal process.

Federal and State Lands

Under the Mineral Leasing Act of 1920, as subsequently amended, the Bureau of Land Management (BLM), a division of the Department of the Interior, is responsible for the management of oil and gas leasing and unitization matters affecting onshore federal lands. The Bureau of Ocean Energy Management (BOEM) is responsible for the management of all offshore leasing and unitization matters as well as all onshore and offshore royalty collections.

The BLM has a formal process for review and approval of unit agreements. When the proposed unit contains less than 10% federal lands, the BLM might approve a non-federal unit agreement. Otherwise, a BLM-approved unit agreement and unit operating agreement must be used. A company making an application to form a unit should expect to provide the BLM with relevant well, geologic, and geophysical information in support of the unit application.

Federal units can sometimes cover as much as 1,000 acres or more. As such, it is fairly common for a federal unit to include not only federal leases but also state and private leases. The proposed unitization must, in such a case, conform to the provisions of all lease forms as well as to state and federal regulations. Each state has its own requirements and forms for consent and ratification. In addition, when state leases are included within the boundaries of the proposed unit, the BLM will require evidence of state approval before officially approving the unit. Unlike unitizing leases on privately owned lands, where the operative provisions are contained in the lease form itself, unitizing federal- and state-owned minerals requires meetings with local federal and state offices as well as a possible agreement to drill one or more wells as consideration for receiving unit approval.

RELEASE

A relinquishment document evidences the surrender, release, or abandonment of a lease.

Eventually, the time comes when an oil and gas lease terminates. It might terminate because it has reached the end of the primary term with no activity taking place that might perpetuate it. In another scenario, the lease terminates after years of production, when wells reach their economic limit and are ready to be plugged and abandoned with no further activity planned. Or it might terminate because the lessee desires to surrender/release the lease prior to the expiration of the primary term.

In some instances, a lease is not deliberately terminated. The most common cause of inadvertent termination is the failure of the lessee to pay a delay rental. In this instance, the lessor might demand that a release be filed in the event he or she wants to lease the minerals to another company (fig. 9.2). If lease covers privately owned minerals, the lessee might attempt to negotiate a new lease. If the lease covers state- or federal-owned minerals, it is quite possible that the lease will terminate with the lessee still responsible for paying the lessor the total amount of delay rentals yet to have been paid. In other words, some leases require payment of delay rentals, whereas others merely give the lessee the option to extend the lease for another year by payment of a delay rental.

The terms of a lease might require that a release be filed in the public records if, at the end of the primary term, no activity has taken place to perpetuate the lease. If the instrument is silent on the matter, it is still common for the lessor to request that a release be filed so as not to cloud title in the event that another company is interested in leasing.

A lease will expire when it has been extended beyond the primary term by wells that have now been plugged and when no further wells are planned. Usually, the lease will terminate before the lessee has completed abandonment and restoration operations. Provisions will require the lessee to properly plug and abandon all wells, remove equipment, and restore the surface to a condition as near as possible to its original one. In this instance, also, a release will be filed in the public records if required under the terms of the lease or if requested by the lessor.

Although leases covering privately owned minerals will contain provisions negotiated between lessor and lessee, leases covering state- or federal-owned minerals generally have fixed terms and provisions. Those terms change nevertheless over time as state and federal regulations are revised. Some state and federal lease forms require the lessee to prepare and submit a *relinquishment* document or *surrender* document to the appropriate state or federal office before it is allowed to terminate a lease prior to the expiration of the primary term. In this case, the lessee would still be required to pay a delay rental until such lease has been properly relinquished or surrendered pursuant to the terms of the lease.

RELEASE OF OIL AND GAS LEASE

STATE OF ________________ §
COUNTY OF ______________ §

KNOW ALL MEN BY THESE PRESENTS, that the undersigned, __________________________, does hereby release, relinquish, surrender, and forever quitclaim to the hereinafter named Lessors, their heirs, successors, and assigns, as their interest may appear, any and all right, title, and interest whatsoever presently owned by the undersigned in the land described herein below by virtue of the following described Oil and Gas Lease(s):

Insofar as said Oil and Gas Lease(s) cover(s) the following described land:

IN WITNESS WHEREOF, this instrument is executed on this ____ day of ____________________, 20_______ .

____
(Signature of Releasor)

____
(Signature of Releasor)

ACKNOWLEDGMENT

STATE OF ________________ §
COUNTY OF ______________ §

This instrument was acknowledged before me on this _______ day of ____________________, 20______ by ______________________________ .

____
(Signature of Notary)

____
(Printed Name of Notary)

My commission expires: ________________

Figure 9.2. A form for a release of an oil and gas lease

The *Federal Register* is a journal that posts notices about rules and regulations of federal agencies.

With regard to BLM leases, it is important to note that while the lease itself might be simple (only running four pages in length), it is subject to changes in federal regulations. The *Federal Register* is the publication where most notices about regulations are announced. Later, the regulations are organized by topic (codified) in volumes that are easier to use; that publication is called the *Code of Federal Regulations*. The *C.F.R.* is continuously revised by the U.S. Department of the Interior, and as regulations change, so can provisions of BLM leases. Its volumes are updated annually, and an online edition is updated daily. Those involved in leasing who do not inform themselves of changes in the law risk penalties or even forfeiture.

SUMMARY

- State laws regulating well spacing and density, along with those prorationing, or limiting production of oil, have led to the creation of the drilling and spacing unit. As a tract is not always adequate for the size requirement of a DSU, pooling, or combining tracts, is often practiced.
- Under certain circumstances, such as when the resources in a formation can only be economically recovered using large-scale operations, it is desirable to combine many tracts of land, a practice known as unitization. That process is more complex and cumbersome than the one for pooling, but it can also yield greater rewards.
- Pooling and unitization can be advantageous overall to lessees and to mineral and royalty owners, as they can make production possible where it would not otherwise be. However, the mineral owners' royalty shares are determined by the acreage they contribute, so those who own tracts with greater production potential might be disappointed by the royalties they receive under the agreement.
- When the pooling or unitization comes about by the mutual agreement of lessors and lessees, it is described as "voluntary." In some cases, when parties do not agree to pooling or unitization, the formation of a drilling unit is imposed by law. In those cases, the terms "forced" or "involuntary" pooling and "compulsory" or "statutory" unitization are used.
- The formalities required for pooling vary according to whether the leases have a pooling and unitization clause giving the lessees authority to form pooling agreements. The formalities also vary according to the requirements of any such clauses. Even without the express authority to pool granted by a lease, pooled units can be formed with the consent of the lessees and the mineral, royalty, and overriding royalty owners.
- The process of forming a unitized field usually involves a multitude of tasks, including persuading many people that the project is economically desirable and drafting agreements. After agreements are executed, an approval and an order for the unit are generally required by the state regulatory agency.

- When the unitization is to take place on public lands, form agreements with the Bureau of Land Management—for onshore tracts—or the Bureau of Ocean Energy Management—for offshore tracts—are required.
- A lease might terminate inadvertently, as when wells have been plugged and abandoned or when, at the end of the primary term, there is no production and the lessee fails to pay delay rentals. Under circumstances such as those, it is advantageous for a mineral owner to secure a release from the lessee so that the property may be leased again.
- Some state and federal leases require the lessee to submit a relinquishment document or surrender document when the lease is terminated before the expiration of the primary term.
- A form lease through the BLM is subject to the rules of the *Code of Federal Regulations*, which is regularly revised. So all parties to BLM leases are advised to keep informed of changes to regulations that might affect their agreements.

References

Alaska Department of Natural Resources—Department of Mining, Land and Water, "Land Ownership in Alaska," *Alaska Department of Natural Resources*, http://dnr.alaska.gov/mlw/factsht/land_own.pdf (accessed October 30, 2012).

American Association of Petroleum Geologists (AAPG), "Oil Flows 'Confidentially' in L.A.," *Oil History: March 2007 Explorer*, http://www.aapg.org/explorer/2007/03mar/oil_history.cfm (accessed July 17, 2012).

Anderson, Owen L., John S. Lowe, David E. Pierce, Jr., and Ernest E. Smith. *Cases and Materials on Oil and Gas Law*. 5th ed. St. Paul: Thomson West, 2008.

Ballem, John Bishop. *The Oil and Gas Lease in Canada*. 4th ed. Toronto: University of Toronto, 2008.

Canadian Centre for Energy Information, "Energy Facts and Statistics," *Centre for Energy: Fast Facts*, http://www.centreforenergy.com/AboutEnergy (accessed July 5, 2012).

Canadian Centre for Energy Information, "Evolution of Canada's Oil and Gas Industry," *Centre for Energy: Centre for Energy Publications*, http://www.centreforenergy.com/shopping/uploads/122.pdf (accessed July 6, 2012).

25 C.F.R. §§ 200.1–227.30 (2012).

43 C.F.R. §§ 3100.0-3–3109.3 (2012).

Exxon Corp. v. Middleton, 613 S.W.2d 240, 245–46 (Tex. 1981).

Fagg v. Texas Co., 57 S.W.2d 87 (Tex. Comm'n App. 1933).

GPS.gov, "Surveying and Mapping," *GPS.gov: Survey and Mapping Applications*, http://www.gps.gov/applications/survey (accessed August 9, 2012).

Greene v. Robinson, 117 Tex. 516, 8 S.W.2d 655 (Tex. 1928).

Jacobus, Charles J., "Legal Descriptions: Metes and Bounds," in *Texas Real Estate Law*, 10th ed. (Mason: Cengage Learning, 2009), 54–56.

La. Rv. Stat. § 30:10 (2012).

Moses, Leslie. *The AAPL Guide for Landmen: From Lease to Release*. Fort Worth: American Association of Professional Landmen, 1970.

Natural Resources Law Center, "Intermountain Oil and Gas Best Management Practices (BMP) Project: Tribal Law," *Oil and Gas Drilling in Colorado, Wyoming, Montana, New Mexico, Utah*, http://www.oilandgasbmps.org/laws/tribal (accessed October 30, 2012).

New Mexico Bureau of Geology and Mineral Resources (NMBGMR), "Oil and Gas Program: Importance of Oil and Gas in New Mexico," *New Mexico Bureau of Geology and Mineral Resources (NMBGMR)*, http://geoinfo.nmt.edu/resources/petroleum (accessed July 17, 2012).

New Mexico Department of Game and Fish, "Oil and Gas Development Guidelines: Conserving New Mexico's Wildlife Habitats and Wildlife," *New Mexico Wildlife*, http://www.wildlife.state.nm.us/documents/oil-andgasguidelines.pdf (accessed October 30, 2012).

New York Times, "'Oil!' and the History of Southern California," *New York Times*, February 22, 2008, http://www.nytimes.com/2008/02/22/timestopics/topics_uptonsinclair_oil.html (accessed July 12, 2012).

Oklahoma Historical Society, "Hot Oil Controversy," *Encyclopedia of Oklahoma History and Culture*, http://digital.library.okstate.edu/encyclopedia/entries/H/HO036.html (accessed July 31, 2012).

Texas State Historical Association, "Oil and Gas Industry," *Texas State Historical Association (TSHA)*, http://www.tshaonline.org/handbook/online/articles/doogz (accessed June 28, 2012).

U.S. Bureau of Indian Affairs (BIA), "Working on Indian Lands," *Indian Affairs*, http://www.bia.gov/WhoWeAre/AS-IA/IEED/DEMD/WIL/index.htm (accessed July 18, 2012).

U.S. Bureau of Land Management (BLM), "Oil and Gas," *U.S. Department of the Interior—Department of Land Management*, http://www.blm.gov/wo/st/en/prog/energy/oil_and_gas.html (accessed October 31, 2012).

U.S. Bureau of Ocean Energy Management (BOEM), "Leasing," *BOEM (Bureau of Ocean Energy Management)*, http://www.boem.gov/Oil-and-Gas-Energy-Program/Leasing/Leasing.aspx (accessed October 31, 2012).

U.S. Bureau of Ocean Energy Management (BOEM), "Oil and Gas Leasing on the Outer Continental Shelf," *BOEM (Bureau of Ocean Energy Management)*, http://www.boem.gov/uploadedFiles/BOEM/Oil_and_Gas_Energy_Program/Leasing/5BOEMRE_Leasing101.pdf(accessed October 30, 2012).

U.S. Bureau of Ocean Energy Management (BOEM), "Outer Continental Shelf," *BOEM (Bureau of Ocean Energy Management)*, http://www.boem.gov/Oil-and-Gas-Energy-Program/Leasing/Outer-Continental-Shelf/Index.aspx (accessed October 30, 2012).

16 U.S.C. § 470bb(4) (2012).

42 U.S.C. § 12511 (2012).

U.S. Energy Information Administration (EIA), "Crude Oil Production," *Crude Oil Production—Petroleum and Other Liquids*, http://www.eia.gov/dnav/pet/pet_crd_crpdn_adc_mbbl_a.htm (accessed June 13, 2012).

Appendix A
Top Oil-Producing States and Federal Offshore Lands, 2009–2011

The table below ranks the top oil-producing states based on thousand-barrels for the years 2009 to 2011. Federal offshore lands are also listed in the ranking. The appendices that follow (B to I) offer specific information on leasing for each of the locations in the table.

States	
1. Texas	1,371,002
2. Alaska	663,785
3. California	604,668
4. North Dakota	345,710
5. Oklahoma	209,067
6. Louisiana	205,589
7. New Mexico	197,791
8. Wyoming	159,224
9. Kansas	121,594
10. Colorado	99,247
Federal Offshore Lands	1,615,727

Source: Adapted from U.S. Energy Information Administration (IEA), "Crude Oil Production." http://www.eia.gov/dnav/pet/pet_crd_crpdn_adc_mbbl_a.htm. Last viewed June 13, 2012.

Appendix B
Leasing in Texas

Since the operators of Spindletop struck oil near Beaumont in 1901, Texas has led the states in oil production. In fact, in the early days of the industry, only Russia rivaled Texas for oil production in the world. Because of the state's status as a top producer, decisions by its courts often stand as precedent in oil and gas law, and the oil industry occupies a central place in its culture and folklore.

For the first decades of the 20th century, exploration and production in Texas happened at a frenzied pace, and few controls were in place. In the East Texas oilfield, in particular, uncontrolled production caused waste, damage to the formation, and a precipitous drop in prices. (Read more about the East Texas field in Chapter 1.)

In the 1930s, Texas lawmakers sought a means to control the volatility of the crude market. The Railroad Commission of Texas (RRC or TRC), an agency whose original mandate was to regulate the railroads, was charged with regulating oil and gas production. After the Commission's first proration orders were ignored and production continued in the field, the governor declared martial law in some counties and sent in the Texas National Guard to prevent the sale of "*hot oil*," oil in excess of production limits. By the 1940s, the commission was able to bring production under its control and stabilize prices. When the Organization of Petroleum Exporting Countries (OPEC) was founded, it used the RRC model of prorationing. By the 1960s, oil production in Texas had declined, world demand had increased, and foreign producers had come to hold more influence over the market. In the 1970s, OPEC displaced the RRC as the primary means of controlling crude prices on a worldwide scale. Today, the Commission continues to enforce environmental regulations in the field (maintaining pollution cleanup programs, for instance) and to maintain safety in pipelines. Its responsibility for regulating natural gas has expanded along with the production of natural gas in the state.

In 1900, Texas was a rural state, characterized by agriculture and ranching. By the end of World War II, owing to economic development brought about largely by oil production, the state had become highly industrialized, with several large cities. Houston is the nexus of a complex system that receives fluids through its port, refines them at plants in outlying towns, and transports them outward to market. Oil companies such as BP America, ConocoPhillips, ExxonMobil, and Citgo have base offices in its Energy Corridor district. Dallas has become a financing center for the oil and gas industry. The economic importance of the industry to the state should not be underestimated, as it continues to provide employment and considerable revenues for taxes.

A particularity of mineral ownership in Texas can be traced back to its colonial history. In original grants of land (patents) from Spain and Mexico, minerals were not included unless express words of designation were used.

When Texas became independent, it adopted this practice for a time, and in certain lands patented between 1895 and 1931, it reserved the minerals. The state continues to hold title to any minerals in those mineral-classified lands. The landowner, who owns a surface estate, is legally considered to be, in taking a mineral lease, an agent of Texas. He or she must share royalties for any producing tracts with the state. The Commissioner of the Texas General Land Office (GLO) in Austin answers inquiries about whether land is mineral-classified. (The address for the GLO's Web site is provided in the resources that follow.) The consideration for those leases must be approved by the Land Office, and leases must be executed on its official forms. (Those forms are available on the GLO's Web site.)

Many tracts of onshore lands are not mineral-classified. Parties to leases for them often begin the drafting process with a Producers 88 lease. (For more on those types of leases, see Chapter 5. Figure 5.1 is an example of a Producers 88 lease.) Today's sophisticated landowners often require amendments (in an addendum) to the form. Clauses added to a form lease might include ones that regulate the use of the surface and the disposal of waste, indemnify a mineral owner for damages caused by operations, restrict the assignability of the lease by the lessee, revise standard pooling rights, specify the time and computation of payments, eliminate warranty of title, grant the lessee the right of first refusal at the end of the lease's term, and release unused acreage or a depth of land (a Pugh clause). (For descriptions of lease provisions, see Chapters 5 and 6.) A few landowners with large holdings and some institutions such as banks have their own custom leases.

Texas owns the land up to 9 nautical miles from its shores. Those lands are leased through the GLO. Between that 9-mile line and the 8,000-foot depth line are lands controlled by the federal government. Offshore leasing for those lands farther and deeper from the coast is a function of the U.S. Bureau of Ocean Energy Management (BOEM). Lessees are determined by a sealed competitive bidding process. The agency then issues standard form leases. (Those form leases are available on the BOEM's Web site. See the resources below for the address.)

Development has taken place in the following regions in Texas: the Gulf Coast, Central Texas (the Austin Chalk formation), the Permian Basin (in West Texas), and East Texas. In recent years, new technologies allowing the profitable recovery of petroleum from shale have led to a flurry of leasing activity at the Barnett, Eagle Ford, and Haynesville formations, in north-central, south-central, and East Texas, respectively.

To learn more about mineral development and about leasing practices in Texas, visit these Web sites:

Bureau of Ocean Energy Management (BOEM)
Gulf of Mexico Outer Continental (OCS) Shelf Region
www.boem.gov

Texas General Land Office (GLO)-Austin
www.glo.texas.gov

Railroad Commission of Texas (RRC or TRC)
www.rrc.state.tx.us

Appendix C
Leasing in Alaska

In nearly every instance that a company wishes to acquire Alaskan oil or gas, it must lease from the federal government, the state of Alaska, or both. Private landowners come far behind the federal and state governments in the size and known producing potential of their holdings. Private ownership is increasing, but much privately owned land remains undeveloped and is therefore still an unknown factor in the estimates of Alaskan oil and gas reserves. The development of private lands will depend, in many cases, on federal action, especially on the construction of transport facilities on nearby federal lands.

The massive federal presence in Alaska is partly due to its history of statehood. In 1867, the United States acquired the lands of Alaska by purchase from Russia. In 1959, when Alaska became a state, the federal government granted the new state 28% ownership of those lands to create an economy for its citizens. Alaska has chosen most of the acreage available for patent, but it still owns less land in its borders with potential for oil and gas production than does the federal government. The federal share of lands in Alaska includes the National Petroleum Reserve-Alaska (NPR-A) and the Arctic National Wildlife Refuge (ANWR); the federal government continues to own nearly two-thirds of all potential onshore oil and gas land in the state.

The federal presence is also partly due to the strategic importance of Alaska during and after World War II. Until the discovery of large oil reserves on the North Slope at Prudhoe Bay in 1968, U.S. military forces provided Alaska's single greatest source of income and employment. With the Prudhoe Bay lease sale in 1969, the basis of Alaska's economy changed dramatically, but the federal government still provides a number of critical jobs for residents.

In the years before the Prudhoe Bay discovery was announced, a series of events took place leading to private ownership of 12% of public lands. In 1966, Alaska natives combined 17 of their regional associations into a statewide organization called the Alaska Federation of Natives (AFN). By 1967, this group had filed claims to lands historically occupied by native peoples. Secretary of the Interior Stewart Udall stopped all disposal of public lands in Alaska until these aboriginal claims could be settled. Settlement was seen as an important factor in the construction of the Alaskan pipeline. Congress passed the Alaska Native Claims Settlement Act (ANCSA) in 1971, granting natives title to 44 million acres plus a cash bonus of nearly a billion dollars.

The transfer of both the land and the money required the creation of special institutions known as Native Corporations, which are now the largest private owners of land in the state. Their goals include the development of any mineral reserves discovered on Native Corporation property.

Since 1980, two factors have encouraged the exploration of both state and federal lands in the state: the completion of the Trans-Alaska Pipeline System (TAPS, sometimes called the Alyeska Pipeline) and the passage of the Alaska National Interest Lands Conservation Act (ANILCA), a law that set aside federal lands as national parks, wildlife reserves, and wilderness areas but allowed mineral development with approval from Congress. Both federal and state procedures for mineral development in Alaska are complex and require detailed information gathering, public hearings, impact studies, and other preliminary steps before a lease sale is finally held.

It should be noted that, despite similarities in procedure, the state and the federal governments have come into conflict from time to time over the leasing of oil and gas lands. Proposed leasing in the Beaufort Sea, for example, has led to jurisdictional disputes. In addition, private groups have goals that can appear to be in conflict with the development of oil and gas. As Alaska has large populations of undisturbed species, environmental policy is very important in the state. In 1989, Prince William Sound was the site of a massive oil spill after the tanker *Exxon Valdez* ran aground. Development of the Arctic National Wildlife Refuge under ANILCA has also been a subject of great controversy, to the point of becoming a national issue over the course of several presidential administrations. Environmental groups will make it likely that, despite the plentiful energy sources to be tapped and the encouragement given to petroleum companies, exploration and development will not occur precipitously. In Alaska, even more than in other states, federal, state, and private interests continue to exercise powerful influences upon one another and to pull—now together, now in opposition—as the state's resources are examined and prepared for leasing.

Leases of privately owned lands in the state tend to be drafted by the companies that are parties to them, and therefore do not take a common form. The same is generally true of leases drafted by Native Corporations, which often have financial terms similar to ones in state leases but also have custom-crafted provisions pertaining to surface estates. Those special provisions might require a lessee to construct assets such as pipelines that can serve as infrastructure to benefit the native people. Parties to leases for Alaska's federal lands complete forms for the Bureau of Land Management, and parties to leases for state lands complete forms through the state's Department of Natural Resources. (Chapter 2 offers information on the bidding process for leases through the BLM; information on leasing through Alaska's DNR is available on the agency's Web site. See the resources that follow for the address of the DNR.)

To learn more about mineral development and leasing practices in Alaska, visit these Web sites:

Alaska Department of Commerce, Community, and Economic Development (DCCED)
www.dced.state.ak.us

Alaska Department of Natural Resources (DNR)
Division of Oil and Gas (DOG)
www.dog.dnr.alaska.gov

Alaska Oil and Gas Conservation Commission (AOGCC)
www.doa.alaska.gov/ogc

Alaska Gas Pipeline Project Office (GPPO)
www.gasline.alaska.gov

U.S. Department of the Interior (DOI)
Bureau of Land Management (BLM)
Alaska Office
www.blm.gov/ak

Bureau of Ocean Energy Management (BOEM)
Alaska Outer Continental Shelf (OCS) Region
www.boem.gov

Appendix D
Leasing in California

Oil seeps existed in the Los Angeles area long before the Southern California Oil Boom of the 1920s. They trapped animals looking for food in prehistoric times, and native peoples used them to tar their canoes. In the early 1920s, discoveries at Huntington Beach, Santa Fe Springs, and Signal Hill made California the biggest producer of crude in the United States. Upton Sinclair's novel *Oil!* (adapted in the 2007 movie *There Will Be Blood*) chronicles in story form the explosive development of the local crude industry and the social phenomena that accompanied it, including political corruption. Oil money created enormous growth, particularly in the city of Los Angeles. It fostered the growth of the movie industry in Hollywood and of the California real-estate industry, as well. With the increased availability of cheap gasoline came a new model for urban development based on the automobile, traffic lights, the construction of major roadways, and suburbs. Oil and gas remain important resources for the economy of California, although restrictions have been placed on drilling to protect human health and the environment.

Leasing in California differs from leasing in other states in several important ways. The first way involves the routine purchase of title insurance for drill sites and the correspondingly larger role played by title companies in checking and reporting on tract titles. The second way involves the lease forms, which are considerably longer and more detailed than forms in other states—so long and detailed, in fact, as to encourage the use of additional short forms to lower recording costs and protect confidentiality. The third way involves environmental regulations and reduced access to lands that are withheld from leasing because of environmental concerns.

In California, the lessee must purchase insurance from a title company that covers the tracts making up a drill site. (Insuring *all* the tracts in an acquired block of leases usually costs more in time and money than lessees are willing to pay.) By the time the drill site is selected, the lessee's landman or lease broker has already made a preliminary check of all the tracts in a block to locate and contact the mineral owners. To conduct this preliminary title check, the landman or lease broker usually does not have to look further than the records of the title company, although county records are also available. That initial check will often be adequate for all tracts except those in the drill site. The lessee needs to investigate the drill site tracts more thoroughly, as those tracts will have to be insured.

Obtaining an oil leasehold report from the title company will give the lessee a list of any problems with the titles he or she is concerned about. The lessee can then arrange to have these defects cured. Curing the titles should remove obstacles in the way of a leasehold title insurance policy.

The lessee will specify how much insurance is needed. On less-important leases, the amount might be only a few thousand dollars. For such an amount, the title company does not always check the chain of title back to the original patent. Larger amounts in the neighborhood of $100,000 or more guarantee a thorough title check, often reviewed by the title company's home office. An insurance policy that protects the lessee against unforeseen title defects can then be issued.

The surface of the land in California is often so valuable that landowners require lease forms with very detailed provisions pertaining to how the surface will be used, including provisions for drilling and equipment placement. Some leases forbid drilling on the leased surface; some specify particular sites to which drilling must be confined and for which a surface rental must be paid. So carefully are the terms laid out that implied covenants are few; many lease forms contain a clause that prevents implied covenants from being read into the lease. The resulting long lease forms are rarely recorded. Instead, petroleum companies often use a memorandum, or memo, giving the essentials (names, dates, and land descriptions), and a sentence or two identifying the short form with its longer counterpart (fig. D.1). A short form thus stands for a particular long form. Recording these short forms is relatively inexpensive and avoids revealing details such as royalty figures to the public. Another notable difference in the agreements between parties in California and in other oil-producing states is in division orders, which are not routine, but rather only executed when the parties anticipate that there might be disagreements, as when an estate presents special problems or fractional interests that are open to question.

California is one of the top oil- and gas-producing states, with much of its production coming from offshore lands. Production also occurs at many large onshore fields, including the Midway-Sunset field and the Kern River field. Additional fields with production potential lie offshore—Dos Cuadras field, Ellwood field, and Wilmington field, for example. However, since a spill in the Santa Barbara Channel in 1969 brought a large oil slick to the coastline, offshore development has been a subject of controversy in the state. The California legislature responded to the spill by halting the leasing of state offshore tracts that same year; there has been a moratorium on the sale of leases for federal tracts off the coast since 1984. Current offshore production takes place at leaseholds that existed before those bans. In addition to concerns about new development offshore, Californians are also concerned with regulating activities such as *fracturing*, a practice that injects chemicals and particulates such as sand into the ground, raising fears of groundwater contamination and instability of the land. These government controls mean that parties interested in exploration and development in California must be prepared to compete for fewer leases and comply with more regulations.

To learn more about mineral development, leasing practices, and state laws and regulations in California, visit these Web sites:

California Department of Conservation (DOC)
Division of Oil, Gas and Geothermal Resources (DOGGR)
www.conservation.ca.gov/dog

Bureau of Ocean Energy Management (BOEM)
Pacific Outer Continental Shelf (OCS) Region
www.boem.gov

California State Lands Commission (SLC)
Mineral Resources Management Division (MRMD)
www.slc.ca.gov

California Laws and Regulations
(Searchable state statutes)
www.leginfo.ca.gov/statute.html

Recording requested by
(When recorded please return to):

____

____

____

Attn:

Space above for Recorder's Use

APN:__________________________________

DOCUMENTARY TRANSFER TAX $ STATED OFF-RECORD

______ Computed on full value of property conveyed

______ Computed on full value less liens and encumbrances remaining at time of sale

____________________________ [Insert Name of Lessee]

MEMORANDUM OF OIL AND GAS LEASE

(Short Form—Subsurface)

THIS MEMORANDUM OF OIL AND GAS LEASE made and entered into as of ______________, 20______, by and between __________________________________, called "Lessor", at ______________________ ________________________ and __________________________________, hereinafter called "Lessee," at ____________________________________.

WITNESSETH:

That in consideration of the sum of Ten Dollars ($10.00) and other valuable consideration, the receipt and sufficiency of which are hereby mutually acknowledged, Lessor has, and does hereby, let, lease and demise unto Lessee the lands described hereafter, with the right and for the purposes of conducting subsurface geophysical operations, exploring and prospecting for and producing and removing oil, gas and other hydrocarbon substances, and uses and purposes incidental thereto, for a Primary Term of ______ years from and thereafter as provided in that certain long form of Subsurface Oil and Gas Lease, ("Lease") between Lessor and Lessee, of same date herewith, all of the terms and provisions of which long form of lease are incorporated fully herein as though written entirely herein, all those certain lands situated in the County of ______________________, State of California, and particularly described as follows, to wit:

[Insert Legal Description]

It is understood and agreed that in the event of a conflict between the terms and conditions set forth in or on this Memorandum of Oil and Gas Lease and of said Lease, the terms and conditions of said Lease shall control for all purposes.

Figure D.1. A form for a memorandum (memo) of oil and gas lease

IN WITNESS OF WHICH, the parties have caused this Instrument to be duly executed as of the date set forth above.

LESSOR: **LESSEE:**

ALL-PURPOSE ACKNOWLEDGMENT

STATE OF CALIFORNIA)
) ss
COUNTY OF)

On ____________________, 20__, before me, ______________________________________,
(Insert Name and Title of Officer Here)

personally appeared ____, to be the person(s) whose name(s) is/are subscribed to the within instrument and acknowledged to me that he/she/they executed the same in his/her/their authorized capacity(ties), and that by his/her/their signature(s) on the instrument, the person(s), or the entity upon behalf of which the person(s) acted, executed the instrument.

I certify under PENALTY OF PERJURY under the laws of the State of California that the foregoing paragraph is true and correct.

WITNESS my hand and official seal.

SEAL

Signature: ___________________________________
(Signature of Notary Public)

STATE OF CALIFORNIA)
) ss
COUNTY OF)

On ____________________, 20__, before me, ______________________________________,
(Insert Name and Title of Officer Here)

personally appeared ____, to be the person(s) whose name(s) is/are subscribed to the within instrument and acknowledged to me that he/she/they executed the same in his/her/their authorized capacity(ties), and that by his/her/their signature(s) on the instrument, the person(s), or the entity upon behalf of which the person(s) acted, executed the instrument.

I certify under PENALTY OF PERJURY under the laws of the State of California that the foregoing paragraph is true and correct.

WITNESS my hand and official seal.

SEAL

Signature: ___________________________________
(Signature of Notary Public)

Figure D.1, cont. A form for a memorandum (memo) of oil and gas lease

Appendix E
Leasing in Oklahoma

Oil and gas have been so integral to the economic development of Oklahoma that it is sometimes called the "state that oil built." While Pennsylvania is credited with the first commercially producing oilwell in the United States (the Drake Well, completed in 1859), Oklahoma should be credited with the first oilwell (completed several years before, near Salina). Even before the Oklahoma and Indian territories were united in statehood, in 1907, men of European extraction had started to flood into the oil-producing areas within those boundaries and establish boomtowns based around production sites. Starting in the 1920s, a series of discoveries brought Oklahoma to the front of the oil-producing states. Many of those discoveries took place on Indian lands, and discoveries on lands of the Osage Indian Nation generated leases sold for unprecedented values. From 1900 to 1935, the Mid-Continent (the region ranging over hundreds of oilfields in Arkansas, Kansas, Louisiana, Oklahoma, and Texas) was the major oil-producing region of the United States, and for most of those years, Oklahoma was the lead oil-producing state in the region.

Oil production followed the same pattern in all states before regulation—overproduction resulting in waste and a catastrophic drop in prices. Production of "hot oil" (oil in excess of that allowed by prorationing orders) continued unabated. In the summer of 1931, Oklahoma's governor, William Murray, responded by calling in the National Guard to stop production in order to artificially raise prices. Around the same time, events to the south paralleled those in Oklahoma, when Texas's Governor Ross Sterling declared martial law and called the National Guard into the fields of his state to control production. By the 1930s, state and federal agencies had finally enacted regulations that slowed production and reduced waste, including regulations affecting well spacing, and the Texas Railroad Commission (RRC or TRC) had begun to affect oil prices throughout the United States and even the world through successful prorationing policies.

Oklahoma has served as a center for development of oil and gas industry technologies such as seismic studies used in exploration and waterflooding techniques used in secondary recovery operations. It has also been an intellectual center for the industry, with its institutes of higher learning and the American Association of Petroleum Geologists (AAPG), which was founded in Tulsa. Several major oil and gas companies have developed in Oklahoma, including Halliburton and Chesapeake Energy. The Arkoma and Ardmore Basins, along with their shelves and platforms, are sites for important oil and gas fields for the United States. And development continues in the state, particularly in the Anadarko Basin—although major investment in new technologies will be required for the deep wells needed to tap its enormous gas reserves.

In recent decades, it was common for mineral owners in Oklahoma to request a Producers 88 lease form with a 40/160/640-acre pooling provision or a Revised 1963 form from Burkhart's. Today, more commonly, oil companies have their own leases. Even though leases are drafted for individual companies by legal staff, they often have similar provisions. Those provisions tend to include the typical ones outlined in Chapter 5 of this book as well as top lease provisions that allow companies to match offers from other companies.

To learn more about mineral development and leasing practices in Oklahoma, visit these Web sites:

Oklahoma Corporation Commission (OCC)
Oil and Gas Division
www.occeweb.com/og/oghome.htm

Oklahoma State Legislature
(Online statutes searchable by keyword)
www.oklegislature.gov

Oklahoma Commissioners of the Land Office (CLO)
Minerals Management Division (MMD)
www.clo.ok.gov

U.S. Department of the Interior (DOI)
Bureau of Land Management (BLM)
Oklahoma Field Office (OFO)
www.blm.gov/nm/st/en/fo/Oklahoma_Field_Office.html

U.S. Department of the Interior (DOI)
Bureau of Indian Affairs (BIA)
Office of Indian Energy and Economic Development (IEED)
Division of Energy and Mineral Development (DEMD)
www.bia.gov

Appendix F
Leasing in Louisiana

Throughout the producing states, mineral leasing is governed by case law as modified by state statutes and administrative rules and regulations. The exception to this pattern can be found in Louisiana. In that state governed primarily by civil law, a statutory code called the *Louisiana Mineral Code* governs the leasing of oil and gas.

Another difference between leasing in Louisiana and leasing in other states—Texas, Mississippi, or West Virginia, for example—arises from how state law conceptualizes mineral ownership. In Louisiana, unextracted minerals such as oil and gas cannot be owned as land can be owned. There is no such thing as a mineral estate separate from a surface estate. What can be owned are mineral rights or interests—that is, rights to explore for, produce, and sell minerals. This distinction does not, of course, prevent people from talking about the sale or purchase of oil and gas as if these minerals could be owned in place.

This distinction affects leasing in Louisiana in various ways. In most states, a mineral sale or reservation is perpetual; in Louisiana, an assignment of mineral or royalty interest or a reservation of mineral or royalty interests in the sale of land will terminate if the interests are not used. When the mineral or royalty rights in the land are owned by someone other than the owner of the land itself, the outstanding mineral rights are considered to be a burden or encumbrance on the full ownership of the land. A mineral or royalty interest that is not owned by the same person who owns the land itself will expire upon the passage of 10 years from the creation of the mineral or royalty right unless operations have been carried out that will interrupt the running of this period. Such operations are the drilling of a well in the case of a mineral servitude, or production in the case of a royalty right. (The mineral servitude confers the same rights as ownership of the minerals themselves in other states, including the right to grant leases and to retain bonuses and delay rentals; the royalty interest is a right to production and royalty only from the land, if applicable.) At the end of the 10-year period, whoever owns the land itself automatically becomes the owner of the mineral or royalty right.

The practical differences that come from Louisiana's history and legal particularities are numerous, but most affect the details of leasing without adding up to major procedural differences of the kind found in California or Alaska. (Procedural differences include, for example, how leases are recorded and the use of different units of measurement such as arpents in land surveys.) Louisiana lease forms, like those used in other states, show a number of variations. Traditionally, forms printed by the M. L. Bath Company of Shreveport have been commonly used. In the Mid-Continent (the oil-producing region of the mid-South of the United States), landmen and attorneys often refer to them as "Bath forms" in the same casual way as they refer to the Producers 88.

Louisiana plays a major role in supplying U.S. energy needs. Much of the oil and gas supplied through Louisiana originates in leases off the coast in the deep waters of the Gulf of Mexico (GOM). As the state only owns lands up to 3 nautical miles from the coast, the bulk of offshore production comes from federal leases. A complex infrastructure in the state consisting of tankers, marine terminals, pipelines, and trucks moves the oil and gas from offshore platforms through the refining process and then to consumers. A small percentage of the crude brought into Louisiana is stored at facilities near Lake Charles and Baton Rouge as part of the U.S. Strategic Petroleum Reserve.

In 2005, Hurricane Katrina caused temporary but significant disturbances in oil distribution and increases in fuel prices. Since then, construction has attempted to restore the infrastructure, particularly the many offshore platforms destroyed during the storm. Within the industry, this effort to rebuild infrastructure has been accompanied by admonitions to upgrade or replace decaying assets, so investment in those assets might be anticipated. At present, demand for offshore leases is most competitive in the deep or ultradeep waters of the GOM, and for onshore leases in parishes where shale formations are present, particularly in the four parishes where the Haynesville formation is located.

To learn more about mineral development and about federal and state leasing practices in Louisiana, visit these Web sites:

Louisiana Department of Natural Resources (DNR)
Office of Conservation and Office of Mineral Resources
www.dnr.louisiana.gov

Louisiana Legislature
(Louisiana laws, including Title 31 of the *Louisiana Mineral Code*)
www.legis.state.la.us

Louisiana Register and *Louisiana Administrative Code*
(Louisiana administrative rules and regulations)
www.doa.louisiana.gov/osr/lac/lac.htm

Bureau of Ocean Energy Management (BOEM)
Gulf of Mexico Outer Continental (OCS) Shelf Region
www.boem.gov

Louisiana Department of Transportation and Development (DOTD)
(Information on the Louisiana Offshore Oil Port, LOOP)
www.dotd.la.gov

Appendix G
Leasing in New Mexico

New Mexico is a state with large energy reserves and—because of its sparse population—relatively low energy requirements. This surplus of energy resources powers New Mexico's economy. Taxes and royalties paid to the state from oil and gas production provide substantial funds for New Mexico's schools, roads, and other public facilities, and the industry is the state's largest civilian employer.

New Mexico's first commercial oilwell came into production in 1924, in the southeastern portion of the state. In late 1920s, the discovery of Hobbs Pool made New Mexico a top oil producer among the states. Today, major production takes place in the San Juan Basin in the northwest of the state and in the Permian Basin in the southeast of the state. (The Permian Basin continues into Texas.) New Mexico has several large refineries, and its large network of pipelines carries oil and gas to markets east and west of the state.

Much of the land in New Mexico is owned by federal, state, or tribal governments. The State Land Office (SLO) manages oil and gas leasing on state lands by its Oil, Gas and Minerals Division (OGMD). Information on the bidding process for obtaining leases to state lands as well as bid application forms are available on the SLO's Web site. (See the resources that follow for the address.) A state statute, the Surface Owners Protection Act (SOPA, enacted in 1978), sets requirements for operators to inform surface owners of potential damage to their estates caused by drilling and to compensate owners in the event that damage occurs.

Sixty percent of the oil and gas production in the state is federal. In some cases, the surface estate is owned by an entity other than the federal government, but the Bureau of Land Management (BLM) nevertheless enforces federal laws, rules, and regulations as they apply to production on those lands. The BLM New Mexico Office holds lease sales as auctions on at least a quarterly basis, and those who obtain leases must submit an Application for Permission to Drill (APD) to the BLM and, in some cases, to the New Mexico Oil Conservation Division (OCD). The primary term of BLM leases is 10 years, and the lease is extended for as long as production is taking place in paying quantities or drilling operations are being seriously conducted.

Indian Lands in New Mexico (and throughout the United States) are managed and administered by the Bureau of Indian Affairs (BIA), an agency of the U.S. government. The bulk of those lands are Tribal Trust Lands (TTL)—that is, lands held in trust by the federal government for the use of a native people. Tribes hold beneficial title to those surface and mineral estates, while the U.S. government holds legal title. The BIA issues standard form leases; there are variants of BIA forms that allow the tribe concerned to be the lessor of the lease. (Forms are available on the BIA's Web site.

See the resources that follow for the address.) Also relevant to the discussion here are allotted lands. Those lands were granted to individual members of tribes under the General Allotment Act (or Dawes Act) of 1887. The BIA has a special set of lease forms for those lands, as well. Because of overlapping jurisdiction on Indian lands, there must often be compliance with federal law and the law of the local tribe to receive permits and approvals for operations.

To learn more about mineral development and leasing practices in New Mexico, visit these Web sites:

New Mexico State Land Office (SLO)
Oil, Gas and Minerals Division (OGMD)
www.nmstatelands.org

U.S. Department of the Interior (DOI)
Bureau of Land Management (BLM)
New Mexico Office (NMO)
www.blm.gov/nm

New Mexico Energy, Minerals and Natural Resources Department (EMNRD)
Oil Conservation Division (OCD)
www.emnrd.state.nm.us/ocd

U.S. Department of the Interior (DOI)
Bureau of Indian Affairs (BIA)
Office of Indian Energy and Economic Development (IEED)
Division of Energy and Mineral Development (DEMD)
www.bia.gov

Navajo Nation Oil and Gas Company (NNOGC)
(Oil and gas development company of the Navajo Nation)
www.nnogc.com

Jicarilla Apache Nation
Oil and Gas Administration
www.jicarillaoga.com

Appendix H
Leasing in the Other Top Ten Oil-Producing States

Visit the Web sites that follow to learn more about mineral development and leasing practices in these top oil-producing states.

North Dakota

North Dakota Industrial Commission (NDIC)
Department of Mineral Resources (DMR)
Oil and Gas Division (OGD)
www.dmr.nd.gov/oilgas

North Dakota Department of Commerce
www.commerce.nd.gov

North Dakota Department of Trust Lands (DTL)
Minerals Management Division (MMD)
www.land.nd.gov

North Dakota Petroleum Council (NDPC)
www.ndoil.org

North Dakota Legislative Branch
(Online statutes organized by chapter)
www.legis.nd.gov/information/statutes/cent-code

U.S. Department of the Interior (DOI)
Bureau of Land Management (BLM)
North Dakota Field Office (NDFO)
Oil and Gas Program (OGP)
www.blm.gov/mt/st/en/fo/north_dakota_field/o_g.html

U.S. Department of the Interior (DOI)
Bureau of Indian Affairs (BIA)
Office of Indian Energy and Economic Development (IEED)
Division of Energy and Mineral Development (DEMD)
www.bia.gov

Wyoming

Wyoming Oil and Gas Conservation Commission (WOGCC)
wogcc.state.wy.us

Wyoming Office of State Lands and Investments (OSLI)
lands.state.wy.us

State of Wyoming Legislature
(Searchable state statutes and Constitution)
legisweb.state.wy.us/LSOWeb/wyStatutes.aspx

U.S. Department of the Interior (DOI)
Bureau of Land Management (BLM)
Wyoming Field Office (WFO)
Oil and Gas Program (OGP)
www.blm.gov/wy/st/en/programs/energy/Oil_and_Gas.html

U.S. Department of the Interior (DOI)
Bureau of Indian Affairs (BIA)
Office of Indian Energy and Economic Development (IEE)
Division of Energy and Mineral Development (DEMD)
www.bia.gov

Kansas

Kansas Corporation Commission (KCC)
Oil and Gas Conservation Division (OGCD)
www.kcc.state.ks.us/conservation

Kansas Legislature
(Searchable statutes)
www.kslegislature.org/li/b2011_12/statute

U.S. Department of the Interior (DOI)
Bureau of Land Management (BLM)
New Mexico-Oklahoma-Texas-Kansas Field Offices
Oil and Gas Program (OGP)
www.blm.gov/nm/st/en/prog/energy/oil_and_gas.html

Colorado

Colorado Oil and Gas Conservation Commission (COGCC)
www.cogcc.state.co.us

Colorado Revised Statutes
(Searchable state statutes)
www.lexisnexis.com/hottopics/colorado

U.S. Department of the Interior (DOI)
Bureau of Land Management (BLM)
Colorado Field Office (CFO)
Oil and Gas Program (OGP)
www.blm.gov/co/st/en/BLM_Programs/oilandgas.html

U.S. Department of the Interior (DOI)
Bureau of Indian Affairs (BIA)
Office of Indian Energy and Economic Development (IEED)
Division of Energy and Mineral Development (DEMD)
www.bia.gov

Colorado Department of Natural Resources (DNR)
State Land Board (SLB)
www.trustlands.state.co.us

Appendix I
Leasing Federal Offshore Lands

Individual states have jurisdiction over submerged lands for a certain distance from their coasts.

- Texas and Florida on its Gulf coast: 9 nautical miles
- Louisiana: 3 imperial nautical miles
- All other states, including Florida on its Atlantic coast: 3 nautical miles

States such as Texas, Louisiana, California, and Alaska have highly profitable offshore operations that bring in significant revenues. State agencies such as the Texas General Land Office (GLO) and the California State Lands Commission (SLC) lease those offshore lands for oil and gas development.

Beyond offshore state-owned lands are those of the Outer Continental Shelf (OCS). The outer limits of the OCS correspond to those of the exclusive economic zone (EEZ), as defined by international law—usually, 200 nautical miles from shore. (The actual limit for any given point can vary according to the topography of the sea floor.) This system creates, starting at the coast, two bands of jurisdiction—one state and one federal—that end where international waters begin. (For a map showing the bands of jurisdiction, see figure 2.4 in Chapter 2.)

The Bureau of Ocean Energy Management (BOEM) of the U.S. Department of the Interior (DOI) administers leases for federal offshore lands. The millions of acres leased by BOEM account for about 24% of domestic oil production and 7% of the domestic natural gas production in the United States. Revenues from bonuses, royalties, and rentals are shared by the federal government with coastal states according to statute.

Until October 2011, the Bureau of Ocean Energy Management, Regulation and Enforcement (BOEMRE) was responsible for all of the functions associated with leasing in the federal zone. After the April 2010 incident involving the *Deepwater Horizon* in the Gulf of Mexico, a decision was made to separate the functions of the bureau by dividing it into three independent agencies. Now, BOEM conducts sales of leases and issues them. Two other agencies carry out the rest of the business associated with offshore leasing: The Office of Natural Resource Revenue (ONRR) collects revenues, and the Bureau of Safety and Environmental Enforcement (BSEE) enforces safety and environmental regulations.

BOEM has regional divisions for Alaska, the Gulf of Mexico (GOM), and the Pacific. Leases come about as the result of a bidding process. First, leases for available tracts are proposed in a series of drafts requiring input from federal agencies and local stakeholders. These drafts form a Five Year

Program for leases that must be approved by the Secretary of the Interior and Congress. Notice of lease sales is posted in the *Federal Register* at least 30 days before the sale date so that sealed bids may be submitted by interested parties. Only qualified bidders may acquire leases: American nationals, resident aliens, corporations, or partnerships. Major oil corporations are sometimes prohibited from jointly bidding on a lease. BOEM, the Attorney General, and the Federal Trade Commission evaluate bids to determine if they are technically and legally adequate. To qualify for competition, bids must additionally meet fair-market value and must not violate anti-trust laws.

In many ways, BOEM leases are like other oil and gas leases. Once a lease is acquired, the lessee pays a bonus; then, when production begins, the lessee pays royalties to the lessor (the government). However, it is not unusual for BOEM leases to include special provisions such as ones:

- Preventing the lessee from selling or assigning the lease interest
- Requiring approval of plans for environmental reasons
- Requiring biological surveys of sensitive seafloor habitats
- Requiring environmental training for personnel involved in operations
- Escalating rentals over time to encourage development of the lease
- Waiving royalty payments temporarily to encourage exploration in a new area or at a greater depth

The provisions of a BOEM lease might appear simple. However, the lessee should remember that activities under the lease must also comply with the rules and regulations in the *Federal Register* (codified in the *Code of Federal Regulations*, or *C.F.R.*) and the laws in the *United States Code*, or *U.S.C.* Statutes in the *U.S. Code* include legislation at the federal level pertaining to health and the environment, such as the Endangered Species Act and the Clean Air Act. Section 1 of the BOEM-2005 Oil and Gas Lease of Submerged Lands Under the OCS Lands Act states that the lease is subject to any relevant statutes or regulations except those that are in direct conflict with express provisions in the instrument. (Lease forms are available on the BOEM Web site. See the resources that follow for the address.) Lessees can keep abreast of developments in the law by consulting the government publications named above on a regular basis. Searchable electronic editions of the publications are available; their online addresses are given below.

To learn more about leasing federal offshore lands, visit these Web sites:

Bureau of Ocean Energy Management (BOEM)
www.boem.gov

Office of Natural Resources Revenue (ONRR)
www.onrr.gov

Bureau of Safety and Environmental Enforcement (BSEE)
www.bsee.gov

Electronic *Code of Federal Regulations* (e-CFR)
www.ecfr.gov

The *Federal Register* (online edition)
www.federalregister.gov

The *United States Code* (online edition)
uscode.house.gov

Appendix J
Leasing in Canada

The oil industries in the United States and Canada have developed in tandem, more or less. There is some debate about whether the first commercially producing oilwell in North America was Edwin Drake's well in Oil Creek, Pennsylvania, or James Williams's well in Oil Springs, Ontario, in the years 1858 and 1859. The first Canadian discoveries took place in Ontario, but greater formations were later discovered in the Western provinces and offshore. The Canadian oil industry, in its early decades, saw the same kind of uncontrolled development as the American industry saw. In 1922, well-spacing rules were put in place, and in 1938, the Alberta Petroleum and Natural Gas Conservation Board (known today as the *Energy Resources Conservation Board*, or *ERCB*) reduced production in the field to encourage conservation and control market volatility.

Canada is a major producer of fossil fuels, ranking sixth in the world for crude oil and third for natural gas. It is the largest exporter of both fuels to the United States. And it is expected to continue to produce: More than 14,000 wells were drilled in Canada in 2011. Technologies allowing the more profitable extraction of bitumen (an extremely heavy form of crude) from sands should allow Canada to exploit the biggest petroleum deposit in the world, the Athabasca oil sands.

The primary producing provinces are Alberta, British Columbia, Saskatchewan, Manitoba, and Ontario. Provincial legislatures have considerable autonomy in handling provincial concerns—or at least, in handling those matters constitutionally defined as falling within their jurisdiction. Consequently, each province has its own statutes and regulations for oil and gas that interact with federal ones regulating the industry.

Some subsurface minerals are privately owned. Rights to minerals in Canada are often determined by legislative act or by whether mineral rights were withheld by the Crown when patents were originally granted. There are more privately held mineral rights in the Eastern provinces than in the Western ones. Minerals of lands outside the provinces belong to the federal government. Those minerals include oil and gas of offshore lands and of the Northern Territories. In addition, there are mineral properties owned by Canada's native peoples, and those lands have their own separate regulations.

Early leases in Canada appear to have been based on agricultural leases. The Producers 88 (in all its permutations) later gained wide acceptance, when it was seen that a "standard" lease was desirable for landowners and operators. (See the section on the Producers 88 lease and figure 5.1 in Chapter 5.) More recently, a truly standard lease used across the provinces has been developed by the *Canadian Association of Professional Landmen* (*CAPL*). At the time of publication of this book, the newest edition of that lease was called the CAPL 1999 Alberta Petroleum and Natural Gas Lease and Grant (or CAPL 99). CAPL was, however, in the process of drafting a new edition. (Any new "PNG"—Petroleum and Natural Gas—form will likely be available for purchase from CAPL in the future. See the resources that follow for CAPL's Web address.) Oil companies continue to produce their own leases. Lessors are advised to read the lease carefully, as familiar language might be used but custom provisions added to the benefit of the company (and the detriment of the lessor). Case law interpreting oil and gas leases in Canada diverges from case law in the United States, so those accustomed to reasoning in U.S. case law should be cautious about applying it to Canadian leases.

Canadian provinces enact new oil and gas legislation from time to time, and anyone interested in leasing mineral rights in Canada must keep abreast of legislation. Administrative agencies make rules and regulations pertaining to mineral development and leasing practices. They also provide information on their Web sites, whose addresses are provided below.

Canada has a national agency for oil and gas:

National Resources Canada (NRCAN)
www.nrcan.gc.ca

The individual provinces have their own oil and gas agencies, as well. These are the ones for the major producing provinces:

Alberta Energy (Ministry of Energy of Alberta)
www.energy.alberta.ca

British Columbia Ministry of Energy and Mines
Oil and Gas Division and Oil and Gas Commission
www.gov.bc.ca

Manitoba Department of Innovation, Energy and Mines
Mineral Resources Division
www.gov.mb.ca/iem/mrd

Saskatchewan Ministry of Energy and Resources
www.er.gov.sk.ca

Ontario Ministry of Natural Resources
Petroleum Resource Centre
www.mnr.gov.on.ca/en/Business/OGSR

This association produces Canada's standard oil and gas lease:

Canadian Association of Professional Landmen (CAPL)
www.landman.ca

This site serves as an unofficial source for Canada's statutes, case law, and regulations:

Canadian Legal Information Institute (CanLII)
www.canlii.org/en

Appendix K
Oil and Gas Lease Interests

TYPES OF INTEREST CREATED BY A LEASE

Royalty Interest

The royalty is the landowner's agreed-upon percentage of the total mineral production of his or her land. It is normally cost-free and continues as long as the lease does, or at least for a period stated in the lease. Clearly, this percentage might turn out to be the landowner's most important economic interest, so he or she might drive a hard a bargain for it, especially if the prospects for production seem good. The traditional ⅛, or 12.5%, royalty, for so many years the typical share of production reserved by the landowner, has been giving way in some parts of the country to a larger figure. It is not uncommon these days for the lease to specify a 3/16 royalty; 1/5, 7/32, or ¼ might be received for a particularly promising tract. Royalty payments are, in most cases, paid by the purchaser of the produced oil even though the lease might provide that the lessee make such payments. Royalty payments for gas produced from leased property are usually paid by the lessee or the operator.

Working Interest

This interest given to the lessee by the oil and gas lease is the operating interest—the one that includes responsibility for all drilling, developing, and operating costs. The lessee, or owner of an oil and gas lease, used to be able to count on a ⅞ share of all the minerals produced. Against that share came all the costs of exploration and development, plus any payments of the kinds mentioned below. Higher royalties for landowners have reduced that once-typical figure somewhat. The working interest can still, of course, be very profitable. It shares with the landowner's interests a certain legal flexibility, too. That is, a lessee can (by state law or by specific lease provision) transfer to other people all or a fraction of the interest in all or a specified part of the property that it has leased. The lessee of a large tract might, for example, find it advantageous to farm out or grant all or a portion of its interest in some part of the leasehold to a third person. That third person would pay the original lessee in money or in an interest in production and agree to drill a well on the property. The lessee can also convey to others (or reserve to itself) payments called "overriding royalties" and "production payments."

Overriding Royalty Interest

This designated percentage of the lessee's working interest, like the landowner's royalty, is free from all production costs except taxes. It comes off the top, and it continues as long as the lease is in effect. Such payments sometimes compensate people who bring good prospects to the attention of an oil company; occasionally, they form part of the lease itself and thus go to the landowner. It was once quite common for landowners to ask for an overriding royalty of, say, ¹⁄₁₆ in addition to ⅛ of total production. Now that mineral owners frequently ask for ³⁄₁₆ royalty, they bargain for an override less frequently. Clearly, ¹⁄₁₆ of a ⅞ working interest plus ⅛ of total production mean fewer dollars than does a flat ³⁄₁₆ of total production.

Production Payment

This payment resembles an overriding royalty in being a cost-free fraction of the working interest. It differs chiefly in its duration. While an override lasts as long as the lease, a production payment ends when a specified amount of money (or number of barrels) has been reached. For instance, a production payment might stop after $100,000—taken from a ¹⁄₃₂ share of the working interest—has been paid.

Net Working Interest

This type of interest is the share remaining to the working interest owners after all royalties, overriding royalties, and production payments have been assigned or reserved to their respective owners. The full working interest owns 100% of the oil and gas wells it brings into production and must pay 100% of all exploring, drilling, and development expenses. If its leasehold is burdened with heavy royalties and other payments out of production, it might be hard-pressed to turn much of a profit.

CALCULATING INTERESTS

Total of Interests

A division order lists all the interest owners in a given unit and expresses their net revenue interests as decimal figures. These figures should add up to 100%. They will include the following:

Royalty owners' revenue interests
Overriding royalty owners' revenue interests
Working interest owners' net revenue interest
Total: 100%

Net Revenues

To calculate the net revenue interest of the various kinds of owners, the formulas shown below are commonly used. The examples assume a drilling and spacing unit of 640 acres made up of individually owned and leased tracts.

Royalty Interest

Calculating royalty is a two-step process.

1. First, calculate the owner's net mineral acres by the following formula:

   Net acres = fraction of ownership × total acres in the tract

For example, if John Smith owns a $\frac{1}{8}$ mineral interest in one quarter of the 640-acre unit, he owns a $\frac{1}{8}$ interest in a 160-acre tract. His net mineral acres can be calculated as follows:

$$\frac{1}{8} \times 160 = 20 \text{ net mineral acres}$$

If Mr. Smith's ownership were expressed as a decimal (based on a percentage) instead of a fraction, the formula would look like this:

$$0.125 \times 160 = 20 \text{ net mineral acres}$$

2. Then, calculate the owner's net revenue interest in the unit with the following formula:

   RI = royalty retained by owner
× net acres owned
÷ total acres in unit

   In Mr. Smith's case, he leases his 20 net acres to the GAS Company while retaining a $\frac{3}{16}$ royalty interest. His net revenue interest will be:

$$\frac{3}{16} \times 20 \div 640 = 0.00585937$$

Overriding Royalty Interest

Calculate the overriding royalty interest by the following formula:

ORRI = overriding royalty
× net acres subject to override
÷ total acres in unit

For example, if Ms. Leggitt receives a $\frac{1}{16}$ overriding royalty on the $\frac{7}{8}$ working interest held by the GAS Company in another quarter of the 640-acre unit, her revenue interest will be as follows:

$$(\frac{1}{16} \times \frac{7}{8}) \times 160 \div 640 = 0.01367187$$

Working Interest

A few more steps are required to calculate working interest.

1. First, determine how many net acres are subject to each retained royalty interest. For example, the GAS Company has 160 acres subject to a $\frac{3}{16}$ royalty (Mr. Smith's) and another 160 acres subject to a $\frac{1}{8}$ royalty (which belongs to Mr. Jones).
2. Next, determine how many net acres are subject to overriding royalties. In this case, the GAS Company has 160 acres subject to Ms. Leggitt's $\frac{1}{16}$ overriding royalty.

$$\text{ORRI} = 0.01367187$$

3. Then, determine the gross working interest on each of the GAS Company's tracts. For example, 160 acres retain a $\frac{3}{16}$ royalty, so the GAS Company is left with a $\frac{13}{16}$ gross working interest in that tract.

Its second tract retains a $\frac{1}{8}$ royalty, leaving the company with a $\frac{7}{8}$ gross working interest. Now use the following formula:

$$WI = \text{gross working interest} \times \text{net acreage} \div \text{total unit acreage}$$

For example,

$$\tfrac{13}{16} \times 160 \div 640 = 0.203125 \text{ WI on first tract}$$
$$\tfrac{7}{8} \times 160 \div 640 = 0.218750 \text{ WI on second tract}$$

4. Now, add the totals from the previous step together.

   0.203125 WI
   0.218750 WI
   0.421875 Total working interest

5. Then, add all the totals from the second step together. In this case, there is only one overriding royalty interest: 0.01367187.

6. Finally, subtract the override total from the working interest total:

   0.42187500
   0.01367187
   0.40820313 Working interest owner's net revenue interest

7. To determine a working interest owner's working interest in the entire 640-acre unit, use the following formula:

   $$WI = \text{total net acres under lease} \div \text{total unit acres}$$

   For example, if the GAS Company has 320 net acres under lease in the 640-acre unit, its working interest in the unit will be as follows:

   $$320 \div 640 = 0.5, \text{ or } 50\% \text{ WI}$$

Total of Working Interests

The total working interests of all the companies involved in the unit add up to 100%. In addition to the GAS Company, two other companies might share in the unit of 640 acres.

LITE Company	28%	
PETRO Company	22%	
GAS Company	50%	
	100%	Total WI

Appendix L
Traditional Units for Measuring Land

Traditional English Surveyor's Measurements

1 surveyor's chain = 100 links of 7.92 inches each
1 rod = 16½ feet
4 rods = 1 chain
1 pole = 1 rod
1 mile = 80 chains, or 5,280 feet
1 acre = 10 square chains, or 43,560 square feet

Equivalents of Various Linear and Square Measurements

Linear Measure

1 inch	equals	.0833 feet
7.92 inches	equals	1 link
12 inches	equals	1 foot
1 vara	equals	33⅓ inches
2.778 feet	equals	1 vara
3 feet	equals	1 yard
25 links	equals	16½ feet
25 links	equals	1 rod
100 links	equals	1 chain
16½ feet	equals	1 rod
5½ yards	equals	1 rod
4 rods	equals	100 links
66 feet	equals	1 chain
80 chains	equals	1 mile
320 rods	equals	1 mile
5,280 feet	equals	1 mile
1,760 yards	equals	1 mile

Square Measure

144 sq. in	equals	1 sq. foot
9 sq. feet	equals	1 sq. yard
30¼ sq. yd	equals	1 sq. rod
16 sq. rods	equals	1 sq. chain
1 sq. rod	equals	272¼ sq. ft.
1 sq. chain	equals	4356 sq. ft.
10 sq. chain	equals	1 acre
160 sq. rods	equals	1 acre
4,840 sq. yd	equals	1 acre
43,560 sq. ft.	equals	1 acre
640 acres	equals	1 sq. mile
1 section	equals	1 sq. mile
1 Twp	equals	36 sq. miles
1 Twp	equals	6 miles sq.

Source: Adapted from *The AAPL Guide for Landmen: From Lease to Release*, 58–59.

Chains and Feet

Chains	Feet	Chains	Feet
1	66	51	3366
2	132	52	3432
3	198	53	3498
4	264	54	3564
5	330	55	3630
6	396	56	3696
7	462	57	3762
8	528	58	3828
9	594	59	3894
10	660	60	3960
11	726	61	4026
12	792	62	4092
13	858	63	4158
14	924	64	4224
15	990	65	4290
16	1056	66	4356
17	1122	67	4422
18	1188	68	4488
19	1254	69	4554
20	1320	70	4620
21	1386	71	4686
22	1452	72	4752
23	1518	73	4818
24	1584	74	4884
25	1560	75	4950
26	1716	76	5016
27	1782	77	5082
28	1848	78	5148
29	1914	79	5214
30	1980	80	5280
31	2046	81	5346
32	2112	82	5412
33	2178	83	5478
34	2244	84	5544
35	2310	85	5610
36	2376	86	5676
37	2442	87	5742
38	2508	88	5808
39	2574	89	5874
40	2640	90	5940
41	2706	91	6006
42	2772	92	6072
43	2838	93	6138
44	2904	94	6204
45	2970	95	6270
46	3036	96	6336
47	3102	97	6402
48	3168	98	6468
49	3234	99	6534
50	3300	100	6600

Source: Adapted from *The AAPL Guide for Landmen: From Lease to Release*, 58.

General Conversion of Traditional Spanish to Customary U.S. Units

1 pole 1 perch 1 rod	=	16½ feet, 5½ yards, 5.94 varas

1 chain	=	100 links, 66 feet, 23.76 varas
1 link	=	7.92 inches
1 mile (statute)	=	1,900.8 varas, 1,760 yards, 5,280 feet, 80 chains, 320 rods, 0.868 min. of latitude
1 acre	=	75.136 varas square, 208.710 feet square, 5,645.376 square varas, 43,560 square feet
1 labor	=	1,000 varas square, 177.136 acres, 1,000,000 square varas, 2,777.777 feet square
1 league	=	5,000 varas square, 25,000,000 square varas, 25 labors, 4,428.4 acres, 13,888.888 feet square
1 league and 1 labor	=	5,099.018 varas square, 25,999,982.402 square varas, 4,605.536 acres, 14,163.917 feet square
1½ league	=	2,214.2 acres, 3,535.533 varas square, 9,820.925 feet square

Spanish Measurements Traditionally Used in Texas

1 league and 1 labor	=	4,605.54 acres	=	26,000,000 square varas (square of 5,000 varas)
1 labor	=	177.136 acres	=	1,000,000 square varas (square of 1,000 varas)
1 league	=	4,428.4 acres	=	25,000,000 square varas (square of 5,000 varas)
½ league	=	2,214.2 acres	=	12,500,000 square varas (square of 3,535.5 varas)
⅓ league	=	1,476.13 acres	=	8,333,333 square varas (square of 2,886.7 varas)
¼ league	=	1,107.1 acres	=	6,250,000 square varas (square of 2,500 varas)
1 section	=	640 acres	=	3,613,040.64 square varas (square of 1,900.8 varas)
½ section	=	320 acres	=	1,806.520.32 square varas (square of 1,344.0 varas)
¼ section	=	160 acres	=	903,260.16 square varas (square of 950.4 varas)
⅛ section	=	80 acres	=	451,630.08 square varas (square of 672.0 varas)
1⁄16 section	=	40 acres	=	225,815.04 square varas (square of 475.2 varas)
4,840 square yards	=	1 acre	=	5,645.376 square varas (square of 75.1 varas)

⅓ league	=	1,476.1 acres, 2.886.7 varas square, 8,019 feet square
¼ league	=	1,107.1 acres, 2,500 varas square, 6,944.444 feet square
1 caballeria	=	108 acres
1 section	=	640 acres, 1,900.8 varas square, 5,280 feet square
1 sitio	=	1 league
1 vara	=	3 geometrical feet, 33⅓ inches
100 feet	=	36 varas
100 yards	=	108 varas
1 minute of latitude	=	1 nautical mile, 1.151 statute miles
1 degree of latitude	=	60 minutes, 60 nautical miles, 69.06 statute miles

To Reduce

Varas to feet, divide by 0.36.
Varas to yards, divide by 1.08.
Yards to varas, multiply by 1.08.
Varas to rods, divide by 5.94.
Rods to varas, multiply by 5.94.
Varas to chains, divide by 23.76.

Chains to varas, multiply by 23.76.

Square varas to acres, multiply by 177.136 and point off six places. (Divide by 5,645.376.)

Square feet to acres, multiply by 22.9568 and point off six places. (Divide by 43,560.)

Source: Adapted from *The AAPL Guide for Landmen: From Lease to Release*, 55–56.

Feet and Varas

1 foot	=	.36 vara	1 vara	=	33⅓ inches
2 feet	=	.72 vara	1 vara	=	2.78 feet
3 feet	=	1.08 varas	2 varas	=	5.56 feet
4 feet	=	1.44 varas	3 varas	=	8.33 feet
5 feet	=	1.80 varas	4 varas	=	11.11 feet
6 feet	=	2.16 varas	5 varas	=	13.89 feet
7 feet	=	2.52 varas	6 varas	=	16.67 feet
8 feet	=	2.88 varas	7 varas	=	19.44 feet
9 feet	=	3.24 varas	8 varas	=	22.22 feet
10 feet	=	3.60 varas	9 varas	=	25.00 feet

French Measurements Traditionally Used in Louisiana

1 arpent = 191.833 feet

1 square arpent = 0.84628 acres

1.1834 square arpents = 1 acre

Arpents and Acres

½ arpent	=	0.4231 acre	37.5 arpents	=	31.7355 acres
1 arpent	=	0.8463 acre	40 arpents	=	33.8512 acres
2 arpents	=	1.6926 acres	45 arpents	=	38.0826 acres
3 arpents	=	2.5388 acres	50 arpents	=	42.3140 acres
4 arpents	=	3.3851 acres	60 arpents	=	50.7768 acres
5 arpents	=	4.2314 acres	70 arpents	=	59.2396 acres
6 arpents	=	5.0777 acres	80 arpents	=	67.7024 acres
7 arpents	=	5.9240 acres	90 arpents	=	76.1652 acres
8 arpents	=	6.7702 acres	100 arpents	=	84.6280 acres
9 arpents	=	7.6165 acres	110 arpents	=	93.0908 acres
10 arpents	=	8.4628 acres	120 arpents	=	101.5536 acres
12.5 arpents	=	10.5785 acres	130 arpents	=	110.0164 acres
15 arpents	=	12.6942 acres	140 arpents	=	118.4792 acres
17.5 arpents	=	14.8099 acres	150 arpents	=	126.9420 acres
20 arpents	=	16.9256 acres	160 arpents	=	135.4048 acres
22.5 arpents	=	19.0413 acres	170 arpents	=	143.8676 acres
25 arpents	=	21.1570 acres	180 arpents	=	152.3304 acres
30 arpents	=	25.3884 acres	190 arpents	=	160.7932 acres
35 arpents	=	29.6198 acres	200 arpents	=	169.2560 acres

Source: Adapted from *The AAPL Guide for Landmen: From Lease to Release*, 55–56.

Appendix M
SI/Metric Units for Measuring Land

General Conversion Factors for U.S. Customary Units to SI Units

American Units	Multiply By	To Obtain SI Units
inches (in.)	25.4	millimetres (mm)
	2.54	centimetres (cm)
feet (ft)	0.3048	metres (m)
yards (yd)	0.9144	metres (m)
miles (mi)	1609.344	metres (m)
	1.61	kilometres (km)
square inches ($in.^2$)	6.45	square centimetres (cm^2)
square feet (ft^2)	0.0929	square metres (m^2)
square yards (yd^2)	0.8361	square metres (m^2)
square miles (mi^2)	2.59	square kilometres (km^2)
acres	0.40	hectares (ha)

U.S. Equivalents of More SI Units

Linear Measurement

10 millimetres	= 1 centimetre	=	0.397 in.	
10 centimetres	= 1 decimetre	=	3.937 in.	
10 decimetres	= 1 metre	=	39.37 in. or 3.28 ft	
10 metres	= 1 decametre	=	393.7 in.	
10 decametres	= 1 hectometre	=	328 ft, 1 in.	
10 hectometres	= 1 kilometre	=	0.62137 mi	
10 kilometres	= 1 myriametre	=	6.2137 mi	

Land Measurement

1 centiare	= $1\ m^2$	= $1,550\ in.^2$
1 are	= 100 centiares	= $119.6\ yd^2$
1 hectare	= 100 acres	= 2.471 acres
$1\ km^2$	= $1,000,000\ m^2$	= $0.3861\ mi^2$

NOTE: Where the International System of Units (SI) is consistently used, the basic unit for large-scale mapping and surveying is the *square kilometre*. Field measurement usually employs the *hectare*.

Figure Credits

All images are copyrighted and may not be reprinted, reproduced, or used in any way without the express written permission of the owner.

Figure		Owner	Web site
1.1	The first page of a form oil and gas lease for Texas from the American Association of Professional Landmen (AAPL)	Copyright © The American Association of Professional Landmen (AAPL). All rights reserved.	www.landman.org
1.2	East Texas saw the consequences of the rule of capture, unchecked by regulation. In that place, contractors established wells side by side in a race to drain the reservoirs, causing a crash in the price of oil and the destruction of the water drive—the natural mechanism of the reservoir that draws in water as oil is drawn out so that pressure is maintained.	The Briscoe Center, The University of Texas at Austin	www.texasbeyondhistory.net
1.3	The water lines of a fracturing operation, or "frac job"	Photo by Bret Boteler. Copyright © EnerMax, Inc. All rights reserved.	www.enermaxinc.com
1.4	In most of the oil-producing nations outside of the United States, rights to minerals are owned by the central government.	The University of Texas at Austin, PETEX	Left and center photos: www.photos.com Right photo: www.thinkstockphotos.com
2.1	In Alaska, land in private ownership outside of native lands makes up less than 1% of the total land. The rest is owned by the state, the federal government, or native peoples.	Copyright © World Resources Institute. All rights reserved.	www.wri.org
2.2	Management of federal lands by U.S. government agencies	Public Domain. Source: O'Connor Center for the Rocky Mountain West, 2002	www.crmw.org
2.3	The Bureau of Indian Affairs administers 56 million acres of land held in trust for Native Americans and Alaskan Natives. The map depicts the largest land units administered by the BIA—ones that are at least 23,000 acres in size.	Copyright © The National Atlas of the United States of America	nationalatlas.gov
2.4	Lands off the shore of the United States are owned by the government: from the shore to 3 or 9 nautical miles out by state government, from 3 or 9 nautical miles out to the 8,000-foot depth line by the federal government.	The University of Texas at Austin, PETEX	www.utexas.edu/ce/petex

Figure		Owner	Web site
3.1	It was once common for English surveying equipment to include a measuring chain. The actual length of the surveyor's chain was used as a measure of distance across land.	The University of Texas at Austin, PETEX	www.thinkstockphotos.com
3.2	Modern equipment used in conducting land surveys includes Global Positioning System (GPS) devices.	The University of Texas at Austin, PETEX	www.thinkstockphotos.com
3.3	This drawing demonstrates how the direction of each boundary line of a property is measured for a metes and bounds description. Comparing an individual property boundary to the lines with a similar bearing on the compass will allow an estimation of the measurement.	The University of Texas at Austin, PETEX	www.utexas.edu/ce/petex
3.4	This simple plat shows the bearings and distances of the property lines as they are typically identified by surveyors. It also shows the conventional abbreviation for place of beginning, POB. Note that the perimeter of the property closes at the place of beginning.	Undisclosed Private Source	www.iammea.org/ggingras
3.5	Small, oddly shaped surveys in a Texas county	Source: The American Association of Professional Landmen (AAPL)	Not available
3.6	A map showing principal meridians and base lines of U.S. public land surveys. States that are not shaded in color on the map are ones that have not historically been part of the Public Land Survey System; land descriptions in those states are often in metes and bounds.	Public Domain. Source: U.S. Geological Survey	www.usgs.gov
3.7	Township numbers are vertical, and range numbers are horizontal. A Congressional township is located at Township 4 North, Range 4 West (in the 4th tier north of the base line and the 4th column west of the meridian).	Source: The American Association of Professional Landmen (AAPL)	Not available
3.8	A plat of a sectioned Congressional township. A hypothetical tract lies in Section 5, and its legal description can be extended to read section 5 T4N R4E.	Source: The American Association of Professional Landmen (AAPL)	Not available
3.9	A subdivided section. An *X* marks the 20-acre tract that can be fully described as W ½ NW ¼ SE ¼ of section 5 T4N R4E, Tornado County, Kansas.	Source: The American Association of Professional Landmen (AAPL)	Not available
3.10	Blocks and lots form regular patterns in urban subdivisions. They are differentiated by numbers on plats.	The University of Texas at Austin, PETEX	www.thinkstockphotos.com

Figure		Owner	Web site
4.1	An abstract of title traces the history of ownership of a property.	The University of Texas at Austin, PETEX	www.utexas.edu/ce/petex
4.2	A landman searching for records at the county clerk's office	Photo by J. G. Domke	www.texpixpublishing.com
4.3	A landman should consider approaching the landowner for information about a land's legal history.	Copyright © Five State Land Services, Inc. All rights reserved.	www.fivestate.com
5.1	A Producers 88 lease form	Copyright © Pound Printing. All rights reserved.	www.poundprinting.com
5.2	A typical lease begins with a title that names the subject of the agreement and a statement of the effective date, the names of the parties, and the consideration promised. In this example, the consideration is stated in the granting clause. (Usually, the bonus stated in the lease is $10.00 rather than the actual bonus, which is kept confidential.)	Proprietor: The University of Texas at Austin, PETEX	www.utexas.edu/ce/petex
5.3	A granting clause, a land description, and a Mother Hubbard clause	Proprietor: The University of Texas at Austin, PETEX	www.utexas.edu/ce/petex
5.4	A habendum clause fixes the primary term of the lease.	Proprietor: The University of Texas at Austin, PETEX	www.utexas.edu/ce/petex
5.5	A royalty clause states the percentage of production to be received by the lessor.	Copyright © L. Rae Connet. All rights reserved.	Not available
5.6	A producing well being shut in with a workover rig	The University of Texas at Austin, PETEX	www.utexas.edu/ce/petex
5.7	A delay rental clause allows extension or termination of the lease if a well is not drilled during the primary term. The rental is paid on an annual basis, usually beginning on the effective date of the lease.	Proprietor: The University of Texas at Austin, PETEX	www.utexas.edu/ce/petex
5.8	A pooling and unitization clause allows the lessee to combine tracts with others in a pool or a unit for the purpose of drilling.	Copyright © L. Rae Connet. All rights reserved.	Not available
5.9	A damage clause addresses how the lessee will compensate the surface owner for such things as losses resulting from accidents. This photo shows the fire that followed an explosion at a drilling rig in Oklahoma.	Copyright © *Enid News & Eagle*. All rights reserved. Photo by Billy Hefton.	www.enidnews.com
5.10	An assignment clause allows the lessee to assign the lease rights to another party and specifies how notice of assignment should be given.	Copyright © L. Rae Connet. All rights reserved.	Not available

Figure		Owner	Web site
5.11	A force majeure clause keeps the lease in force even though delays specified in the lease prevent the lessee from meeting its obligations.	Proprietor: The University of Texas at Austin, PETEX	www.utexas.edu/ce/petex
6.1	An aerial photo of a ranch. A photo such as this one could be marked to indicate areas to be protected from operations.	Copyright © GeoSouthern Energy Corporation. All rights reserved.	Not available
6.2	There can be lease provisions that protect domestic animals or compensate the owner in the event that animals are harmed by operations carried out on the land.	The University of Texas at Austin, PETEX	www.thinkstockphotos.com
6.3	A recordation stamp	Public Domain. Source: Atascosa County Clerk	Not available
6.4	A sample ratification of an oil and gas lease. (The names that appear in the document are fictitious.)	Public Domain. Source: Adapted from a ratification of oil, gas and mineral lease from the Atascosa County Clerk	Not available
7.1	A sample form for a title opinion	Proprietor: The University of Texas at Austin, PETEX	www.utexas.edu/ce/petex
7.2	A runsheet mapping the ownership of mineral rights	Ted W. Walters & Associates, L.L.P.	www.twalters.com
7.3	A sample division order	Public Domain	Not available
8.1	The AAPL joint operating agreements for offshore operations are available through the Web site for the OCS Advisory Board (www.ocsadvisoryboard.org).	The University of Texas at Austin, PETEX	www.thinkstockphotos.com
9.1	The areas outlined in red on the map represent tracts that have been pooled to form drilling and spacing units.	Public Domain. Source: Texas General Land Office	www.glo.texas.gov
9.2	A form for a release of an oil and gas lease	Public Domain	Not available
D.1	A form for a memorandum (memo) of oil and gas lease	Public Domain	Not available

Glossary

A

AAPG *abbr*: American Association of Petroleum Geologists.

AAPL *abbr*: American Association of Professional Landmen.

abandon *v*: to cease producing oil and gas from a well when it becomes unprofitable. Any well may be abandoned after it has proven nonproductive. Several steps are involved in abandoning a well: Part of the casing might be removed and salvaged; one or more cement plugs are placed in the borehole to prevent migration of fluids between the different formations penetrated by the borehole; then, the well is abandoned. In most oil-producing states, it is necessary to secure permission from official agencies before a well may be abandoned.

absolute ownership *n*: theory that minerals such as oil and gas are fully owned in place before they are extracted and reduced to possession. Despite this theory, title to oil and gas might be lost by legitimate drainage and by the rule of capture. Also called ownership in place. Compare *rule of capture*, *nonabsolute ownership*.

abstract-based title opinion *n*: a title opinion based on a complete abstract of title plus other relevant documents. Compare *stand-up title opinion*.

abstract company *n*: a private company in the business of preparing abstracts of title and performing related services. Also called abstract plant.

abstract of title *n*: a collection of all of the recorded instruments affecting title to a tract of land. Compare *base abstract*.

abstract plant *n*: see *abstract company*.

acknowledgment *n*: the process by which a public officer such as a notary public confirms the identity of a person who signs a document and the authenticity of his or her signature on the document.

acquired (federal) lands *n*: land owned by the United States, acquired by deed or otherwise. Such land has never been in the public domain or has been in the public domain at one time and been disposed of, later being reacquired by purchase, condemnation, donation, or exchange.

acre *n*: a traditional unit for measuring the area of tracts of land in areas of the United States settled by the English. One square mile is approximately equal to 640 acres; an acre is approximately equal to 0.4 hectares.

acreage *n*: a number of acres; an area or amount of land.

acreage contribution *n*: acreage owned in the vicinity of a test well being drilled by another party and contributed to the driller of the well in return for information obtained from the operation. The assignment of land is usually made on completion of the well.

addendum *n*: an addition to a written document, as to a written agreement. It usually supplements the document (if there are omissions), clarifies ambiguous or confusing terms, or makes corrections. Addendum (sg); addendums or addenda (pl).

administrator *n*: a person appointed by the court to administer the estate of someone who dies intestate (without a valid will). Compare *executor*.

adverse possession *n*: a method of asserting title to property against other claimants, including the record owner. The claim through adverse possession must include certain acts (as required by statute) over an uninterrupted interval of time. To meet the requirements of most state statutes, the possession must be "open," "notorious," and "hostile." See *affidavit of adverse possession.*

AFE *abbr*: authorization for expenditure.

affiant *n*: a person who swears to an affidavit. See *affidavit.*

affidavit *n*: a written affirmation of fact made and sworn to before a notary public or other authorized official. See *affidavit of adverse possession; affidavit of death and heirship; affidavit of identity; affidavit of nonproduction; affidavit of use, occupancy, and possession; corroborating affidavit.*

affidavit of adverse possession *n*: an affidavit by which a person who occupies or uses a tract of land makes a claim to it against the owner of record. A person who occupies and uses land might be able to make a claim of adverse possession and prevail over the owner of record if he or she can meet the requirements of certain statutes, which vary by state.

affidavit of death and heirship *n*: an affidavit by which it can be established that an owner has died and another person is a legal heir to his or her property. This kind of affidavit serves a purpose when there have not been any probate proceedings to establish the same facts.

affidavit of identity *n*: an affidavit by which the identity of a person is established, especially if the person is known under more than one name.

affidavit of nonproduction *n*: an affidavit in which a lessor or the lessor's bank attests that there is no production at a property. If it is established that there is no production at a property and that the lessee is not paying delay rentals, there are grounds to terminate the lease and a new lease can be taken for the property.

affidavit of use, occupancy, and possession *n*: an affidavit attesting to a present owner's possession of property. It is useful in circumstances where there has been a gap in the chain of title (as when records have been destroyed), and the present owner wishes to find support for a claim to the property. Requirements for such an affidavit include signatures from disinterested witnesses and evidence that the present owner has been in continuous possession of the property for a certain period of time.

allotted land *n*: Indian land designated for use by a specific individual, although the title is still held by the United States and leasing is subject to the control of the Bureau of Land Management. Compare *tribal land.*

American Association of Petroleum Geologists (AAPG) *n*: an association of geologists, geophysicists, students, academics, and people in business. Its missions include encouraging professional conduct, fostering scientific research, and promoting the science of geology—particularly the area of geology concerned with the exploration and production of hydrocarbons. Web site address: www.aapg.org.

American Association of Professional Landmen (AAPL) *n*: an organization of over 17,000 landmen and other types of land professionals in the United States and Canada. Its missions include promoting standards of professionalism, advancing the stature of its members, and encouraging sound stewardship of energy and mineral resources. Web address: landman.org.

AMI *abbr*: area of mutual interest.

anniversary date *n*: the date, usually 1 year from the effective date of the lease, by which rentals must be paid to maintain the lease in effect in the absence of drilling or production.

APO *abbr*: after payout. Commonly used in land departments.

area of mutual interest (AMI) *n*: a geographic area where two or more parties (such as two oil and gas companies) have exploration rights. The term is used in contracts, where the location is described, along with the duration of the agreement and the rights of each party (namely, how the interests will be divided between the parties).

area of mutual interest (AMI) provision *n*: a contract provision concerning an area of mutual interest (AMI). The provision defines the location of the AMI, the rights of each party (namely, what percentage of the resources belong to each party), and the length of the agreement. It might also incentivize the parties to share information. See *area of mutual interest (AMI)*.

arm's length transaction *n*: a transaction that takes place, often between parties with shared or opposing interests, where the parties agree to act independently and without a special relationship with each other. These types of transactions are arranged so that neither party can influence the other unfairly, as in a case, for example, where one party might pressure the other to sell property at a lower price than its market value. Arm's length transactions are carried out to ensure that a transaction is legally valid and the purchase price is fair.

arpent *n*: a unit of measurement of length that has traditionally been used for surveying land in areas of the United States settled by French speakers. One arpent is approximately equal to 191.8 feet.

assign *v*: to transfer a right or title in property, usually by written agreement. See *assignee*.

assignee *n*: the party assigned rights and duties under a contract. See *assign*.

assignment *n*: a transfer of rights and interests in property or rights under a contract—for example, the transfer of an oil and gas lease from the original lessee to another party.

assignment clause *n*: a clause in any legal instrument that allows either party to the instrument to assign all or part of his or her interest to others.

attest *v*: to verify or witness; to authenticate by signing.

attorney-in-fact *n*: a person acting under a power of attorney agreement; a person designated to legally act as fiduciary, or agent, on behalf of the principal (the person for whom the power of attorney agreement is made).

authorization for expenditure (AFE) *n*: an estimate of costs prepared by a lease operator and sent to nonoperators for their approval before work is undertaken. An AFE is normally used in connection with well-drilling operations.

B

back-in *n*: an option right reserved by the granting company of a farmout to convert an overriding royalty to working interest once specified conditions have been met. Compare *election at casing point*.

bank draft *n*: a written order drawn up by a bank in the form of a check that authorizes payment by another bank to a named person from an account that the first bank has made a deposit in. This form of payment is seen as more secure than a personal check. Also called draft. See *five-day draft, sight draft*.

base abstract *n*: an abstract of title that contains full and complete copies of all recorded instruments from the sovereignty of the soil to the date the abstract is completed as set forth in the abstractor's certificate.

base line *n*: in the Public Land Survey System used in the United States, an imaginary line on an east-west orientation similar to a line of latitude. The term is often to refer to the principal base line, which is a base line intersecting the principal meridian and dividing the townships between the north and the south. Compare *meridian*.

bearing *n*: in metes and bounds property surveys, the direction of a survey line. The bearing of such survey lines is indicated by the cardinal points of the compass and is measured in degrees of a circle (360). For greater precision, minutes ($^1/_{60}$) and seconds ($^1/_{3600}$) can be added to the degree measurement.

bequeath *v*: to make a gift of personal property (as opposed to land) by means of a will. Compare *devise*.

BIA *abbr*: Bureau of Indian Affairs.

BLM *abbr*: Bureau of Land Management.

BOEM *abbr*: Bureau of Ocean Energy Management.

bonus (consideration) *n*: a cash payment by the lessee for the execution of an oil and gas lease by the mineral owner, usually expressed as dollars per acre. Occasionally, an oil payment or overriding royalty might be reserved as a bonus by a lessor in addition to regular royalty.

bottomhole contribution agreement *n*: a type of support agreement by which one company offers to make payments to another in exchange for drilling information if the drilling reaches a certain depth, the reason for the agreement being that the first company needs information from a certain depth for its own use. In the event that the second company is unable to drill to that depth, the first company will make no payment. If the second company judges that it is likely to drill to the specified depth, it might seek out the agreement to offset the cost of drilling. See *support agreement*.

bottomhole letter *n*: a letter contract providing for a contribution to the cost of drilling a well to a specified depth, regardless of whether the well is a producer or a dry hole.

BPO *abbr*: before payout. Commonly used in land departments.

Bureau of Indian Affairs (BIA) *n*: an agency within the U.S. Department of the Interior (DOI) that is responsible for managing land held in trust for American native peoples, including Native Americans and Alaskan Natives. It is charged with making improvements to the lands that provide economic opportunities to the native peoples while protecting the integrity of the lands and the culture of the owners. Web address: www.bia.gov.

Bureau of Land Management (BLM) *n*: an agency within the U.S. Department of the Interior (DOI) that is responsible for managing the nation's public lands and resources in ways that best serve the American people. The resources on public lands under the BLM include recreation; forestry; fish and wildlife; range; timber; minerals; watershed; wilderness; and natural, scientific, and cultural resources. Web address: www.blm.gov.

Bureau of Ocean Energy Management (BOEM) *n*: an agency within the U.S. Department of the Interior (DOI) that is responsible for managing the exploration and development of the nation's offshore resources. It administers oil and gas leases in the Outer Continental Shelf (OCS). It is charged with balancing economic development, energy independence, and environmental protection. Web address: www.boem.gov.

C

Canadian Association of Professional Landmen (CAPL) *n*: a Canadian association of land professionals. It promotes professional development among its members, provides information about the industry, and sells products useful to land professionals, including standard form leases. Web site address: www.landman/ca.

CAPL *abbr:* Canadian Association of Professional Landmen.

caption *n*: an indication, next to a signature in a document, of the capacity in which the party is signing. A caption might indicate, for example, that the signer is the guardian of the estate of a minor.

capture *n*: see *rule of capture*.

carried interest *n*: a fractional interest in oil and gas properties that belongs, for example, to a working interest owner or unleased landowner who agrees to a joint operation without being willing to pay a share of the costs of the operation. An interest might be carried until the well pays out, at which point it might stop or might continue for the life of production.

carved-out interest *n*: an interest in oil and gas created out of a greater interest and assigned by the owner. Examples are the grant of an overriding royalty interest out of a working interest and the grant of an oil payment out of a working interest.

case law *n*: see *common law*.

casing point *n*: 1. the depth in a well at which casing is set, generally the depth at which the casing shoe rests. 2. the objective depth in a drilling contract, either a specified depth or the depth at which a specific zone is penetrated. When the depth is reached, the operator makes a decision about running and setting a production string of casing.

certified copy *n*: a copy made from records in a recorder's or county clerk's office, certified by the recorder or county clerk as being the exact copy of the paper on file or of record.

cessation of production clause *n*: in an oil and gas lease, a clause that provides the lessee with the right to begin new operations within a stated time period should production cease.

C.F.R. *n*: *Code of Federal Regulations.*

chain *n*: a unit of measurement for length that has traditionally been used for surveying land in areas of the United States settled by the English. One chain is approximately equal to 66 feet or 20.1 metres.

chain of title *n*: the sequence of recorded transfers (links) in title from the original patent to the present time.

civil law *n*: a modern legal system derived historically from Roman law. Characteristically, written laws are the primary source of law in the system. Civil law is often seen in opposition to common law, where legal doctrines developed in cases are often the primary source of law. The legal system in Louisiana is strongly influenced by the Napoleonic Code, which means that it is largely based on civil law.

cloud (on title) *n*: a claim or encumbrance that, if upheld by a court, would impair the owner's title to the property.

***Code of Federal Regulations* (*C.F.R.*)** *n*: a collection of the rules and regulations of the executive departments and federal agencies of the Unites States. The rules and regulations are announced as they are passed in the *Federal Register*. Later, they are codified, or organized by subject for ease of use, in the *Code of Federal Regulations*. The *C.F.R.* is composed of 50 titles that represent diverse areas of federal regulations, including Energy, Mineral Resources, and Protection of Environment. The printed *Code* is updated once per year, with individual volumes updated on a rolling basis; an online edition is also available. Web address: www.ecfr.gov.

commercial quantities *n*: an amount of oil and gas production large enough to enable the operator to realize a profit, however small. To keep a lease in force, production must be in quantities sufficient to yield a return in excess of operating costs, even though drilling and equipment costs might never be recovered. Also called paying quantities.

common law *n*: a system of law based on court decisions, or judicial precedent, rather than on legislated statutes, executive decrees, or administrative regulations. Common law began in England and was later used in English colonies. It is still applied in the United States, although Louisiana law is largely based in civil law, which is Roman in origin and brought to the state by way of Spanish and French law. Also called case law.

community property *n*: property held jointly by husband and wife and acquired after marriage. Several states have community-property systems; common-law states, however, regard the property of each spouse acquired after marriage (subject to some conditions) as being separate and under the unique control of the individual. In states that do not have a community property system, married couples may elect to share property under a recognized scheme such as joint tenancy, tenancy by the entirety, or tenancy in common. See *joint tenancy (with a right of survivorship), tenancy by the entirety, tenancy in common.*

competitive leasing *n*: a procedure based on competitive bidding used to acquire oil and gas leases to federal lands within areas designated by the U.S. Geological Survey (USGS) as known geologic structures (KGS) or on offshore federal lands.

completed well *n*: a well on which drilling and completion operations have been finished. The well might be completed as a dry hole, a well capable of producing oil or gas, a disposal well for salt water, or another type of special-purpose well.

compulsory unitization *n*: unitization that proceeds without the willing cooperation of all the affected parties. The unitization is authorized by order of a state regulatory agency in accordance with state statutes. Also called statutory unitization.

Congressional township *n*: the square, 6 miles on each side, that is the major unit of land of the Public Land Survey System used in the United States.

consideration *n*: a promise or an act of legal value bargained for and received in return for a promise; an essential element of a contract. In oil and gas leases, consideration may be payment in money or in kind; it must often be "serious" (rather than nominal) consideration. Compare *bonus (consideration)*.

construction *n*: in contract law, the interpretation given by a court to a writing—for example, an interpretation of an ambiguous legal instrument or statute.

continuous drilling clause *n*: in an oil and gas lease, a clause designed to keep drilling operations going steadily after the primary term has expired. In some clauses, designated intervals between completion of one well and commencement of the drilling of another might require the operator to develop the leased land up to its allowable density. Also called continuous development clause, development clause.

contract *n*: an agreement between at least two parties that can be enforced by law and that names obligations for each party and the consideration offered in exchange. (See *consideration*.) A drilling contract covers the cost of drilling the well, the distribution of expenses between operator and contractor, the type of equipment to be used, and other factors.

contract area *n*: the lands and interests governed by a joint operating agreement (JOA); the leaseholds where development and operations are to take place under the agreement. Also called prospect area.

convey *v*: to transfer title to property from one party to another, usually by means of a written instrument such as a deed.

co-owners *n*: see *cotenants*.

COPAS *abbr*: Council of Petroleum Accountants Societies, Inc.

correlative rights *n pl*: the right of each owner of property in a pool to produce without waste his or her just and equitable share of the oil and gas.

corroborating affidavit *n*: an affidavit provided by a witness who attests to the veracity of a statement by another witness. In the case of an affidavit of use, occupancy, and possession, it is sometimes preferable to obtain separate corroborating affidavits from witnesses attesting to the affiant's claims, rather than having the witnesses sign the affidavit of use, occupancy, and possession itself. See *affidavit of use, occupancy, and possession*.

cotenants *n*: persons who hold possessory interest, from title or a lease, in the same piece of land. Those who hold interest from title are also called co-owners. Tenants in common and joint tenants are types of cotenants. See *tenancy in common, joint tenancy (with a right of survivorship)*.

Council of Petroleum Accountants Societies, Inc. (COPAS) *n*: an organization of the oil and gas industry's accounting professionals in the United States and Canada. It develops standard procedures for accounting in the industry with the aim of increasing the efficiency of oil and gas companies. Web site address: www.copas.org.

county clerk n: an elected county official with many duties, including keeping records to property titles. Records for a given piece of property, such as mineral deeds, leases, and liens, can be found at the county clerk's office.

coverall clause *n*: see *Mother Hubbard clause*.

cure (a title) *v*: to remedy defects and omissions that could make the present owner's claim to property questionable. To cure a title, a title examiner might require additional facts not evident in the material examined. The curative material is usually obtained in recordable form.

curtesy *n*: the right of a husband, in some states, to a life interest in all his wife's inheritable lands. The right comes into effect upon her death, provided that the couple has children capable of inheriting. Compare *dower*.

D

damage *n*: an injury or another type of loss to a person or property, including domestic animals. Compare *damages*.

damage clause *n*: in an oil and gas lease, the clause specifying that the lessee will be liable to the surface owner for damage to growing crops or other specified items.

damages *n*: 1. compensation in the form of money claimed by a person who has suffered a loss or injury. 2. such compensation ordered by a court in response to a claim. Compare *damage*. See *liquidated damages*.

deed *n*: a legal document that conveys title to real property. Compare *deed of trust*.

deed of trust *n*: an instrument used to transfer legal title to real property as security for the repayment of a loan or the fulfillment of some other obligation; a type of three-party mortgage commonly used in many states, including Alaska, California, Colorado, Oklahoma, and Texas. See *real property*. Compare *mortgage, trust, deed*.

delay rental *n*: money payable to the lessor by the lessee for the privilege of deferring the commencement of drilling operations to keep the lease in force. Such a payment may be made monthly, quarterly, or annually.

delay rental clause *n*: see *drilling and delay rental clause*.

density *n*: see *well density*.

Department of the Interior (DOI) *n*: a department of the U.S. federal government set up to provide a framework for a complete and balanced national energy plan through coordination and administration. It is responsible for long-term, high-risk research and development of energy technology, the marketing of federal power, energy conservation, the nuclear weapons program, energy regulatory programs, and a central energy data collection and analysis program. The Bureaus of Indian Affairs, Land Management, and Ocean Energy Management are under the Department of the Interior, and it is charged with the administration and leasing of public lands, including lands held in trust for Native Americans. Web address: www.doi.gov.

depletion allowance *n*: a reduction in U.S. taxes for owners of an economic interest in minerals to compensate for the lower value of the property as the mineral(s) are exhausted.

depth limitation *n*: in an oil and gas lease, a provision limiting drilling to a certain depth from the surface.

de-risk *v*: in business, to reduce the risk of an investment. In the oil and gas industry, many strategies are employed to de-risk investments, such as support agreements, where one company offers support in drilling a well in the form of payment in exchange for information obtained from the drilling conducted by another company.

descent and distribution laws *n*: the laws in a state that determine the disposition of real and personal property to heirs in the absence of a will. Also called law of descent and distribution, laws of intestacy, intestate succession statutes.

description *n*: an exact description of real property with details that allow the identification of the property in legal documents such as deeds, mortgages, and mineral leases. It locates the property geographically and names boundaries and any other features that are of legal interest, such as easements. See *real property*.

determinable fee *n*: an interest in property that will end at the happening or nonhappening of a particular event. In some states, an oil and gas lease is considered to create a determinable fee in real estate.

determination of ownership (judicial) *n*: see *transfer of ownership (judicial)*.

development clause *n*: see *continuous drilling clause*.

development well *n*: a well drilled in proven territory to complete a pattern of production.

devise *v*: to make a gift of real property—for example, land—by means of a will. See *real property*. Compare *bequeath*.

disclaimer *n*: a renunciation of a legal right or claim. One type of disclaimer is a renunciation of any claim of title to property. Surface tenants, for example, often sign disclaimers (in the form of tenant consent agreements) relating to the mineral estate and title of land leased for oil and gas exploration.

divided interest *n*: a fractional interest in property. In the case of minerals, when the interest is conveyed, the new owner has a 100% interest in the designated fraction of the described tract. For example, a divided interest in an 80-acre tract results in a 100% interest in 20 specific, describable acres out of that tract; the owner does not have a ¼ interest in all 80 acres with the other owners. Compare *undivided interest.*

division order *n*: a document directing the purchaser of oil or gas to pay the interest owners according to the proportions set out in the instrument. The purchase might require execution by all owners of interest in the property.

division order opinion *n*: a statement of opinion by a title examiner on the state of a title to land, or to mineral, royalty, or working interest in a producing tract of land. This opinion, usually in letter form, forms the basis of payment to all affected owners and must recite all of the owner's interest. Compare *title opinion, drill site opinion.*

DOI *abbr*: Department of the Interior.

dower *n*: the right of a wife, in some states, upon the death of her husband to a life interest in his inheritable lands. Compare *curtesy.*

draft *n*: see *bank draft.*

drilling and delay rental clause *n*: in an oil and gas lease, the clause that allows the lease to expire after a given period of time (often 1 year from the date of the lease) unless drilling begins or delay rentals are paid. Also called delay rental clause and "unless" clause.

drilling and spacing unit (DSU) *n*: a unit of the size required or permitted by statutory law or by regulations of a state conservation body for drilling an oil or gas well. Also called proration unit.

drilling block *n*: a lease or a number of leases on adjoining tracts of land that constitute a unit of acreage sufficient to justify the expense of drilling an exploration well.

drill site opinion *n*: the written statement of opinion by a title examiner on the status of the title to a drill site, usually in letter form. Compare *title opinion, division order opinion.*

dry hole *n*: any well that does not produce oil or gas in commercial quantities. A dry hole might flow water, gas, or even oil, but not in amounts large enough to justify production.

dry-hole clause *n*: in an oil and gas lease, a clause that allows the operator to keep the lease if a dry hole is drilled (in other words, if the wellbore does not produce oil in commercial quantities). The operator has a specified period of time in which to drill a subsequent well or begin paying delay rentals.

dry-hole contribution agreement *n*: a type of support agreement by which one company offers to make payments to another in exchange for drilling information in the event that the well drilled is a dry hole. If the well is productive, however, the first company makes no payments and still receives the drilling information. The second company seeks out the agreement as a way to offset its costs for the event that the hole is dry. See *support agreement.*

dry-hole letter *n*: a form of support agreement in which the contributing company agrees to pay so much per foot drilled by another company in return for information gained from the drilling. The contribution is paid only if the well is a dry hole in all the formations encountered.

DSU *abbr*: drilling and spacing unit.

E

easement *n*: a limited right to use another's land for a specific purpose—to access an adjacent property that is landlocked or to install utility lines, for example.

election at casing point *n*: an elective decision to participate or not in the completion attempt on a well. The completion includes the cost of running completion production casing and other costs. The decision is made when the operator is ready to run casing and complete the well.

encumbrance *n*: a claim or a charge attached to a property—for example, a mortgage or a lien for unpaid taxes.

Energy Resources Conservation Board (ERCB) *n*: a tribunal that regulates the energy resources of the Canadian province of Alberta. It regulates the development and transportation of energy resources with the aim of promoting the economy while protecting human health and the environment and conserving the resources of the province. Web site address: www.ercb.ca.

entailed *adj*: for the purpose of inheritance, limited to specified heirs, such as lineal (direct) descendants. The practice of entailing property has been abolished in most states of the United States.

entirety *n*: see *tenancy by the entirety*.

Environmental Protection Agency (EPA) *n*: the major agency of the United States federal government charged with protecting human health and the environment by enforcing federal statutes. Its headquarters are in Washington, D.C., but it has regional offices. Web address: www.epa.gov.

EPA *n*: Environmental Protection Agency.

ERCB *abbr*: Energy Resources Conservation Board.

escheat *n*: a reversion of property to the state when a person with no heirs dies intestate.

estate *n*: the nature and extent of a person's ownership, right, or interest in land or other property.

estoppel *n*: a bar to asserting a claim contrary to one that has been legally established as true. Generally, the party prevented from making the claim has established the truth of the matter by its own previous representations.

et al. *abbr*: and others (Lat. *et alii*). Commonly used in oil and gas leases.

et ux. *abbr*: and wife (Lat. *et uxor*). Commonly used in oil and gas leases.

et vir *abbr*: and husband (Lat. *et vir*). Commonly used in oil and gas leases.

examination of title *n*: a thorough inspection of the recorded documents pertaining to a tract's history of ownership. Title examinations are performed by attorneys who look for gaps, ambiguities, or any doubtful points in the chain of title that would cast a cloud on the present owner's claim to the property. The examiner will then set forth in a written opinion the facts and instruments that, in his or her judgment, are necessary to make the title marketable or legally defensible.

execute *v*: to complete a legal instrument by the required actions—for example, by signing and delivering the instrument. The term might describe only signing a document, or it might describe a process that includes signing and delivering a document to the named grantee, lessee, or assignee.

executive rights *n*: in regard to mineral rights and interests, the right to execute oil and gas leases. Executive rights might not include the right to bonus or rentals.

executor *n*: the person named in a will to carry out its provisions.

exhibit *n*: see *rider*.

exploration well *n*: a well drilled either in search of a new, as yet undiscovered, pool of oil or gas or to greatly extend the limits of a known pool. It involves a relatively high degree of risk. Exploratory wells might be classified as

(1) wildcat, drilled in an unproved area; (2) field extension, or step-out, drilled in an unproven area to extend the proven limits of a field; or (3) deep test, drilled within a field area but to unproven deeper zones.

F

farmee *n*: the legal party that has a lease farmed out to it. By a farmout agreement, a farmee acquires the right to drill in order to receive an interest in the lease.

farm-in *n*: an agreement identical to a farmout, with the operator as the third party (farmee). See *farmout agreement*.

farm in *v*: to accept, as an operator, a farmout. See *farmout agreement*.

farmor *n*: the individual or company that farms out a lease.Under a farmout agreement, the farmor does not pay to drill, as that is the obligation of the farmee.

farmout agreement *n*: an agreement by which the owner of a lease (farmor) assigns the leasehold interest or some part of it to a third party (farmee) who agrees to drill a well within the expiration date of the primary term of the lease. A farmout is distinguished from a joint operating agreement (JOA) by the fact that the party farming out does not incur any of the drilling costs. The primary characteristic of a farmout is the obligation of the third party to drill one or more wells on the farmout acreage in order to receive an interest in the lease.

farm out *v*: for a lessee, to agree to assign a leasehold interest to a third party (farmee), subject to stipulated conditions. See *farmout agreement*.

federal lease *n*: an oil and gas lease on federal land issued under the Mineral Leasing Act. Federal leases usually provide step-scale or sliding-scale royalty; a flat discovery royalty of ⅛ might also be specified.

fee *n*: see *fee simple absolute*.

fee holder *n*: one who holds an estate in land in fee simple. See *fee simple*.

fee in surface *n*: an estate in the surface of land, created when the owner separates or severs his or her mineral interests from the surface of the land. See *sever*.

fee simple *n*: an estate in land on which there are no restrictions or limitations as to the heirs who may inherit.

fee simple absolute *n*: an estate in land of absolute ownership, whose owner has the unqualified rights to dispose of it (as by will) and to profit from its resources. It might, however, be subject to eminent domain, taxation, police power, and escheat. Also called fee.

fee tail *n*: an estate in land to which there is a fixed line of inheritable succession limited to the issue of the body of the grantee or devisee and to which the regular and general succession of heirs at law is cut off.

fee tail female *n*: an estate in land limited by a deed or will that conveys ownership to a person and his or her female heirs only. Male heirs are not capable of inheriting the estate.

fee tail male *n*: an estate in land limited by a deed or will that conveys ownership to a person and his or her male heirs only. Female heirs are not capable of inheriting the estate.

fiduciary *n*: a person who serves to act for the benefit of another in all matters connected with a specified undertaking. Because of the nature of the relationship with a fiduciary, he or she is bound by the duties of good faith and candor, and must promote the interests of the person who is to benefit from the relationship rather than his or her own. Fiduciary obligations exist, for example, between a trustee and the beneficiaries of the trust.

fief *n*: a feudal estate; in Medieval England, an estate in land offered by the Crown to a tenant and to be held, for a time, in exchange for goods or services. Also called fee.

file for record *v*: to send an instrument to the county clerk for recording.

five-day draft *n*: a draft or order for payment that must be picked up within five days after it arrives at the drawer's bank. For example, if a lessee pays a lessor a cash bonus by means of a sight draft, the lessee must pick up that draft within five days after it arrives at his or her bank from the lessor's bank.

foot/feet (ft) *n*: a unit of measurement of length that has traditionally been used in surveying land in areas of the United States settled by the English. One foot is approximately equal to 0.3 metres.

forced pooling *n*: pooling of leased tracts undertaken without the willing cooperation of all the parties. Forced pooling might occur as the result of an order from a state regulatory agency, initiated by a petition of one or more of the parties affected. Also called statutory pooling, involuntary pooling.

force majeure clause *n*: in a contract, the clause that excuses the lessee from timely performance of his or her obligations should certain events beyond the lessee's power to control occur. It usually also contains a statement that the contract is subject to state and federal laws. More generally, force majeure means a force or event that cannot be anticipated or controlled.

foreign grant *n*: a conveyance of land by a sovereign state to a company or an individual. Lands of territories that became states of the United States were originally owned by Spain, Mexico, France, England, Russia, the Kingdom of Hawaii, and various native peoples. Those sovereign powers made grants of land over time. Some pieces of property, to have a complete chain of title, must have records to the original foreign grant. Compare *patent*.

four-corner rule *n*: a legal rule holding that an instrument such as an oil and gas lease must be interpreted by what appears on the face of document—that is, what is contained in the document's four corners. Interpretation is made without any knowledge of the circumstances under which the instrument came into being provided by outside evidence (such as testimony of witnesses). In addition, the instrument is construed as a whole, without reference to any one part more than another.

frac *adj*: related to fracturing. See *fracturing*.

fracing *n*: see *fracturing*.

fracturing *n*: the practice, in the oil and gas industry, of inducing a mixture of fluids and particulate solids into a rock layer under pressure in order to cause fractures in the rock. After cracks form, solids in the fracturing fluids prop the cracks open so that hydrocarbons can flow more easily to the surface. Also called hydraulic fracturing.

Freestone rider *n*: see *Pugh clause*.

G

General Land Office *n*: see *Texas General Land Office*.

general warranty clause *n*: a warrant of title from the grantor for all claims. Compare *special warranty clause*.

GLO *abbr*: Texas General Land Office.

good title *n*: see *marketable title*.

grantee *n*: one to whom property is conveyed. Compare *grantor*.

granting clause *n*: a clause in an oil and gas lease that specifies the rights and interests granted by the lessor to the lessee. Such rights usually involve searching, drilling for, and producing oil and gas.

grantor *n*: one who conveys property. Compare *grantee*.

guardian *n*: a person appointed by a court for the purpose of managing property and rights for another person who is considered incapable of doing so—for example, a minor child, an insane person, or a mental incompetent.

H

habendum clause *n*: in an oil and gas lease, the clause that fixes the duration of the lessee's interest in the primary term and typically extends the interest into the secondary term on the condition that production is taking place on the property. Also called term clause.

HBP *abbr*: held by production. Commonly used in land departments.

hectare (ha) *n*: a metric unit of measurement of area approximately equal to 2.5 acres.

hereditaments *n*: any property that can be inherited—real or personal.

homestead property *n*: property such as land, a house, outbuildings, and tools owned and used by a family that cannot be seized to pay general debts.

"hot oil" *n*: (from the era when prorationing was new to the petroleum industry) oil in excess of limits set on production by individual states; oil above quotas illegally tapped and transported.

I

implied covenant *n*: an obligation or benefit not specified in an agreement but held by the courts to be implied in it. For example, one implied covenant in an oil and gas lease is an obligation on the part of the lessee to drill an initial well.

incompetent *n*: a person judged by the court to be incapable of managing his or her own affairs by reason of insanity, low IQ, deteriorating mental condition caused by disease, or another reason. Also called non compos mentis (not of sound mind).

independent *n*: a nonintegrated oil company or an individual whose operations are in the field of petroleum production, excluding transportation, refining, and marketing.

initial well *n*: a well that is required to be drilled under a contract such as an operating agreement or a farmout agreement.

interest (in land) *n*: a legal share of real property; a right or a claim to real property. The term refers to the extent of ownership of property in terms of what percentage is owned, over what time period, and with what rights (to transfer, to sell, to encumber, etc.). It is often used to speak about forms of ownership other than the fee, such as tenancies or community property, where owners share property. See *real property*, *tenancy by the entirety*, *tenancy in common*, *community property*.

International System (SI) of Units *n*: a decimalized system of units of measurement devised around base units that include the metre and the kilogram. It is derived from the metric system.

intestate *adj*: without leaving a valid will. When a person dies intestate, the state distributes his or her property according to statute. See *descent and distribution laws*.

involuntary pooling *n*: see *forced pooling*.

J

JOA *abbr*: joint operating agreement.

joint operating agreement (JOA) *n*: a contract by which two or more co-owners of the operating rights in a tract of land join together to share the costs of exploration and possible development.

joint tenancy (with a right of survivorship) *n*: a type of special property ownership by two or more persons whose joint title is created by the same deed or will. Each of the tenants owns an undivided interest in the property. Upon the death of a joint tenant, the survivors receive the deceased joint tenant's remainder. See *right of survivorship*. Compare *tenancy in common, tenancy by the entirety, community property.*

joint venture *n*: a business undertaking, usually of more limited scope and length than a partnership, in which control, profits, losses, and liability are all shared.

L

landman *n*: a professional in the petroleum industry who negotiates with landowners for oil and gas leases, options, minerals, and royalties and with producers for joint production operations. The term is gender-neutral and is used to refer to a woman in the profession, as well.

landowner *n*: one who owns land.

lease *n*: 1. a legal agreement between a landowner, as lessor, and a company or individual, as lessee, that grants the right to occupy or use the property in exchange for some kind of consideration such as rent. (See *consideration*.) In the case of an oil and gas lease, an agreement is formed between a mineral owner (lessor) and a company, an individual, or individuals who wish to produce minerals on the land (lessee). It allows the lessee to exploit the premises for minerals or other products in exchange for royalty payments and a bonus. (See *oil and gas lease*.) 2. the area where production equipment is located on property that is subject to an oil and gas lease.

lease bonus *n*: see *bonus* (*consideration*).

lease broker *n*: an independent landman who might work with several operators or companies.

leasehold *n*: the estate in real property created by a lease. A leasehold is held by a lessee, usually for a fixed period of time. See *real property*.

leasehold interest *n*: all or a fractional part of the interest of a lessee (grantee) under an oil and gas lease. Such interest includes the right on the part of the lessee to search for, drill, and produce oil and gas from a lease tract subject to royalty payments. Also called working interest, operating interest.

lease purchase agreement *n*: in mineral leasing, an agreement between companies for the purchase by one company of a block of the other's leases. Lease brokers and companies also make lease purchase agreements.

legal description *n*: see *description*.

legal effect clause *n*: in an oil and gas lease, the clause that binds the parties and declares the lease effective for the lessor when he or she signs the instrument.

legal person *n*: an entity recognized by the law as having some of the rights, duties, and liabilities that a natural person, or human being, has. Companies, corporations, and cooperatives are considered to be legal persons.

lessee *n*: the recipient of a lease (such as an oil and gas lease), who holds the property and can use it.

lesser interest clause *n*: in an oil and gas lease, a provision allowing a lessee to reduce rents and royalties proportionately if, after an examination of title, it is discovered that the lessor does not own all the minerals of the estate. Also called proportionate reduction clause.

lessor *n*: the conveyor of a lease (such as an oil and gas lease), who allows the lessee to hold the property and use it.

letter agreement *n*: a legally binding agreement in the form of a letter. It is a type of contract, and might consist of an exchange of letters between parties.

liability *n*: a debt or obligation.

life tenant *n*: someone who holds the exclusive right to possess and use property during his or her lifetime but who cannot devise or bequeath the property. Compare *remainderman*.

line n: see *base line*.

link *n*: a unit of measurement for length that has traditionally been used for surveying land in areas of the United States settled by the English. One link is approximately equal to 0.66 feet or 0.2 metres.

liquidated damages *n*: monetary compensation (damages) awarded by a court or agreed-upon in advance, as in a contract, in the event that a party breeches a contract, a person is injured, or property is damaged.

lis pendens *n*: notice that a suit has been filed in a court of law and that the property owned by the defendant may be liable to judgment.

location *n*: the well site.

location damages *n pl*: compensation paid to the surface owner for actual and potential damage to the surface and crops in the drilling and operation of a well.

log *n*: see *well log*.

M

marketable title *n*: a title apparently free from defects, which can be sold or successfully defended in court. See *encumbrance*.

"market value at the mouth of the well" *n*: a determination of the price of gas based on the price the market will bear prior to any cost reduction for treating or transporting the gas. Mineral owners might ask for royalty payments based on "market value at the mouth of the well" as a way of ensuring that the payments are on par with those received by lessees. Also called wellhead price.

memorandum (memo) of oil and gas lease *n*: a form that takes the place of an oil and gas lease in the public records and provides only the elements required to put the public on notice. Those elements include the names of the parties and the description of the land. Memos are designed to allow the parties to keep confidential terms of the lease such as the bonus and royalty.

meridian *n*: in the Public Land Survey System used in the United States, an imaginary line on a north-south orientation similar to a line of longitude. The principal meridian is the line dividing the ranges between east and west that intersects the base line. Compare *principal meridian, base line*.

metes and bounds *n pl*: a method of delineating the boundaries of a piece of land by measuring from a well-marked reference point and following the boundaries of the land all the way around to the beginning point again. The description relies heavily on reference to natural objects (such as roads and streams) or to artificial ones (such as markers placed by the surveyor).

The method situates and measures the land for surveys, which can be used in deeds and other transfers.

metre *n*: the basic unit of length of the International System (SI) of Units and the metric system. One metre is approximately 3.28 feet.

metric system *n*: a decimalized system of units of measurement devised around base units that include the metre and the kilogram. The system most currently used internationally, the International System (SI) of Units, is derived from the metric system.

mile(s) (mi) *n*: a unit of measurement for length, depth, and height that has traditionally been used for surveying land in areas of the United States settled by the English. One mile is equivalent to 1.6 kilometers.

mineral *n*: broadly, a naturally occurring homogeneous substance that is obtained from the ground for human use such as, stone, coal, salt, sulfur, sand, petroleum, water, and natural gas.

mineral acre *n*: the full mineral interest and rights in 1 acre (0.4 hectares) of land.

mineral-classified *adj*: in Texas, a class of land whose owner shares mineral rights with the state. At the time tracts of land were patented to individuals, the land commissioner designated some as mineral-classified, meaning that the state owned the rights to all minerals. (See *patent*.) Today, the owner of such a tract is considered an agent of the state and shares the proceeds from production on the land with the state.

mineral deed *n*: the legal instrument that conveys minerals in the land along with the rights to search for and produce them.

mineral estate *n*: rights and interest in the minerals found on or beneath the surface of land, created when the owner severs his or her interest in the property. See *sever*.

minerally classified *adj*: see *mineral-classified*.

mineral owner *n*: where interests in land have been severed, the owner of the rights and interests in a mineral estate. Compare *surface owner*.

minimum royalty *n*: a royalty payment amount to be made regardless of the rate of production. The excess of such payments over regular royalty is chargeable against future production, if any, accruing to the royalty interest.

mining partnership *n*: a form of joint venture very similar to an oil and gas joint operating agreement (JOA). Profits, losses, operations, and ownership are all shared, and the partners are jointly as well as severally (separately) liable.

mortgage *n*: 1. a conveyance of title to property as security for the repayment of a debt (such as a loan) or the performance of an obligation. 2. A legal document such as a contract specifying the terms of a mortgage. Compare *deed of trust*.

Mother Hubbard clause *n*: a clause in an oil and gas lease that includes in the leasehold lands that might be owned by the lessor and inadvertently omitted from the legal description. These lands are usually oddly shaped bits adjoining the described tract. Also called coverall clause.

N

NARO *abbr*: National Association of Royalty Owners.

National Association of Royalty Owners (NARO) *n*: a nonprofit trade association whose members include mineral and royalty owners, specialized professionals, and corporations. It provides services to oil and gas royalty owners. Its goals are to promote exploration and production of minerals in the United States while protecting the interests of mineral owners through education and advocacy at the state and federal levels of government. Web address: www.naro-us.org.

net revenue interest *n*: the portion of oil and gas production money out of which operating and development costs are paid; the portion remaining after deduction of royalty interests.

net working interest *n*: the share of production remaining to the working interest owners after all royalties, overriding royalties, production payments, and other reservations or assignments have been deducted.

nonabsolute ownership *n*: in oil and gas law, the view that minerals cannot be owned in place. In some states, such as Louisiana, the landowner owns the surface of the land along with the rights to explore, drill, and reduce subsurface minerals to possession. Also called nonownership, nonownership in place. See *rule of capture*. Compare *absolute ownership*.

non-consent/consent *n*: a provision in a joint operating agreement (JOA) that allows parties who consent to later operations to penalize parties who do not consent. The penalty can be arranged in various ways but, to be effective, it must assume the productiveness of the proposed operation. The parties who do not consent are said to go non-consent.

nonexecutive royalty owner *n*: one who owns a severed portion of a royalty interest but does not execute leases, participate in bonuses or rentals, or have rights of exploration and production. Such owners are said to have nonexecutive rights. Also called nonparticipating royalty owner.

nonownership *n*: see *nonabsolute ownership*.

nonownership in place *n*: see *nonabsolute ownership*.

nonparticipating royalty owner *n*: see *nonexecutive royalty owner*.

notary (public) *n*: a public officer authorized to perform certain legal functions such as taking affidavits and witnessing and authenticating the execution of agreements. The purpose of the notary is to prevent fraud. Notaries are commissioned for a term in a particular state.

O

OCC *abbr*: Oklahoma Corporation Commission.

OCS *abbr*: Outer Continental Shelf.

offset drilling rule *n*: a rule applied by the courts—especially in states that have adopted nonabsolute ownership views of oil and gas—stating that a landowner whose property is being drained of migratory resources by wells on neighboring tracts can defend those assets by drilling wells of his or her own and producing as quickly as possible. Compare *rule of capture*.

offset well *n*: a well drilled on an adjacent tract of land on which there is a producing well. See *offset drilling rule*.

oil and gas lease *n*: 1. an agreement between a mineral owner (lessor) and a company, an individual, or individuals (lessee). It allows the lessee to exploit the premises for minerals or other products in exchange for royalty payments and a bonus. Compare *lease*. 2. the area where production equipment is located on property that is subject to an oil and gas lease.

oil payment *n*: a nonoperating interest in oil and gas from one or more leases, providing to its owner a fractional share of the oil and gas produced, free of the costs of production, and terminating when a specified dollar amount or volume of production has been realized. Oil payments might be created and reserved when a lease or royalty interest is assigned, or might be carved out of a leasehold or royalty interest and assigned to another party.

Oklahoma Corporation Commission (OCC) *n*: an agency of the state of Oklahoma that regulates public utilities, transportation by rail and pipeline, the safety of petroleum storage tank systems, and oil and gas drilling. Web address: www.occ.state.ok.us.

operating agreement *n*: see *joint operating agreement (JOA)*.

Outer Continental Shelf (OCS) *n*: the submerged land between areas subject to state mineral ownership and a depth of roughly 8,000 feet, beyond which mineral exploration and development are not, at present, feasible. Boundaries of the Outer Continental Shelf are set by law: For example, the state of Louisiana owns 3 miles seaward from the shoreline, while Texas owns land 9 miles from the shoreline. Generally, the name is used to describe federally controlled areas.

overconvey *v*: to convey (intentionally or by mistake) a larger fraction of interest in real property than the owner actually has a right to convey. See *real property*.

overriding royalty *n*: an interest carved out of the lessee's working interest, entitling its owner to a fraction of production free of any production or operating expense, but not free of production or severance tax levied on production. An overriding royalty can be created by grant or by reservation. Commonly, an override is reserved by the assignor in an assignment such as a farmout agreement. An override's duration corresponds to that of the lease from which it was created.

ownership in place *n*: see *absolute ownership*.

P

paid-up lease *n*: an oil and gas lease that, when first acquired, is paid up through the primary term. All delay rentals are paid along with the cash bonus, and no further action is required during the primary term.

parol evidence *n*: evidence given verbally rather than in writing.

patent *n*: in the case of land, an instrument by which a government conveys an estate of land to a company or individual. A patent results when a foreign land grant is documented and officially published by a sovereign. Compare *foreign grant*.

paying quantities *n*: see *commercial quantities*.

payment in kind *n*: payment in goods, services, or a combination of those things, instead of money.

payout *n*: 1. the point at which the operator of a well has recovered the costs of exploring, drilling, completing, and operating a well and can begin to show a profit. 2. the time required to show a profit.

personal property *n*: all property except that which is considered to be real property; moveable property such as vehicles, furniture, and other personal effects. Compare *real property*.

place of beginning (POB) *n*: The point at which a metes and bounds property survey begins. The perimeter of the property is then traced back to the place of beginning using measurements of direction in degrees and of distance. Also called point of beginning.

plat *n*: a map of a particular tract, group of tracts, or area of land that shows its defining features, such as boundaries and roads.

PLSS *abbr*: Public Land Survey System.

POB *abbr*: place of beginning.

point of beginning *n*: see *place of beginning (POB)*.

pooling *n*: the combining of small or irregular tracts into a unit large enough to meet state spacing and prorationing regulations for drilling. See *forced pooling, statutory pooling, voluntary pooling*. Compare *unitization*.

pooling agreement *n*: in the oil and gas industry, an agreement, usually initiated by a lessee and requiring the signatures of affected owners, to pool two or more tracts of land when a lease does not grant the lessee the authority to form pooled units.

pooling and unitization clause *n*: in an oil and gas lease, the clause that permits the lessee to form units by pooling or unitization.

potential *n*: the maximum volume of oil or gas that a well is capable of producing, calculated from well test data.

power of attorney *n*: a legal instrument that authorizes one person to act for another, with broad legal authority or a limited authority to make decisions only on certain matters. It ends upon the death of either of the parties.

preferential right of purchase *n*: a prior right of purchase reserved to buy an oil and gas interest by meeting the terms of a proposed sale of the interest to any other party.

primary term *n*: the specified duration of an oil and gas lease—for example, 3 years. The lease specifies conditions that will cause the lease to continue into the secondary term, such as production in paying quantities. Compare *secondary term*.

principal meridian *n*: in the Public Land Survey System used in the United States, the imaginary line on a north-south orientation dividing the ranges between east and west and intersecting the base line. It is one of many meridians in the survey system. Compare *meridian, base line*.

producer's form *n*: see *standard form*.

Producers 88 *n*: see *standard form*.

production payment *n*: a cost-free percentage of the working interest that ends when a specified amount of money or number of barrels has been reached.

proportionate reduction clause *n*: see *lesser interest clause*.

prorationing *n*: a system, enforced by a government agency or by agreement between operators, that limits the amount of petroleum that can be produced from a well or a field within a given period of time.

proration unit *n*: see *drilling and spacing unit (DSU)*.

prospect *n*: a lease or other right in a particular geographical area believed to have production pontential. Additional geological and geophysical work might be required before a test well is drilled there.

prospect area *n*: see *contract area*.

provision *n*: a clause of a legal instrument or a law addressing a particular matter; a stipulation.

public domain land *n*: generally, lands owned by the U.S. government. Also called federal lands.

Public Land Survey System (PLSS) *n*: the current name for the method of measuring land adopted by the United States in 1785. Under this system, the land is measured in squares called Congressional townships, which are approximately 6 miles wide and 6 miles long. The squares are located at the intersections of columns called "ranges" and tiers called "townships." Also called rectangular survey system.

Pugh clause *n*: in an oil and gas lease, a clause that releases nonproducing acreage (horizontal release) or zones (vertical release) at the end of the primary term or some other specified period. Under such a clause, nonproductive or untested zones and acreage that are outside a producing pooled unit must be released if drilling or exploration does not occur by the end of the specified time. Also called Freestone rider.

Q

quitclaim deed *n*: a deed that conveys any rights or interests that a person might have in property without warranting title. It merely transfers whatever title there might be without representing that the title is valid.

R

Railroad Commission of Texas *n*: see *Texas Railroad Commission* (*TRC* or *RRC*).

range *n*: in the Public Land Survey System used in the United States, the name given to the columns of land running north and south. Congressional townships are placed in ranges at 6-mile intervals. Compare *township*.

ratification *n*: approval and confirmation of a contract or other legal instrument, usually by means of a second written instrument. Ratification is useful when a previous act was not legally binding, as when a third party without authority to act as agent executed a contract.

ratify *v*: in contract law, to review and approve a previous agreement. It may consist of confirming a contract that has already been executed but that is, because of a defect, not legally binding. In other cases, an individual may confirm an agreement undertaken on behalf of a group. The purpose of ratification is to make an agreement legally binding.

real property *n*: 1. land, including resources buried beneath the surface of land, and any property affixed to land, such as buildings. 2. rights and interests attached to real property. The rights attached to property include those to transfer it, to lease it to other parties, to use its resources to make a profit, and to encumber it (with loans). The term "interests" is used to described the extent of rights in real property—for example, whether two people sharing ownership of the same property have the right to inherit each other's interest upon death. See *interest* (*in land*).

reassignment obligation *n*: a part of a farmout agreement or other assignment that stipulates an obligation to reassign earned acreage back to the farmor or assignor before the farmee or assignee allows the lease to expire on the acreage.

record *v*: to enter a legal instrument into a book or the public record, usually in the county clerk's office. Recording amounts to legal notice to all persons of the rights or claims specified in the instrument.

recovery (operations) *n*: a stage of oil or gas production after the initial phase of extraction, where a fluid such as water is injected into the formation to maintain pressure and push hydrocarbons toward the wellbore.

rectangular survey system *n*: see *Public Land Survey System* (*PLSS*).

reform *v*: to rewrite a contract, guided by principles of equity. Contract reformation is a legal remedy carried out by court order. Parties who believe that the written form of an oil and gas lease does not express what was intended or agreed upon might sue in hope that the court will agree with them and reform the lease to express the intentions of the parties. Courts are hesitant to reform contracts, and at least one of the parties must show that a mistake or fraud has occurred.

release *n*: a statement filed by the lessee of an oil and gas lease indicating that the lease has been relinquished.

release clause *n*: see *surrender clause.*

relinquishment (document) *n*: a legal instrument evidencing the surrender, release, or abandonment of a lease or interest in a lease.

remainderman *n*: someone who holds a future interest in property and who will come into possession when the present possessory interest ends (as upon the death of a life tenant). Compare *life tenant.*

reversionary interest *n*: a future interest created by law when an estate is, for example, leased. The reversion is not conveyed but is retained to take effect later in favor of the grantor or his or her heirs. See *term minerals.*

revocation provision *n*: in a division order, a provision allowing all parties to revoke the agreement, usually with a certain number of days' written notice. See *division order.*

rider *n*: a provision in a lease given as a separate attachment. Also called an exhibit or allonge.

right of survivorship *n*: under joint tenancy, the automatic transfer of the interest of a deceased cotenant to the surviving cotenants; the right of the surviving cotenants to succeed to the interest of the deceased. The same right exists under tenancy by the entirety, which is a joint tenancy of married couples, but the right does not exist under tenancy in common. See *joint tenancy (with a right of survivorship), tenancy by the entirety, tenancy in common.*

right-of-way *n*: 1. the legal right to pass over public land and privately owned property established by usage or contract. 2. the land over which the right exists. The width of a right-of-way varies according to contract specifications and individual easements, but it is generally between 50 and 100 feet.

rod *n*: a unit of measurement for length that has traditionally been used for surveying land in areas of the United States settled by the English. A rod is approximately equal to 16.5 feet, 5.5 yards, or 5.0 metres.

royalty *n*: the part of oil, gas, and minerals or their cash value paid by the lessee to the lessor or to one who has acquired possession of the royalty rights, based on a percentage of the gross production from the property free and clear of all costs except taxes.

royalty clause *n*: in an oil and gas lease, the clause that establishes the percentage of production paid to the lessor.

royalty deed *n*: the legal instrument that conveys a share of oil or gas production. Unlike a mineral deed, a royalty deed does not create a severance of the estate.

RRC *abbr*: Texas Railroad Commission.

rule of capture *n*: a rule applied by the courts that gives title to oil and gas produced from a tract of land to the party having reduced it to possession—in other words, to the first party to acquire it by production. The rule has been modified a great deal by state regulatory agencies. See *nonabsolute ownership.* Compare *absolute ownership, offset drilling rule.*

runsheet *n*: a landman's list and brief description of all the documents in the history of ownership of a given tract of land. Compare *takeoff.* See *chain of title.*

S

secondary recovery operations *n*: see *recovery (operations)*.

secondary term *n*: the term of an oil and gas lease that follows the primary term. If one of the conditions specified in the instrument is present, such as production in paying quantities, operations, or the payment of shut-in royalties, the lease is usually extended into the secondary term. Compare *primary term*.

section *n*: a unit of land measurement in the Public Land Survey System used in the United States. Each 6-mile square, or Congressional township, is divided into 36 sections. A section is usually 1 square mile, or 640 acres. See *Congressional township*.

seismic option agreement *n*: an agreement, usually between a petroleum company and a landowner, that permits seismic exploration of land for a specified price per acre. Once the data has been obtained, the petroleum company can often, by the terms of the agreement, lease selected acreage again for an agreed upon price.

sever *v*: 1. in oil and gas law, to separate or remove a resource such as oil or gas from real property so that it is considered personal property. 2. to divide an estate in land so that there is a surface estate and a mineral estate. See *real property*.

severance *n*: the separation of a mineral or royalty interest from other interests in that land given by grant or reservation.

shut in *v*: 1. to close the valves on a well so that it stops producing. 2. to (temporarily) close in a well in which a kick has occurred.

shut-in payment *n*: see *shut-in royalty*.

shut-in royalty *n*: payment to royalty owners in lieu of production, rentals, or other types of consideration on a shut-in gas well that is capable of producing but does not have a market. Also called shut-in payment.

shut-in royalty clause *n*: a clause in a lease specifying the payments that must be made on a gas well capable of producing but shut in for lack of a market or pending connection with a pipeline. It holds the lease in force, although the clause might specify that payments will only hold the lease for the lessee for a period of time—2, 3, or 5 years, for example—so that the lessor is able to negotiate for higher shut-in royalties under a new lease periodically.

shut-in well *n*: usually, a gas well shut in for lack of a market or pending connection with a pipeline.

SI *abbr*: International System (SI) of Units.

sight draft *n*: a draft or order for payment that must be picked up on the day that it arrives at the drawer's bank. For example, if a lessee pays a lessor a cash bonus by means of a sight draft, the lessee must pick up that draft on the same day that it arrives at his or her bank from the lessor's bank.

simultaneous filing *n*: a noncompetitive procedure similar to a drawing used to grant oil and gas leases on federal lands that have not been leased before.

sovereign *n*: in the case of land, the government that holds and is capable of transferring title.

spacing *n*: see *well spacing*.

special warranty clause *n*: a warranty of title from the grantor for him or her and his or her lessees, assigns, etc. but no further back in the chain of title. Compare *general warranty clause*.

standard form *n*: an oil and gas lease form traditionally used in the Midcontinent and Gulf regions and originally based on the Producers 88 form from an Oklahoma printing company. There is a great diversity of such forms presently, as the original form has been heavily revised and the provisions customized, to the degree that courts do not actually recognize a "standard form" for leases. Also called Producers 88, Standard Form 88, Producers Special, producer's form.

stand-up title opinion *n*: a report prepared by a title examiner who works from a runsheet checked at the county courthouse before deciding whether or not additional documents are needed. It can be less costly and time-consuming to prepare a stand-up opinion than an abstract-based title opinion because the first does not require an abstract of title, which might not be available. Compare *abstract-based title opinion.*

statute law *n*: law enacted by a legislative body, rather than law derived from constitutions, judicial decisions, executive orders, or administrative regulations. Compare *common law.*

statute of frauds *n*: the statutes in force in all states of the United States (based on the English Statute of Frauds and Perjuries of 1677) that require certain contracts to be evidenced in writing and signed by the party to be charged. Contracts for the sale or transfer of an interest in land fall under the statute of frauds, so they must be in a signed writing.

statutory pooling *n*: see *forced pooling.*

statutory unitization *n*: see *compulsory unitization.*

subordination *n*: in the case of an oil and gas lease, a supplementary agreement that resolves the priority of rights to the leased property and subordinates an earlier instrument—for example, a mortgage—to the oil and gas lease.

support agreement *n*: an agreement, usually between petroleum companies, by which one contributes money to another's drilling operation in return for information gained from the drilling. See *dry-hole contribution agreement, bottomhole contribution agreement.*

surface estate *n*: rights and interests in the surface of land, created when the owner severs, or separates, his or her interests in the property.

surface owner *n*: owner of the rights and interests in a surface estate (where interests in an estate in land have been severed). Compare *mineral owner.*

surrender clause *n*: in an oil and gas lease, the clause that specifies the procedure to be followed should the lessee wish to surrender all or part of his or her leased interests. Also called release clause.

surrender (document) *n*: a legal instrument evidencing the relinquishment or release of a lease or interest in a lease.

T

takeoff *n*: a report, usually prepared by an abstract company, listing and briefly describing the documents relevant to the title of a given piece of property. A takeoff is less expensive to prepare than a complete abstract of title and is similar to a landman's runsheet. Compare *runsheet.* See *chain of title.*

tenancy by the entirety *n*: a joint tenancy created between spouses when the nature of ownership of their shared property is not specified in a document such as a deed or will that coveys the property. This type of shared ownership is recognized in several states where community property is not recognized. See *joint tenancy (with a right of survivorship), right of survivorship.* Compare *tenancy in common, community property.*

tenancy in common *n*: a type of shared ownership. Under tenancy in common, two or more cotenants possess equal or unequal shares in a property, and there is no right of survivorship. (See *right of survivorship.*) This type of shared ownership is recognized in several states where community property is not recognized. Compare *joint tenancy (with a right of survivorship), tenancy by the entirety, community property.*

tenant *n*: 1. one who occupies or holds real property. See *real property, life tenant.* 2. in the case of joint tenancy, tenancy by the entirety, and tenancy in common, one who shares ownership of real property with another or with others. See *joint tenancy (with a right of survivorship), tenancy by the entirety, tenancy in common.*

tenants in common *n*: cotenants under a tenancy in common. See *tenancy in common.*

term *n*: see *primary term, secondary term.*

term clause *n*: see *habendum clause.*

term minerals *n pl*: severed minerals acquired for a certain time and, usually, as long thereafter as production continues.

tertiary recovery operations *n*: see *recovery (operations).*

Texas General Land Office (GLO) *n*: the agency of Texas charged with managing state-controlled lands and the minerals contained in them. Its headquarters are in Austin, Texas. Web address: www.glo.texas.gov.

Texas Railroad Commission (TRC or RRC) *n*: an agency of the state of Texas that regulates many industries, especially the oil and gas industry. It was originally established to regulate the railroads but it no longer does so. The RRC issues drilling permits, sets proration schedules, and regulates the size of drilling and spacing units (DSUs). Also called Railroad Commission of Texas. Web address: www.rrc.state.tx.us.

tight hole *n*: a well about which information is restricted for security or competitive reasons and such information given only to those authorized to receive it.

title *n*: 1. the legal right to control and dispose of property. 2. the basis of that right, which can be proven. 3. evidence of such a right in the form of legal documents such as deeds.

title check *n*: a preliminary survey of records affecting the title to a property conducted by a landman or lease broker to quickly determine, for the purpose of assessing whether a lease should be initiated and with whom, whether there are likely to be leases or encumbrances and which parties own interests in the property. Compare *examination of title.*

title opinion *n*: the written opinion of a title examiner on the status of the title to a given piece of property, usually stating whether the property has a marketable title. See *abstract-based title opinion, stand-up title opinion.* Compare *drill site opinion, division order opinion.*

top lease *n*: a lease acquired while a mineral lease to the same property is still in effect. The top lease replaces the existing lease when it expires or is terminated.

township *n*: in the U.S. Public Land Survey System, the name given to the tiers of land running east and west. Compare *range.*

transfer of ownership (judicial) *n*: a transfer by the court of an interest in real property. When ownership of land is concerned, a judicial transfer of ownership usually involves the appointment of a receiver by the court. The receiver can then act, for example, to execute an oil and gas lease on the property. The situation might arise when the landowner is missing or unknown, after foreclosures, or after tax sales. Also called determination of ownership (judicial).

transfer order *n*: an agreement concerning change of production ownership, indemnifying the pipeline company or purchaser.

TRC *abbr*: Texas Railroad Commission.

tribal land *n*: land within an Indian reservation or owned by an Indian tribe, group, or band.

trust *n*: a right in property held by one party at the request of another for the benefit of a third party. The settlor establishes the trust; the trustee holds the property and manages it; the beneficiary is said to benefit from the relationship. Compare *deed of trust*.

trustee *n*: the party that holds and manages the property in a trust for the benefit of another. A trustee has duties specified by the terms of the trust.

turnkey contract *n*: a drilling contract that calls for the payment of a stipulated amount to the drilling contractor upon completion of the well. In a turnkey contract, the contractor furnishes all material and labor and controls the entire drilling operation, independent of supervision by the operator. A turnkey contract does not as a rule include the completion of a well as a producer.

U

undivided interest *n*: where ownership of property is shared, a fractional interest in it. For example, a ¼ undivided interest in an 80-acre tract amounts to a ¼ interest in the entire 80 acres, or 20 net undivided mineral acres. Compare *divided interest*.

unit agreement *n*: an agreement, when there is a unitization, that pools the interests of the parties and acts as a grant by the royalty owners to the working interest owners of the tracts of land so that the tracts can be developed as a single unit. Compare *unit operating agreement*.

***United States Code* (*U.S.C.*)** *n*: a compilation of the federal laws of the United States. It is codified, or organized by subject for ease of use. Currently, the *U.S. Code* is composed of 51 titles that represent diverse areas subject to the laws of Congress, including Conservation, Mineral Lands and Mining, and Public Lands. The official printed *U.S. Code* is updated every six years; an online edition is also available. Web address: uscode.house.gov.

unitization *n*: the combining of many leased tracts on a field-wide or reservoir-wide basis to facilitate large-scale operations such as secondary recovery. Compare *pooling*.

unit operating agreement *n*: an agreement, when there is a unitization, between the working interest owners concerned, by which they establish a committee to oversee unit operations and decide on the sharing of costs. Compare *unit agreement*.

unleased owner *n*: a mineral owner who has not leased his or her property.

"unless" clause *n*: see *drilling and delay rental clause*.

U.S. Bureau of Indian Affairs (BIA) *n*: see *Bureau of Indian Affairs*.

U.S. Bureau of Land Management (BLM) *n*: see *Bureau of Land Management*.

U.S. Bureau of Ocean Energy Management (BOEM) *n*: see *Bureau of Ocean Energy Management*.

U.S.C. *n*: *United States Code*.

U.S. Department of the Interior (DOI) *n*: see *Department of the Interior*.

V

vara *n*: a unit of measurement of length that has traditionally been used for surveying land in areas of the United States settled by Spain or Mexico. One vara is approximately equal to 33.3 inches.

voluntary pooling *n*: pooling of leased tracts willingly undertaken by all the parties involved, both working interest owners and royalty owners. Compare *forced pooling*.

voluntary unitization *n*: unitization that is accomplished with the willing cooperation of the affected parties, both working interest owners and royalty owners. Compare *compulsory unitization*.

W

warrant (title) *n*: 1. to guarantee the security of a title. 2. to promise to compensate the grantee if he or she is evicted for reason of title.

warranty clause *n*: in an oil and gas lease, the clause that assures title to the leased property. See *general warranty clause, special warranty clause*.

warranty deed *n*: a deed in which the grantor transfers legal title to another and warrants the title. The grantor warrants title in several ways in the deed: first, by promising he or she is the lawful owner and has the right to convey the property, second, by warranting that the property is free from encumbrances, and third, by promising to defend title for the grantee (compensate in the event of loss). See *warranty clause, general warranty clause, special warranty clause*.

well density *n*: the ratio between the number of wells drilled in a field and the acreage. Under a 40-acre spacing pattern, the well density is one well per 40 acres. Compare *well spacing, prorationing*.

wellhead price *n*: see *"market value at the mouth of the well."*

well log *n*: A systematic recording of the data, such as a driller's log, mud log, electric well log, or radioactivity log. Many different logs are run into wells to discern various characteristics of the downhole formation.

well permit *n*: an authorization, usually granted by a governmental conservation agency, to drill a well. A permit is also sometimes required for deepening or remedial work. Also called drilling permit.

well spacing *n*: the number and location of wells over an oil or gas reservoir, limited by state regulations. Compare *well density, prorationing*.

windfall profit tax *n*: a federal excise tax on crude oil, which has a different rate for oil in a number of categories—for example, newly discovered oil, stripper oil, stripper oil produced by independents, and so on. The tax rate is determined at a percentage—for instance, at 25%—of the difference between a base price and a market price. There are a variety of exceptions and exemptions.

working interest *n*: the interest in oil and gas that includes responsibility for all drilling, developing, and operating costs. Also called operating interest, leasehold interest.

Y

yard(s) (yd) *n*: a unit of measurement of length that has traditionally been used for surveying land in areas of the United States settled by the English. One yard is approximately equal to 0.9 metres.

Index

AAPG. See *American Association of Petroleum Geologists (AAPG).*
abandonment, 126
absolute ownership, 8
abstract-based opinions, 93–94, 103
abstract companies, 45, 46–47, 54, 103. See also *abstract plants; title companies.*
abstract plants, 46–47, 94. See also *abstract companies; title companies.*
abstracts of title, 45–46, 54, 103
accounting procedure, 100, 115, 116–117
acknowledgment
  as part of lease, 61, 80
  purpose of, 79, 80, 86
  requirements of, 88, 96
acquired lands, 22, 23, 25, 28
acts of God, 78
addendums/addenda, 55, 79, 135
administrative law, 7
administrators and executors, 15–16
adverse possession affidavits, 96, 97–98
AFE. See *authorization for expenditure (AFE).*
affiant, 96–97
affidavits
  adverse possession, 96, 97–98
  corroborating, 97
  in curing titles, 96
  death and heirship, 96
  identity, 96
  nonproduction, 96, 97
  for title opinions, 94
  use, occupancy, and possession, 96, 97
agencies. See *federal agencies; state agencies.*
agreements to explore and develop
  about, 105–106
  farmout agreements, 110–111
  joint operating agreements (JOAs), 113–116
  letter agreements and formal contracts, 112–113
  support agreements, 107–109
  summary, 117
Alabama, 21, 35
Alaska
  federal lands, 24, 136–138
  land ownership, 20
  leasing agency for state lands, 21
  leasing in, 136–138
  native lands, 25, 136–138
  offshore lands, 152, 136–138

ranking as a top oil-producing state, 133
state regulatory agency, 52
aliens (noncitizens), 24, 153
allotted land, 23, 25–26, 149
American Association of Petroleum Geologists (AAPG), 42, 144
AMI. See *area of mutual interest (AMI)*.
animal protection (provision), 82, 83–84, 88
annual rental, 12, 24, 27, 49, 50, 51, 54
antitrust laws, 125
area considerations, 50–51
area of mutual interest (AMI), 112, 115, 116
Arizona, 21, 30
arm's length transaction, 67
arpents (unit of measurement), 30–31, 39, 146, 164
assign (transfer), 24
assignees, 77
assignment clause, 61, 77
attorney-in-fact, 16, 85
attorney's forms, 55, 59
authorization for expenditure (AFE), 115, 117

base abstracts, 47–48, 94
base line, 35, 36, 40
bearing of survey line, 32, 33, 39
bequeath (personal property), 4
BIA. See *Bureau of Indian Affairs (BIA)*.
BLM. See *Bureau of Land Management (BLM)*.
blocks and lots, 38
BOEM. See *Bureau of Ocean Energy Management (BOEM)*.
bonus
authorization to pay by landman or lease broker, 44, 49
Bureau of Land Management (BLM) lease sales figures, 24, 27
as concern of landman, 50, 54
as concern of landowner, 51, 54
confidentiality of, 63, 86
defined, 62
method of payment, 86–87, 90
with paid-up leases, 70
parties receiving payment of, 12
variations in figures from state to state, 50
bonus drafts, 87
bottomhole contribution agreements, 106–107, 109, 117
bound, defined, 32
boundary descriptions, Pennsylvania, 65
Bureau of Indian Affairs (BIA), 23, 25–26, 28, 145, 148, 149, 150, 151
Bureau of Land Management (BLM)
approved unit operating agreements, 125
competitive leasing, 23–24
federal lands in individual states, 137–138, 145, 150–151
form agreements, 129
as information source, 46
leases, 128–129
lease sales, 24
as mineral owner, 10
noncompetitive leasing, 24
onshore federal lands, 22–23, 28, 125
SI (International System of Units) conversion, 31
as source of records on Indian lands, 26
as source of records on public lands, 46
tribal and allotted lands, 26
unit and unit operating agreements, 125
Bureau of Ocean Energy Management (BOEM), 125
jurisdiction over offshore lands, 22–23, 28
Outer Continental Shelf (OCS), 26–28
SI (International System of Units) conversion, 31
as source of records on federal lands, 46
by-products, 60, 67

California
Bureau of Land Management (BLM) lease sales, 24
community property, 13
foreign grants (grant-based land titles), 30, 34
leasing agency for state lands, 21, 152
leasing in, 139–143
offshore operations, 152
procedural differences in leasing, 146
ranking as a top oil-producing state, 133
state regulatory agency, 52
U.S. Public Land Survey System (PLSS), 34
Canada
accounting procedure, 116
Canadian Association of Professional Landmen (CAPL), 155–156
CAPL 99 form lease, 114
leasing in, 155–156
mineral ownership in, 19
caption, 85
capture, 8–9
case law, 4, 7, 8, 12, 17, 146, 156
cessation of production clause, 61, 72
C.F.R. See *Code of Federal Regulations (C.F.R.)*.
chain of title, 92, 96, 97, 103, 140
chains (unit of measurement), 30, 39, 161–163
civil law, 4, 146

clerk of court for the parish (source of public records in Louisiana), 47
cloud on title, 96, 103, 126
Code of Federal Regulations (*C.F.R.*), 23, 26, 28, 128–129, 153, 154
Colorado, 21, 30, 52, 133, 151
commencement of drilling, 70
commercial/paying quantities, 66
common/case law, 4, 7, 8, 12, 17, 146, 156
community property, 13
compensatory royalty payments, 82, 83
competitive leasing, 23–24
complete/base abstracts, 46–47, 48, 94
compulsory/involuntary unitization, 123, 125, 128
confidential terms, 62, 63, 86, 90, 139
Congressional townships, 35–37, 40
conservation laws, 8, 9, 100, 106, 120
consideration, 55, 61, 70, 76, 80, 125, 135
  bonus as consideration, 50, 62
  confidentiality of bonus, 63
  defined, 62
  nominal, 62
  as requirement of contract, 62, 79
  serious, 62
  types of, 62
constitutional law, 7
continuous drilling clause, 61, 72
contract area, 113, 115, 116
controlling date, 60
co-owners/cotenants, 12–13, 17, 61, 88, 90
co-ownership/cotenancy, 12–13, 17
COPAS. See *Council of Petroleum Accountants Societies, Inc.* (*COPAS*).
correlative rights, 9, 51
corroborating affidavits, 97
cost recovery, 111, 115, 123
cotenancy/co-ownership, 12–13, 17
cotenants/co-owners, 12–13, 17, 61, 88, 90
Council of Petroleum Accountants Societies, Inc. (COPAS), 116
county clerk's office, 26, 45, 47, 54
coverall clause/Mother Hubbard clause, 61, 65
curing titles
  affidavits used in, 96–98
  documents other than affidavits used in, 98–99
  of leased properties, 91
  methods of, 103
  after title examination, 94
  well permit application after titles have been cured, 100

damage, 11, 25, 53, 76, 80, 134, 148
damage clause, 61, 76
date
  controlling date, 60
  effective date, 60, 61, 63, 71, 80
  date of acknowledgment, 60, 61
  date of execution, 60, 61, 80
  date of recordation, 60
  undated leases, 60
day-after-sale offer, 24
death and heirship affidavits, 96
deeds of trust, 98–99
deep wells, 53, 144
defects in titles. See *curing titles.*
delay rental clause, 61, 70, 71
delay rentals, 62, 66, 70, 72, 77, 92, 97, 122, 126, 129, 146
density (well), 43, 51, 53, 54, 72, 120, 128
Department of the Interior (DOI), 22–23, 25, 128, 138, 152
depth limitations, 65
descent and distribution laws, 15
description (legal)
  about, 29–30
  importance of completeness, 39
  methods of, 32–38
determinable fee, 4
development agreements, types, 106
development/continuous drilling clause, 72
devise (real property), 4, 5, 62
disclaimers, 98–99
division orders
  in California, 140
  defined, 92, 100
  execution of, 100–102
  paying process, 104
  purpose of, 102, 104
  revocability/revocation provision, 102
  sample, 101
  signing of, 102
division order (title) opinions, 92–93, 100, 103
DOI. See *Department of the Interior* (*DOI*).
domestic animals, 82, 84, 88
draft payments, 62, 87, 90
drilling and delay rental clause, 61, 70

drilling and spacing unit (DSU)/proration unit, 113, 117, 120–121, 123, 128
drilling/well permit, 12, 100, 103
drill or pay, 70
drill site opinion, 92–93, 103
dry-hole clause, 61, 72
dry-hole contribution agreements, 106–108
DSU. See *drilling and spacing unit (DSU)/proration unit.*

EEZ. See *exclusive economic zone (EEZ).*
effective date, 60, 61, 63, 71, 80
elements of a lease. See *lease elements; special terms and provisions.*
encumbrances, 93, 100, 103, 146
English
- origins of American law, 8, 14
- units of measurement (in land descriptions), 30–31, 39

entailed (property), 4
Environmental Protection Agency (EPA), 10
equipment installation/placement, 11, 82, 88
estates, 4–5
European units of measurement (in land descriptions), 30–31
examination of title, 44, 54, 92–95. See also *preliminary title checks.*
- title examiners, 92
- title opinions, 92–95

exclusive economic zone (EEZ), 7, 152
exclusive rights, 5, 8, 12, 62
execution of lease, 85, 88
- acknowledgment, 86
- date of, 60, 61, 80
- recording of executed lease, 86–87
- variations in proper execution, 85–86

executors and administrators, 15–16
exploration, 22, 23, 42, 49, 50, 53, 66
exploration agreements, 105–117
- types of, 106

exploration costs, 106, 111, 113, 117
exploration rights, 1, 5, 8, 11, 62, 111
Exxon Corp v. Middleton, 102

Fagg v. Texas Co., 59
farmee, 106, 110, 111
farmor, 106, 110
farmout agreements, 106–107, 110–113, 117
- defined, 106, 107, 110, 117
- forms of, 112

federal agencies, 10, 26, 45, 46, 55, 79, 128, 152. See also *Bureau of Indian Affairs (BIA); Bureau of Land Management (BLM); Bureau of Ocean Energy Management (BOEM); Environmental Protection Agency (EPA).*
federal lands, 10, 20, 126, 128, 129, 135. See also *Bureau of Indian Affairs (BIA); Bureau of Land Management (BLM); Bureau of Ocean Energy Management (BOEM).*
- about, 22
- acquired lands, 25, 28
- in Alaska, 136–137
- competitive leasing, 23–24, 28
- federal offshore lands, 152–154
- Indian lands, 25–26, 28
- lease forms, 56
- leasing authorities for, 23
- in Louisiana, 147
- management of, 22
- in New Mexico, 148–148
- noncompetitive leasing, 24–25, 28
- offshore lands, 26–28
- public domain lands, 23–24, 28
- unitization of, 125

Federal Onshore Oil and Gas Leasing Reform Act of 1987, 23
Federal Register, 128, 153, 154
federal regulations, 25, 26, 43, 112, 125, 126, 128
fee, 4, 14
- fee in surface, 5
- fee simple, 4, 5, 8, 11, 17
- fee tail, 4

fiduciaries, 15, 18
fief, 4
final negotiations
- about, 81
- special terms and provisions, 81–84

Final Notice of Sale (FNOS), 27
financing exploration and drilling, 91
five-day draft, 87
Five Year Program, 26–27
Florida
- foreign grants (grant-based titles), 30
- jurisdiction over submerged coastal lands, 26, 152
- leasing agency for state lands, 21
- U.S. Public Land Survey System (PLSS), 35

FNOS. See *Final Notice of Sale (FNOS).*
forced/involuntary pooling, 13, 122–123, 128
forced pooling laws, 123
force majeure clause, 61, 78

force majeure provision, 112
foreign grants (grant-based land titles), 30
form leases. See also *standard leases.*
AAPL Form 610 Model Form Operating Agreement-1956, 114
AAPL Form 610-1989 Model Form Operating Agreement, 114
about, 55, 79
attorney's forms, 59, 81
Bath forms, 56
farmout agreement forms, 112
landowner's forms, 59, 81
model forms, 114
from private companies, 56, 80
Producers 88, 56–58, 80
state and federal, 56, 80
Texas form lease sample, 6
types of, 55, 80
frac fluids, 84
fractional interests, 64–65, 140
fracturing, 10, 78, 106, 107, 140
free gas, 82, 83, 88
Freestone riders, 82–83, 122
French units of measurement (in land descriptions), 29–31, 39, 146, 164

gas marketing, 67
gas purchase, 83
gas royalties, 67
General Land Office. See *Texas General Land Office (GLO).*
general warranty clause, 78
geologists and geophysicists, 41–42, 49, 53
GLO. See *Texas General Land Office (GLO).*
GOM. See *Gulf of Mexico (GOM).*
good title, 44, 92, 102, 104. See also *marketable title.*
grant-based land titles (foreign grants), 30
grantees, 4, 47, 60, 103
granting clause, 61, 62–64, 80
grantors, 47, 60
Greene v. Robinson, 14
guardians, 15, 16, 18
Gulf of Mexico (GOM), 27, 135, 147, 152

habendum clause, 61, 66
hectares, 31, 165
helium, 60, 64
homestead property, 13
horizontal drilling, 106
horizontal Pugh clause, 83. See also *Pugh clause.*
hydraulic fracturing, 106. See also *fracturing.*

identity affidavits, 96
implied rights/covenants/obligations, 62–63, 83, 140
Indian lands, 22, 23, 25–26, 28, 144, 148, 149
initial well, 111–113
international law, 7, 152
International System (SI) of Units, 31, 165. See also *metric system.*
Interstate Oil Compact Commission, 120
intestacy, 15
involuntary/compulsory unitization, 123, 125, 128
involuntary/forced pooling, 13, 122–123, 128

joint operating agreements (JOAs)
2002 710 AAPL Joint Operating Agreement (Shelf), 114
2007 810 AAPL Joint Operating Agreement (Deepwater), 114
cost sharing, 111, 113, 117
farmout agreements, 111
model forms, 114
pooling agreement, 122, 123
reasons for, 105–107, 117
special provisions, 115–116
joint tenancy (with a right of survivorship), 12
judicial determination of ownership, 17
judicial transfer, 17

Kansas, 21, 52, 83, 133, 144, 151

land department, 43, 100
land description, 39, 64. See also *description (legal).*
landman
authority of, 49, 54
compared to lease broker, 44
concerns of, 49–50
gender-neutral term, 2
responsibilities of, 43, 44–48, 87, 90, 91, 92, 94, 96–99, 103, 106, 113
role in negotiations with landowner, 49–51
title checks, 54
land measurement and land description
about, 29–30

description completeness, 39
methods of description, 32–38
units of measurement, 30–31
summary, 39–40
land negotiator, 2
landowners
as agents of the state, 14, 18
cotenants, 12–13, 17
defined, 3
gas marketing by, 67
as information source, 45, 48, 54
lessors, 11, 17
life tenants and remaindermen, 12, 17
married persons, 13, 17
mineral owners, 11
representatives of mineral owners, 15–17, 18
rights of, 11, 17
surface owners, 11
types of estates they own, 11–13, 17
unqualified, 5, 17
landowner's forms, 59
land professional, 2
laws of descent and distribution, 15
lease. See also *form leases.*
compared to other commercial leases, 1
defined, 1
release of, 76, 77, 97, 99, 126–129
right of landowner to execute, 11
"standard" forms, 5, 59
lease brokers
compared to landmen, 44, 53–54
responsibilities of, 44, 49, 50, 53–54, 94, 139
lease elements
acknowledgment, 61, 79, 80, 86, 88, 96
assignment clause, 61, 77
cessation of production clause, 61, 72
consideration, 55, 61, 70, 76, 80, 125, 135
continuous drilling clause, 61, 72
damage clause, 61, 76
date, 60, 61, 63, 71, 80
defined, 62
delay rental clause, 61, 70, 71
description (legal), 29–30, 32–38, 39
drilling and delay rental clause, 61, 70
dry hole clause, 61, 72
effective date, 60, 61, 63, 71, 80
force majeure clause, 61, 78
granting clause, 61, 62–64, 80
habendum clause, 61, 66
lease forms. See *form leases.*
legal description, 29–30, 32–38, 39
legal effect clause, 61, 79
lessor's signature, 61, 79
Mother Hubbard clause/coverall clause, 61, 65
parties' names, 60–61
pooling and unitization clause, 61, 72–75
preamble, 61, 80
proportionate reduction clause, 61, 65, 78
provisions, 59, 61, 79, 80
royalty clause, 61, 67–68
shut-in royalty clause, 61, 69
signature block, 61
signature of lessor, 61, 79
surrender clause, 61, 76
title, 60, 61, 63, 80
unitization clause, 61, 72–75
warranty clause, 61, 65, 78
lease forms. See *form leases.*
leasehold, 62
lease memorandum/memo, 86, 90, 140, 142–143
Lease Sale Notice, 20, 24
leasing authorities for federal lands, 23
leasing preparations
preliminary explorations, 41–44
preliminary negotiations, 49–53
preliminary title checks, 44–48
summary, 49, 53–54
legal description
about, 29–30
importance of completeness, 39
methods of, 32–38
legal effect clause, 61, 79
legal guardians, 15, 16, 18
legal person, 16
lessee
advice for, 12, 16, 17, 20, 23, 24, 25, 56, 60
defined, 17, 60
obligations of, 11, 12, 61, 62, 66, 76
rights of, 11, 12, 62, 77
lesser interest clause, 65
lessor
advice for, 60
defined, 11, 17, 60
obligations of, 62
rights of, 62
lessor's signature, 61, 79
letter agreements and formal contracts (for farmouts), 112–113
liability, 112
life tenants, 12, 17
links (unit of measurement), 30, 39, 161
liquidated damages, 112
Louisiana
arpents (as unit of measurement), 31, 164
Bath forms, 56

civil law, 4
clerk of court for the parish (as source for public records), 47
division orders, 102
forced pooling, 123
foreign grants (grant-based land titles), 30
jurisdiction over submerged coastal lands, 152
lease (Bath) forms, 56
leasing agency for state, 21
leasing in, 146–147
legal documents in, 47
marital status, 60
Napoleonic Code, 4
ranking as a top oil-producing state, 133
royalty payments, 51
rule of capture, 8
serious consideration, 62
state regulatory agency, 52
varas (as unit of measurement), 31
Louisiana Revised Statute 30:10, 123

marital property ownership, 13
marketable title, 92, 103–104. See also *good title.*
market value clause, 82–83
married persons, 13, 17, 85, 96
memorandum/memo of oil and gas lease, 86, 90, 140, 142–143
meridians, 35–36, 39, 40
mete, defined, 32
metes and bounds
example of, 33
method of, 29, 32, 39
natural objects, 34
in South and Southwest, 34
methods of description
history of, 32
metes and bounds, 32–34
urban subdivisions, 38
U.S. Public Land Survey System (PLSS), 35–38
metres, 31, 65, 165
metric system, 31. See also *International System (SI) of Units.*
Mexico, 14, 30, 134
"mineral," as ambiguous term, 60
mineral-classified (lands), 14, 18, 19, 23, 59, 135
mineral estate, 5, 7, 10, 11, 17, 19, 23, 47, 53, 64, 146, 148
mineral leasing, types of law affecting, 7
Mineral Leasing Act for Acquired Lands, 25
Mineral Leasing Act of 1920, 23, 125
mineral owners, 11, 17, 83, 85, 100, 104, 120, 123, 128, 129, 158. See also *representatives of mineral owners.*
mineral ownership
Bureau of Land Management (BLM), 10
in Canada, 155–156
limitations on, 3–5, 7–10, 17
rights to, 5–6
in Texas, 8–9, 14, 18, 19, 134–135
theories of, 8
minerals in place, 8
Mississippi, 21, 35, 146
model forms, 114, 117
Montana, 21, 26
mortgages/mortgage instruments, 48, 98–99
Mother Hubbard clause/coverall clause, 61, 64–65

Napoleonic Code, 4
National Association of Royalty Owners (NARO), 41
national parks, 22, 25, 28, 137
Native Americans, 25. See also *Indian lands.*
negotiations. See also *preliminary negotiations.*
final, 81–84
for special provisions, 88
Nevada, 21, 30
New Mexico
Bureau of Land Management (BLM), 23
federal lands, 23
foreign grants (grant-based land titles), 30
leasing agency for state lands, 21
leasing in, 148–149
ranking as a top oil-producing state, 133
state regulatory agency, 52
nonabsolute ownership, 8
noncompetitive leasing, 23–24
nonexecutive royalty owners, 122
nonjoining co-owners, 13
nonownership in place, 8
nonparticipating royalty owners, 75, 122
nonproduction affidavits, 96, 97
notary public, 61, 79–80, 86, 88, 96
notice
of public lease sales, 24, 26–27, 153
in public records, 86, 88, 90
of regulations, 20, 128

OCC. See *Oklahoma Corporation Commission (OCC).*
OCS. See *Outer Continental Shelf (OCS).*
offset wells, 72, 82, 83, 88

offshore lands
  Bureau of Ocean Energy Management (BOEM), 22, 23, 26–28
  federal jurisdiction, 22–23, 26
  leasing of, 26–28, 152–154
  Outer Continental Shelf Lands Act of 1953, 26–27
  Outer Continental Shelf (OCS), 26, 28
  in ranking with top oil-producing states, 133
  state jurisdiction, 26
Ohio, 21, 35
oil and gas lease. See *lease.*
oil and gas lease form. See *form leases.*
oil, gas, and associated liquid hydrocarbons lease, 1
oil, gas, and mineral lease, 1
Oklahoma
  damage to surface estate, 11
  federal lands, 23
  Indian lands, 26
  leasing agency for state lands, 21
  leasing in, 144–145
  Producers 88, 56
  ranking as a top oil-producing state, 133
  regulations in, 9, 43
  reservations in, 26
  rule of capture, 8
  state regulatory agency, 52
Oklahoma Corporation Commission (OCC), 9, 43, 52
onshore public domain lands, 22, 23–26, 28, 125, 136. See also *Bureau of Indian Affairs (BIA); Bureau of Land Management (BLM).*
operation rights, 11
Outer Continental Shelf Lands Act of 1953, 26
Outer Continental Shelf (OCS), 26, 28, 152
overproduction, 8, 120, 144
overriding royalty/royalties, 111, 157–160
ownership. See also *privately owned land.*
  of federal lands, 1, 22–28
  of Indian lands, 25–26, 28
  of minerals. See *mineral ownership.*
  of offshore lands, 26–27, 28
  of state lands, 1, 20–21, 28
ownership in place, 8

paid-up lease, 66, 70
patenting, 14
paying/commercial quantities, 66
payments in cash, 62
payments in kind, 62
payout, 111
Pennsylvania, 21, 60, 65, 144, 155
per-acre bonus, 27
permit form, 100
permit (well/drilling), 12, 100, 103
persons acting under powers of attorney, 15, 16, 18
place/point of beginning (POB), 32–33, 39
plat, 30, 33, 37
plat map approval, 82
plugging and abandonment, 82, 84, 88, 111
POB. See *place/point of beginning (POB).*
point/place of beginning (POB), 32–33, 39
pooled units, 75, 120, 122, 128
pooling
  about, 119–122
  compared to unitization, 119, 123
  defined, 72, 119
  forced/involuntary, 123
  procedures to form a pooled unit, 122, 123
  voluntary, 120–122
pooling agreement, 122
pooling and unitization clause, 73–74
pooling clause, 72–75, 120
power of attorney, 16, 18
preamble, 61, 80
preliminary negotiations
  about, 49
  area considerations, 50–51
  bonus, rental, and royalty, 49–53
  landman concerns, 49–50
  landowner concerns, 51–53
  offer evaluation, 51–53
primary term length, 49–51, 54
  tract size and spacing, 51–53
  summary, 49, 54
preliminary title checks
  abstract companies, 46–47
  county clerk offices, 47
  information sources, 45
  landowners, 48
  purpose of, 44
  state and federal agencies, 46
  title companies, 46–47
preparations for drilling, producing, and selling
  about, 91
  curing titles, 96–99
  examining titles, 92–93
  executing division orders, 100–102
  permitting and drilling, 100
  summary, 103–104

primary term
  in Bureau of Ocean Energy Management (BOEM) bids, 27
  defined, 24, 49, 66
  in delay rental clauses, 71
  in habendum clause, 66
  length of, 49–51, 54
  in paid-up leases, 70
principal meridian, 35, 36
private company lease forms, 55
  Producers 88, 56
  Producers 88 lease form sample, 57–58
  Producers 88, revised versions, 56, 59
private law, 7
private leases, 62, 125
privately owned land, 3–18
  in Alaska, 20
  economic constraints, 10
  landowners and types of estates they own, 11–13, 17
  landowners as agents of the state, 14, 17
  lease filing, 87
  legal limitations, 3, 7–10
  limitations on mineral ownership, 4, 7–10
  ownership types, 4
  private ownership, 3–18
  representatives of mineral owners, 15–17, 18
  rights to mineral ownership, 5
  types of ownership, 4
  unitization, 124–125
Producers 88, 55–59, 79
Producers 88 lease form sample, 57–58
Producers 88, revised versions, 55–56
proportionate reduction clause, 61, 65, 78
proposals (well), 115
prorationing, 120, 128, 134, 144
proration unit, 120. See also *drilling and spacing unit (DSU)/proration unit.*
prospect area, 113. See also *contract area.*
prospects, 42, 53, 106
provisions. See *lease elements; special terms and provisions.*
public domain lands. See *federal lands.*
public lands. See also *federal lands; state lands.*
  leasing authorities for, 22
  unitization of, 125, 129
Public Land Survey System (PLSS), 29, 35–38, 39, 40
public records, 16, 46–47, 54, 60, 79, 80, 86, 87, 90
Pugh clause, 75, 82–83, 88, 122, 135

quitclaims, 98–99, 103

ranges, 35–36, 39
ratification, 13, 88–90, 98, 99, 122, 125
ratify, defined, 12
recordation, 60, 87. See also *recording.*
recordation stamp, 87
recording, 16, 86–88
recovery methods, 63, 75, 124, 144
release clause, 76
release (of lease), 76, 77, 97, 126–129
Relinquishment Act, 14
relinquishment (document), 126, 129
remainderman, 12, 17
rental, 12, 24, 27, 49, 50, 51, 54
rental receipts, 98
representatives of mineral owners
  attorneys-in-fact, 15, 16
  executors and administrators, 15–16
  fiduciaries, 15
  guardians, 15, 16
  persons acting under powers of attorney, 15, 16
  representatives of unknown or missing heirs, 15, 17
  trustees, 15, 16
representatives of unknown or missing heirs, 15, 17
Republic of Texas, 14
reservations, 26
Restricted Joint Bidders (list), 27
revocation provision, 102
right(s)
  to benefit from land, 5, 8
  to bequeath property, 4
  to build roads, 11
  to convey land, 5
  to devise property, 4
  to enter property, 5, 11, 63
  to explore, 1, 5, 8, 11, 62, 111
  implied, 63
  to install equipment, 11
  to lease land, 5, 7, 11, 16
  of life tenant to possess and use property, 12
  of mineral-classified landowner, 14, 135
  of mineral ownership, 1, 5, 14, 23
  to minerals in Canada, 155
  to minerals in Louisiana, 146
  to produce, 5, 62
  of remainderman to come into possession of property, 12
  to sever an estate, 5
  of survivorship, 12
  to water, 83
rods (unit of measurement), 30, 39, 161, 163

royalties/royalty payments, 43, 50–51, 62, 67. See also *compensatory royalty payments; overriding royalty/royalties.*
  calculating, 158–159
  defined, 11, 67, 157
  in Louisiana, 146
  under pooling and unitization, 72, 75, 120, 122
royalty clause, 61, 67–68
royalty owners. See also *nonparticipating royalty owners.*
  division orders, 100–102, 104
  National Association of Royalty Owners (NARO), 125
  obligations of, 75
  payments to, 69, 104
  pooling and unitization, 120, 122, 124–125, 128
  signatures of, 124
rule of capture, 8–9
runsheet, 44, 54, 94–95, 103

secondary recovery operations, 124. See *recovery methods.*
secondary term, 66, 72
Secretary of the Interior, 25–27, 136, 153
seismic studies, 28, 42, 53, 116, 144
serious consideration, 62
sever (an estate), 5, 11, 17
shale plays, 50, 106
shut-in payments/royalties, 69
shut-in royalty clause, 61, 69
sight draft, 87
signature block, 61, 80
signatures
  captions to accompany, 85
  conventions regarding, 79, 85
  of cotenants, 12, 17, 90
  of lessee, 61
  of lessor, 61, 79, 85, 86
  of notary, 61, 86
  of owners for pooling and unitization, 122, 124
  of representatives, 85
  of spouses, 13, 17
SI (International System of Units) conversion, 31
site reclamation and well plugging, 64, 82, 84, 88, 126
site restoration, 64, 82, 84, 88, 126
spacing (well). See *well spacing.* See also *drilling and spacing unit (DSU)/proration unit.*
Spain, 14, 30, 134
Spanish units of measurement (in land descriptions), 29–31
special terms and provisions
  accounting procedure, 115, 116
  animal protection, 82, 83–84
  area of mutual interest (AMI), 112, 115, 116
  authorization for expenditure (AFE), 115, 117
  compensatory royalty payments, 82, 83
  equipment placement, 82
  free gas and gas purchase, 82, 83
  market value clause, 82, 83
  negotiations for, 81, 88
  offset wells, 82, 83
  plat map approval, 82
  proposals (well), 115, 117
  Pugh clause, 82, 83
  site reclamation, 82, 84
  water, 82, 83–84
  well plugging, 82, 84
special warranty clause, 78
standard leases, 5, 49, 54, 61, 70, 75, 79, 155. See also *form leases.*
stand-up (title) opinions, 93–94, 103
state agencies. See also *Texas Railroad Commission (TRC or RRC); Oklahoma Corporation Commission (OCC).*
  permits from, 100, 103
  responsibility to lease state lands, 20–21, 28, 152
  responsibility to regulate mineral production, 8, 9, 10, 17, 120, 128, 144
  rules and regulations, 7, 9, 10, 43, 51, 113, 122, 125, 128
  as sources of information, 42, 45–46, 52
state lands, 19–21, 28, 125, 137, 141, 148, 150, 152
statute of frauds, 45
statute/statutory law, 4, 7, 17, 146
statutory pooling laws, 123
subdivided section, 36–38
subdivisions, 38–40
subordination, 98, 99
substitute well, 109, 111
sulfur, 60, 64, 67
support agreements
  about, 107
  bottomhole contribution agreements, 106, 109, 117
  dry-hole contribution agreements, 106, 108, 117
surface estate, 5, 11, 17, 19, 135, 137, 146, 148
surface owners, 11, 14, 17, 18, 19, 43, 53, 76, 83, 148
surrender clause, 61, 76
surrender (document), 61, 76, 126, 129

takeoff, 46, 94
tax certificates, 47, 94, 98

tax partnership provisions, 112
tax payment proof, 47, 94, 98
tax receipts, 47, 94, 98
tenancy by the entirety, 12–13
tenancy in common, 12
term. See *primary term; secondary term; terminology.*
term clause, 66
termination (of lease), 67, 71, 76, 97, 126, 129, 146
terminology
  "fee,"4
  of granting clause, 62
  "Indian lands," 25
  "landman" as gender-neutral term, 2
  legal, 4
  "mineral" as ambiguous term, 60
  oil and gas lease, defined, 1
  "standard" forms, 5, 59
  statute of frauds, 45
Texas. See also *Texas General Land Office (GLO); Texas Railroad Commission (TRC or RRC).*
  absolute ownership, 8
  adverse possession claims, 98
  conservation laws, 8
  delay rental payments, 70
  designated units, 122
  division orders, 102
  foreign grants (grant-based land titles), 30
  form oil and gas lease, 6
  history of mineral production in, 8–9, 14, 120, 134
  jurisdiction over submerged coastal lands, 26
  leasing agency for federal lands, 23
  leasing agency for state lands, 21
  leasing in, 134–135
  metes and bounds land descriptions, 34
  mineral-classified lands, 14, 18
  mineral ownership theories, 8
  ranking as top oil-producing state, 133
  Relinquishment Act, 14
  royalty payments, 51
  rules and regulations, 20, 53, 120
  Spanish units of measurement (in land descriptions), 30–31
Texas General Land Office (GLO), 14, 20, 21, 56, 135, 152
Texas Railroad Commission (TRC or RRC), 9, 43, 52, 53, 144
Texas Register, 20
Texas Trust Act, 16
title. See also *good title; lease elements (title); marketable title; preliminary title checks.*
  about, 3, 5, 8, 39, 78, 86, 100, 102, 136, 148
  checking, 44–48, 49, 53–54, 139–140
  curing, 96–99, 103
  examining, 92–95, 103–104
  insurance, 139
title companies, 45–47, 139–140. See also *abstract companies; abstract plants.*
title examiners, 46, 92–94, 100, 103–104
title opinions
  about, 92–93
  abstract-based (title) opinions, 94
  division order title opinions, 92, 100, 104
  drill site title opinions, 92, 103
  sample form, 93
  stand-up (title) opinions, 94
townships. See also *Congressional townships.*
  colonial, 32, 35
  (tiers), 35–36, 39
tribal land, 23, 25–26
trust, 16, 25, 148
trustees, 15–16, 18
types of law affecting mineral leasing, 7

unit agreements, 123–125
United Nations Convention on the Law of the Sea, 7
United States (U.S.) Code, 25, 153, 154
  defined, 25
unitization
  about, 119–120, 123–124, 128
  of Bureau of Land Management (BLM) lands, 125, 128
  compared to pooling, 119, 123
  compulsory/statutory, 123, 125, 128
  defined, 75, 119, 128
  of federal and state lands, 125
  habendum clause, 75
  pooling and unitization clause, 61, 72–75
  of private lands, 124–125
  state regulatory agency approval of, 125
  unitization clause, 61, 72–75
  voluntary, 123, 124–125, 128
unitization clause, 61, 72–75
unitized field, 124, 128
unit operating agreement, 124–125
units of measurement (in land descriptions), 30–31
unqualified landowner, 5, 17
urban subdivisions, 38, 40
U.S. Department of the Interior (DOI). See *Department of the Interior (DOI).*
use, occupancy, and possession affidavits, 96, 97
U.S. public lands, leasing authorities, 22

U.S. Public Land Survey System. See *Public Land Survey System* (*PLSS*).
Utah, 21, 30

varas (unit of measurement), 30–31, 39, 161, 163–164
vertical Pugh clause, 83. See also *Pugh clause.*
Veterans Land Board, 20
voluntary pooling, 120–122, 128

warranty clause(s), 61, 65, 78
water rights, 83–84
water wells, 83
well density, 43, 51, 53, 54, 72, 120, 128
well/drilling permit, 12, 100, 103
well logs, 42, 105
well plugging, 82, 84, 88, 111, 113, 126, 129
well proposals, 115
well spacing. See also *drilling and spacing unit* (*DSU*)/*proration unit.*
  about, 43, 51, 53, 54, 72, 100, 119
  compared to well density, 51
  defined, 7, 51
  history, 9, 120, 144, 155
West Virginia, 8–9, 21
working interest, 100, 110–111, 115, 157–160
working interest owners, 100, 104, 110, 115, 116, 122, 124
Wyoming
  federal lands, 23
  leasing agency for state lands, 21
  leasing in, 150–151
  ranking as a top oil-producing state, 133
  reservations, 26
  state regulatory agency, 52